All My Yesterdays

All My Yesterdays

James Marsden

ATHENA PRESS
LONDON

All My Yesterdays
Copyright © James Marsden 2007

ISBN 10-digit: 1 84748 145 0
ISBN 13-digit: 978 1 84748 145 0

First Published 2007 by
ATHENA PRESS
Queen's House, 2 Holly Road
Twickenham TW1 4EG
United Kingdom

Printed for Athena Press

Author's Note

The genealogical history of the Marsden family and the family members that appear in this novel are real, as are the events surrounding them.

Other characters that appear are not true portraits or caricatures of the persons mentioned and are an amalgam of factors drawn from the author's memory and imagination, with in most instances their identity disguised to avoid any possible embarrassment to them or their surviving families.

Throughout the work the author intended no slight or criticism, only to portray life as experienced by him over a period of seventy-five years between 1932 and 2007.

Preface

The Marsden Family of South Wales and Pembrokeshire

The earliest record of the Marsden name can be traced back to around 1070 and the townships of Greater and Little Marsden situated about five miles from Burnley on the borders of Lancaster and Yorkshire. *The Genealogical Memoirs of the Family of Marsden* by Benjamin Marsden, James Aspinall Marsden and Robert Sidney Marsden, published in 1914, records its history up until that time and identifies the many branches of the family established as members moved to the various regions of the UK and Ireland.

This book also records the Marsden arms, first recorded in 1378 and appearing in a deed dated at Leicester on 12 June 1415. In 1733 James Marsden of Manchester applied to the Heralds College for a grant of arms for him and his descendants and this appears on the cover to this work over the motto, which translates as 'War is the ultimate victor'. Since then there have been additions and minor variations to the arms with a motto of '*ne timeas recte faciendo*' (fear not where acting rightly) being used.

The first recording of the family's presence in South Wales and Pembrokeshire was in relation to a William Marsden, who apparently spoke Welsh and was the regular marriage witness for the parish of Penrith. William married in 1772 and he and his wife Mary had six children – John, William, Godfrey, Hannah, Thomas and Robert. Although little is known of the first five born, the marriage of the youngest son, Robert to Mary Jenkins of the Parish of Penrith and Castellan, in the County of Pembrokeshire, was solemnised at the parish church of the Chapelry of Castellan on the tenth day of July 1817 and involved Mary Jenkins obtaining the consent of Friends which would suggest that she had Quaker connections.

In November 1820 Robert Marsden was recorded as being witness to the marriage of Margaret Jenkins, the widowed mother of his wife Mary, to a widower David Evans at the parish church of Castellan, the marriage once again requiring the consent of friends, further suggesting the Quaker connection.

Although it is unclear as to how many children Robert and Mary had, Robert's death is recorded in the burial records of Whitechurch Parish Church as being on 8 March 1832 at the age of thirty-five years, his place of residence at that time being Blaenffos in the county of Pembrokeshire. On 3 March 1846, Robert Marsden was recorded as being the father of John Marsden – born in 1823 – at John's marriage to Martha James at St Brynnach Parish Church, Nevern in the county of Pembrokeshire.

John Marsden was a farmer and following his marriage to Martha James lived at Penbwcle, Morfa, in the parish of Nevern. Penbwcle was a typical farm cottage of the time, located within the boundaries of Ffynnon-ddwfn Farm. As the family grew, they were forced to move to an adjacent and larger cottage known as Pencnwc, with Penbwcle falling into disrepair and eventual ruin. John and Martha lived at Pencnwc until Martha's death in 1900 and John's death in 1909. Both were buried at St Brynnach Church, Nevern. John and Martha Marsden had eight children:

- Maria Marsden, born at Nevern in 1847, married a John Morris in 1888, and following residence at 28 Beauchamp Street, Cardiff, died at that address in 1920.

- William Marsden, born at Nevern in 1849, married in 1876 to a Catherine Williams in Pontypridd. Although there is no record of the date of his death, the 1891 census registers him at the time as living at 2 Bryn Eirw Terrace, Hafod, Pontypridd.

- Mary Marsden, born at Nevern in 1850, married in 1880 at Pembroke. There is no record of the date of her death.

- James Marsden, born at Nevern in 1851, married Martha James at St Brynnach Church, Nevern in 1875, and died at Nevern in 1939.

- Ann Marsden, born in 1858 at Nevern, married in 1883, there is no record of her husband's name or the date of her death.

- John Marsden, born in 1859 at Nevern, married Margaret Anne Davies at Cardigan in 1891, and died at Kenfig Hill in 1940.

- David Marsden, born at Nevern in 1866, married Elizabeth Howells at an unknown venue and date. There is no record of the date of his death.

- Martha Pattie Marsden, born at Nevern in 1871. At the age of fourteen years parish records show that she christened her illegitimate daughter Martha Marsden at St Brynnach Church on 12 April 1885. Following the death of her father at Pencnwc in 1909, she moved to Cardiff to be with her sister Maria. There she met and married a David Walter Jones in Cardiff in 1917, and following residence at 7 and later 28 Beauchamp Street, Cardiff, died a widow at Kenfig Hill in 1949 and was buried in Cardiff.

For the purpose of this preface the following account relates to James Marsden, who continued the family tradition of farming, and his brother John Marsden, who became a master mariner.

As previously mentioned, James Marsden was born in March 1851 in the Parish of Nevern, Pembrokeshire. In April 1875 he married Martha James, born in October 1850, at St Brynnach Parish Church, Nevern.

Following their wedding, the couple left Pembrokeshire with James becoming a tenant farmer at Park Farm, Llangennech, Carmarthenshire, where their five children were born. The family returned to the parish of Nevern in September 1891 to take up the farming tenancy of Ffynnon-ddwfn Farm, and to be close to James's aging parents at Pencnwc. Following the death of his mother and father, James bought Ffynnon-ddwfn and farmed there until his death in 1939.

James and Martha's children were:

- Catherine Jane Marsden, born 25 May 1876 at Llangennech and moved with the family to Pembrokeshire in

1891. She moved to Cardiff in 1956 to live at 107 Claude Road, Roath, and died in May 1970 at the age of ninety-four years. She did not marry and had no children.

- James Robert Marsden, born on 19 May 1877 at Llangennech and moved with the family to Pembrokeshire in 1891. In 1895 he married Elizabeth Thomas, and bought and farmed Wenallt Farm at Velindre, Pembrokeshire. He gave up farming in 1952 and moved to Newport where he died in June 1954. His wife, Elizabeth, died in 1958. There were no children from the marriage.

- John Llewellyn Marsden, born 27 January 1879 at Llangennech and moved with the family to Pembrokeshire in 1891. He later qualified as a marine engineer and died on 4 December 1917 by drowning, following an accident while his ship was docked at Barry Docks, South Wales.

- Martha Ann Marsden, born on 12 March 1881 at Llangennech and moved with the family to Pembrokeshire in 1891. On 20 November 1922 she married David James a master mariner from Newport. She died on 4 July 1934 age fifty-three years. Captain James committed suicide the following year while at sea. There were no children from the marriage.

- Thomas Owen Marsden, born on 8 August 1890 at Llangennech and moved with the family to Pembrokeshire in 1891 where he later farmed with his father on the family farm. In 1932 he married Alice Muriel Lawrence, born on 20 January 1914 at 160 Tyntila Road, Llwyn-y-pia, Ystrad Rhondda. Their one child, James John Marsden, was born on 30 October 1932 at Nevern. Following the death of Alice Muriel on 28 May 1956, Thomas Owen Marsden and his sister Catherine Jane Marsden left Pembrokeshire to live with James John Marsden at Cowbridge and later at Claude Road in Cardiff. Thomas Owen Marsden died on 10 March 1972.

- James John Marsden, left Nevern in 1952 to study at the University College of South Wales and Monmouthshire and at the Welsh School of Medicine. He married Judith

Margaret Llewellyn of Cardiff in 1956, and after four years, living and working in Cowbridge in the Vale of Glamorgan, returned to live in Claude Road, Cardiff in 1960. There were two children from the marriage, David Lawrence Marsden, born on 28 January 1959 in Cardiff, and Julia Ann Marsden, born on 24 November 1962 in Cardiff.

James and Judith were divorced in 1978, and Judith died on 1 January 2001.

On 26 July 1980 James John Marsden married Maria Salome Leca, a Portuguese National living in Keppoch Street, Cardiff, at the Cardiff Registry Office with the couple moving to Brecon, Powys in January 1981. There were no children from the marriage.

In 1992 James and Maria returned to Cardiff to live at Cranmer Court, in the City of Llandaff on the outskirts of Cardiff.

In 1983 David Lawrence Marsden married Sandra Burbidge at Leicester Register Office. Their only son, Carl Marsden, was born on 17 December 1991. The family lived in Huncote, Leicestershire until they divorced in 2002. David Marsden now lives in Loughborough with a partner, Melissa Offspring. They have twin girls – Charlotte Marsden and Megan Marsden, born on 22 March 2004.

Julia Ann Marsden married Peter Woolcock, on 21 May 1987 and the couple are now living at Woodlawn Way, Cardiff. They have no children.

- John Marsden, born on 1 December 1859, trained and qualified as a master mariner and following his marriage to Margaret Ann James, born on 30 November 1867, the couple moved from the parish of Nevern to Cardiff, where they lived at 107 Claude Road, Roath. This move was after the 1881 Census, which has no record of the family being in Cardiff. In the late 1920s the family moved to Kenfig Hill where John Marsden died on 31 March 1940, and Margaret Ann Marsden died on

2 February 1941. There were six children from the marriage:

- John George Marsden was born on 29 October 1892. He followed his father and qualified as a master mariner. He died of drowning while on active service on 15 March 1917. He was not married.

- Andrew Llewellyn Marsden was born on 14 January 1895. He died on 9 December 1912 at the age of seventeen years.

- Eloda Keziah Marsden was born on 2 December 1901. She qualified as a pharmacist and established a retail pharmacy business at Pisgah Street, Kenfig Hill, when the family moved from Cardiff. She died on 7 September 1936 at the age of thirty-five years. She was not married.

- Lois Eudora Marsden was born in February 1903. She qualified as an optician and practised alongside her sister at Kenfig Hill. She was not married and died on 2 November 1982.

- Bertram (Berti) Marsden was born in 1904. He qualified as an engineer and following his marriage moved to the outskirts of Pontypool, Monmouthshire. He had one son, Kelvin Marsden. He died in 1964.

- Edward (Eddie) Marsden was born in 1906 and followed his father in qualifying as a master mariner. Following his marriage he lived at Kenfig Hill were his only son, Duncan Marsden, was born. Eddie died in 1968.

- Kelvin Marsden was born in 1934. He married and had two children; Veronica Marsden and Richard Marsden. The family now live in Porthcawl.

- Duncan Marsden was born in 1944. Following his education at Cowbridge Grammar School and Llandaff Technical College, he moved to the Midlands to work and where he married and brought up two children. Following early retirement he now lives in Porthcawl.

The following chapters trace the life and times of one member of the Marsden family; his successes and failures, his loves and losses, and attempts to capture in words 'all his yesterdays'.

James Marsden

Chapter One

It was a Sunday evening in October 1932. The chill wind drove the rain against the wooden-framed windows of the westerly-facing, stone-built farmhouse, built in the mid-1800s as part of the Llwyngwair Manor estate. The house stood proud, overlooking the farmyard and the various farm buildings which formed the nucleus of the 200-acre farm known as Ffynnon-ddwfn (Deep Well) situated in the parish of Nevern in the county of Pembrokeshire. In one of the four bedrooms Alice lay on the iron bedstead waiting for the next contraction and the pains which had wracked her body for the past three to four hours. Her sister-in-law, Catherine Marsden, wiped the perspiration from her brow and whispered that she should not worry as the midwife was on her way.

Alice, the only daughter of Edith and John Lawrence, was born on 20 January 1914 in Ystrad Rhondda, and following her schooling at Gelli Junior School and Beddau Senior School, was obliged due to her mother's illness to entered Garth Olwg Cottage Home for Children in June 1923. Following the split-up of Edith and John's marriage in 1919 and the death of Alice's day-old twin brother and sister in January 1920, Edith became ill and spent a great deal of her life in and out of the Llwyn-y-pia Hospital. Four years later Edith died at Parc Gwllt Care Home, Bridgend, from influenza and endocarditis at the age of thirty-one.

On 28 May 1928 Alice, who was now nearing her fifteenth birthday, was discharged from the Cottage Home into the care of Miss Catherine Marsden who had travelled from Pembrokeshire in search of a domestic servant to work in the family home and farm.

At fifteen years of age Alice was a striking girl of medium build with an olive skin, raven black hair and deep brown eyes that were constantly smiling. Indeed, her pleasant manner and disposition made her immediately popular with the family and fellow servants. One member of the family who found her very attractive was Tom, the youngest son of James and Martha Marsden, who, following their return from Carmarthenshire in 1891, firstly to become tenants and later owners of the farm that lay north of Newport and some two miles west of the village of Nevern, and although Tom had not had previous girl friends he was smitten with Alice.

James Marsden was a tall, lean, handsome man with snow-white hair and a close-clipped moustache, who even at the age of eighty was active in both the local community and on his beloved farm. His wife Martha, who had presented him with five children, had died in July 1923 – a loss from which he never fully recovered. The eldest of the children was Catherine Jane, followed by Robert, then Jack and Martha and finally Tom. Tom could be described as the 'runt' of the family – he was short, of slight build and due to spending much time horse riding, had developed a curved spine that made him appear even shorter. By May 1928, Robert had married and with his wife Elizabeth was farming on their own farm in Velindre; Martha had married a local master mariner – Captain David James – and was living in Newport, while Jack had been tragically drowned at sea during the 1914–1918 World War. Catherine had not married, and in the tradition of the times, ran the family home for her father, assisted by a kitchen maid, with her youngest brother Tom running the farm assisted by a young live-in farm hand called Ruben, who had come from a boys home; and a local part-time, middle-aged labourer called Davy who lived with his unmarried sister in a small cottage adjoining the farm.

It was into this household that Alice came in May 1928 as a domestic servant. Alice proved to be a very willing and capable worker, being able to undertake most of the domestic duties required without instruction or supervision. Outside the routine of farm life, other activities, of which there were few, were centred on the local church at Nevern and the various social activities organised by the families and young people who attended church. Foremost among these were the Annual Harvest Thanksgiving Service, held on completion of the harvest in late

September or early October; the Christmas 'Social' that usually took place in the village church hall in late December; and the odd Eisteddfod or Singing Festival, usually held at one of the many chapels in the area.

Another feature of farm life at that time was the weekly visit undertaken by the family to the nearest town of Newport to purchase those items of food and clothing that were not grown or provided by the farm. Such visits were invariably undertaken by Catherine accompanied, upon her arrival, by Alice and Catherine's brother Tom, who drove the pony and trap that was the sole means of transport at the time. While Catherine and Alice visited the various shops, friends, and distant relatives in the town, Tom would park the trap in the coach yard adjoining the Golden Lion tavern, stable the horse in its stables and then adjourn to the bar room, to return at an agreed time for the journey home. Alice and Tom soon struck up a friendship, with Alice undertaking more and more work on the farm in addition to her household duties. This work she loved and her presence had a beneficial effect on Tom and the other farm workers, since she was always cheerful, happy, had a good sense of humour, and was a very hard worker. It was not, however, until after her sixteenth birthday in January 1930 that Alice and Tom became lovers. In January of the following year they were married at the parish church of St Brynnach, Nevern – the venue of James and Martha's marriage in 1875 prior to their leaving Pembrokeshire to take up the tenancy of Park Farm, Llangennech. Alice was aged seventeen, and Tom twenty-five years her senior, at forty-two years of age. Alice became pregnant almost immediately, much to the delight of James Marsden and the family, since the marriage of Robert to Elizabeth and Martha to David had not resulted in any children, and with Jack having died and Catherine unmarried, this pregnancy appeared to be the only way that the family would gain a foothold in the next generation.

On that particular Sunday, the local midwife, Nurse Price, had finished her washing-up following Sunday lunch. Her husband Jack was enjoying his after-lunch sleep in an armchair in front of the wood fire that burned in the black cast-iron grate with adjoining oven that had cooked the lunch. The Prices' lived in a small white-washed cottage overlooking the Newport Estuary that saw the River Nevern join the Irish Sea. Jack, a small, weather-beaten retired sailor, spent most of his time during the summer months ferrying locals and visitors across the estuary in a small rowboat, which he also used for some inshore fishing. At four o'clock it was already dusk with the westerly wind and rain making it particularly unpleasant, causing most locals to be in their homes. The sound of horse's hooves on the gravel leading to the front of the cottage caused Jack to wake up with a start, while the knocking on the front door confirmed that they had a visitor, and one who appeared to be in a hurry. Nurse Price hurried to the door to be confronted by a very wet Tom and the news that Alice was in labour and in need of her skills as a midwife. While Jack offered Tom the customary cup of tea, Nurse Price hurried off to change into her nurse's uniform and ensure that her black leather bag contained all the necessary requirements for a birth. Nurse Price was a short, round woman with a cheerful face and a calm disposition. Once she was satisfied that her crisp, starched blue uniform was in place and that her blue nurse's cap was at the right angle she ushered Tom out of the front door, gave Jack a peck on the cheek and bustled around to the rear of the house to where her car, a black late twenties Austin 7 'Top Hat' saloon, was parked. Having squeezed behind the wheel of the little two-door vehicle, she pressed the starter and carefully made her way out onto the road that connected the row of houses facing the estuary to the main town of Newport. The wind and rain were now lashing the countryside as Nurse Price drove the little car towards Deep Well Farm and the anxious Marsden family.

Having negotiated the long, winding and now muddy driveway boarded by trees that led to the farmyard, Nurse Price heaved herself out of her car and struggled up the path to the front door. Why, she thought, should babies choose such terrible weather to make their arrival? The door was opened by James, who immediately directed her up the stairs that led to the bedroom where Alice, attended by Catherine, was still suffering the contractions which by now were becoming more frequent and more painful.

Downstairs in the large square farmhouse living room Tom, who had had a change of clothes, waited with his father James for the sounds that would announce the birth. His wet clothes hung steaming on a wooden clothes horse in front of the wood fire that crackled in the black cast-iron grate with adjoining oven and hob. Above the fireplace was a mantle that supported two brass candlesticks, a brass spill box and two china greyhounds. Two armchairs fronted the fire while the remaining chairs, which doubled as dining chairs, were scattered around the large square central dining table. On the smoke-tinted walls hung two pictures of hunting scenes and in pride of place above the mantle a framed Valedictory Address that had been presented to James upon his family leaving Llangennech in September 1891. None of the chairs were occupied that night since both Tom and his father were too busy pacing backward and forwards anxiously waiting for news from upstairs. Slowly the hands of the grandfather clock that stood near the door leading to the hall and stairs, moved towards nine o'clock and then, at long last, the long-awaited cry of the newborn was heard. Catherine appeared in the hall doorway to announce, 'It's a boy.'

Chapter Two

I weighed in at eight pounds and six ounces, and immediately made my presence felt by crying the remainder of Sunday night and the best part of Monday morning. My mother had experienced a difficult delivery and Nurse Price doubted her ability to have more children, a view that was bourn out with the passage of time.

The room where I was born and where I slept for the next eighteen years was at the rear of the house, and was initially shared by my mother, father and myself. It was furnished with an iron-framed double bed with a straw mattress, on top of which was a feather-filled second mattress. White linen sheets topped by hand-made quilts completed the bedding, with the number of quilts varying with the seasons and depending how cold it was. The only other bedroom furniture consisted of a large oak wardrobe with matching chest of drawers. The stained floor-boards were uncovered except for a small rush mat on each side of the bed. My first bed was in the form of a carved wooden cradle that had a wooden hood and rockers. This occupied a corner of the room and as I grew was replaced by a single iron bedstead.

Growing up in a farm environment in the 1930s and early 1940s was an experience that few who have not lived through it can visualise. My first public appearance was my christening that took place at St Brynnach Church on 20 January 1933, my mother's birthday. My mother, father, grandfather and my aunty Catherine, all dressed in their best Sunday clothes, drove to the church in the horse and trap to be met at the church by my uncle Robert and his wife Elizabeth, together with other family friends who wanted to see the new addition to the family. I was christened James Lawrence, thereby combining elements from both my mother's and father's families. Following the registering of the christening by the parish parson, all present set off on the return journey to the farm where modest refreshments had been prepared. There then followed the ceremony of entering the baptism in the leather-covered brass-bound family Bible which always rested at the end of the long dining table that occupied the centre of the dining room and was where my grandfather spent many a Sunday afternoon reading chapters from its various books.

That visit to St Brynnach marked the first of many, since from that time onwards I attended church on most Sunday mornings accompanied by my mother, my aunt, or both. My father rarely went to church since in his view the women attended to view the clothes and hats of other ladies in the congregation and the men only attended because they had to. My first recollections of the world at large was my mother taking me for walks through the leafy, flower-decked hedgerows, with the hum of bees collecting pollen, birds singing and me in my pushchair, since in the early days I was a slow walker. As the months and years passed I experienced events that will always be in my memory and reflects the saying, 'life is a collection of memories'.

By the age of five I was a constant companion of my grandfather, who as the years went by restricted his activities on the farm to those he enjoyed and were in keeping with his advancing years. Among these were carpentry and gardening. He was a most competent carpenter, and this work that involved making wooden gates, styles, and doors for the farm was undertaken in a room in one of the farm's outbuildings, which was dominated by an enormous wooden bench that had been part of a ship wrecked off the Pembrokeshire coast. To this bench had been fixed a vice and various blocks of wood to assist planning. For hours I would sit on this bench watching my grandfather convert strips of rough timber into functional objects, how he made the various joints, and how such joints were pegged, since he rarely used nails.

His interest and knowledge of gardening bordered on the professional and I was fascinated and privileged in those early years to observe the ways he pruned shrubs, planted seeds, vegetables and flowers. Every morning at dawn my grandfather could be seen in the garden or orchard, where he would eat a selection of fruit or vegetables that were in season – raw onions, raspberries, strawberries, blackcurrants, apples were all on his list.

This selection was followed two hours later by a full breakfast of bacon and eggs. This style of living would appear to have suited my grandfather, since apparently he had never had a day's illness in his eighty-plus years and up until the age of eighty, he acted as church warden to St Brynnach Church, was a regular churchgoer and a member of the parish council.

My other companion at this time was the part-time farm labourer Davy Jones. He was a short, stocky man with red hair and a large, drooping moustache. Davy had never married and lived with his spinster sister. He had a great sense of humour and was constantly making me laugh, as he went about his work, which was very varied, since Davy was an all-rounder when it came to farm work.

These early years on the farm taught me many things, including the farmer's dependency on nature and the changes brought about by the seasons. Winter on the farm in those days was a difficult time with heavy rain and the resulting muddy conditions curtailing many activities. Cattle required housing and feeding indoors to avoid their hooves breaking up the sodden grassland; sheep had to be fed regularly out in the fields since grass would be at a premium. If the snow came these conditions could worsen and on many occasions the farm would be cut-off from the outside world, with the only means of travel to the nearest village being on horseback. The collection of milk from the farms was also affected by heavy snowfall, resulting in the uncollected milk having to be made into butter and cheese or if there was a surplus, fed to the pigs. Spring would see the lambing season when the flock of around a hundred sheep required constant attention, with multi-births requiring some lambs to be brought into the house to be fed from a bottle and kept warm. My first introduction to a lamb was when, its mother having died, this particular lamb that had become a member of the family followed my mother around the house and farm, and decided to butt me from behind, resulting in my taking a dive which I did not take kindly to.

Spring was also the time for ploughing those fields designated for the sowing of cereals and root crops, and the fencing off from grazing areas of grassland designated for hay that would be ready to cut and harvest by early summer. The smell of newly-mown hay was to me unforgettable and tossing and turning the hay on a sunny day was a wonderful experience. Once the cut hay was declared dry, a task undertaken by my father with much deliberation, the weather forecast for the following day would be checked on the battery-operated radio, and the hay would be gathered into 'stooks' ready to be harvested the following day. Haymaking in those days was a social affair with farmers from adjoining farms coming to assist in loading the hay onto the horse-drawn cart which could be two-wheeled or four-wheeled, the latter being referred to as a 'gambo'. One man would be on the cart placing the hay to achieve the maximum load, while two or three others would pitch the hay onto the cart with pitchforks, while another would lead the horse, ensuring that the cart stopped at appropriate intervals. There were usually two such carts, one in the field while the other was being unloaded in the hay yard to form a hayrick. Hay was transferred from the cart to the hayrick by means of a twenty-to-thirty-foot-high wooden mast supported by guy ropes. The mast in turn supported, through a series of ropes and pulleys, a four-prong metal grab located at the end of an arm that rotated round the mast. A horse harnessed to one end of the rope and pulley system effected the lifting of the grab full of hay from the cart to be swung onto the hayrick. The releasing of the hay by the grab was effected by a pull-rope operated from the ground, and many a time the release would be effected when the grab was directly above the men building the hayrick, covering them with hay, much to the amusement of the pull-rope operator.

Once all the hay had been gathered and the hayricks completed, all the workers would be invited into the house for a meal washed down with home-made beer. Such a supper would normally not end until late, with those from other farms who had come to help, leaving in a cheerful mood. During the next few days the hayricks would be inspected at morning and night for signs of overheating due to fermentation. Such inspections involved a long metal rod being inserted into the middle of the hayrick, left for a time and then checked for warmth. Provided the hay had been harvested at the correct time and without excessive moisture, the heat generated would be within acceptable limits and the hay would make excellent winter fodder.

Once the internal temperature of the hayrick was deemed normal the hayrick would then be ready for thatching. This involved cutting a considerable amount of reeds, which were in plentiful supply growing around a pond adjoining the farmyard. After allowing these a few weeks to dry, they were tied into small bundles that made up the individual units of the thatch. The thatch would then be held down by rows of twine anchored at intervals by hazel sticks that were cut from the hedgerows and pointed to make easy access into the hay. Thatching was a skilled task at which both my grandfather and father were experts. Once the thatch was in place the ridge and eves would be trimmed with shears so that the finished product looked like a small thatched cottage but without a door or windows.

July also saw the gathering of the potato crop, which although not extensive resulted in much backache among the workers. The rows or drills of potato plants that would by now be past their flowering stage were opened by means of a horse-drawn plough, exposing the potatoes. These were then gathered by hand and bagged. The potatoes would then be transferred into the store to be spread over the floor to complete the drying process, and then covered with a layer of straw. These potatoes would be used throughout the year.

By the time the hay harvest was completed and the hayricks thatched, the cereal crops of oats, barley and wheat that had been sown in the spring had assumed the golden colours of harvest time. The grain-bearing heads were inspected to ascertain whether the grains were firm and fully developed, at which time the binder that had laid idle since the previous autumn, had to be brought out and serviced in readiness for harvesting.

I always viewed the binder as a great invention. To see this horse-drawn machine with its rotating vanes, canvas conveyor belts and rattling chains cut a field of oats or barley and deposit the crop as sheaves of equal size and weight, was always a source of wonder to me.

As the binder threw out a constant stream of sheaves there were usually three or four workers following who gathered the sheaves and placed them in upright 'stooks', each of four to six sheaves, so that by the time the cutting was completed all the sheaves were in stooks that stood in rows across the field. This system ensured that the grain heads were exposed to the wind and sun and would thoroughly dry before the final stage of harvesting.

Another feature connected with the binder and which I well remember was rabbits. Cutting any crop with a binder involved starting by following the hedges of the field and working towards the centre. As this progressed the area of crop left standing got smaller and smaller. Any rabbits, and in those days they were plentiful, that had been in the field were gradually driven by the noise of the binder towards the centre, until they were eventually forced to make a dash for safety, at which time the farm dog, a black and white sheepdog called Juno, had a great time chasing the rabbits and occasionally catching one, which usually ended up as the next day's lunch.

The next stage in the harvesting of cereals was similar to that of the hay harvest. Once the stooks were deemed dry and the grain heads fully ripe and hard, horse-drawn carts and farmers from adjoining farms would gather, and all the stooks would be transferred from field to farmyard to form 'ricks'. These ricks resembled hayricks, but with all the sheaves laid out in layers with the cut ends facing outwards, and the grain ends facing inwards. Since sheaves were more manageable than loose hay, the ricks were usually built with considerable skill and could vary in shape, some being square and some round. Since these ricks had a short life span, they were rarely thatched and stood waiting for the threshing machine to arrive.

The arrival of the threshing machine was to any small boy an unforgettable event and could be likened to the arrival of a monster on the farm. At the time, a contractor visiting all farms in the area upon request undertook the threshing of cereal crops. The threshing machine itself was a large, steel-framed, wooden, four-wheeled structure painted two-tone red and pulled by a very large steam traction engine that bellowed smoke and steam and in addition to conveying the thresher from farm to farm, provided the power, via a belt driven system, to the threshing machine. Seeing this monster entering the farmyard for the first time was the event of the year and one that I shall never forget. On the day of the threshing farmers from the adjoining farms again came to help. Some to pitch the sheaves of corn, barley, or wheat from the ricks onto the top of the threshing machine, where two other operatives removed the string holding the sheaves before feeding them into the thresher, where high-speed metallic revolving drums separated the grain from the straw. The grain emerged at one end of the machine to be collected in sacks, while the straw and the husks emerged from the opposite end, with the former made into a straw rick that would be used for winter feed when mixed with hay, or as animal bedding. Following a successful day's threshing all participants were invited into the farm kitchen for a meal washed down with much homemade beer.

During the next few days the sacks of cereals were emptied onto the floor of the grain store, with the grain turned occasionally to complete the drying process and to avoid any mould developing or the grain heating.

Once the hayricks had been thatched, the threshing was over, the cereal crops were in the store and the fruits from the garden and orchard had been gathered, it was time to look forward to the annual Harvest Thanksgiving Service. I recall going with my mother and aunt to St Brynnach Church to assist with the decoration ready for the services. Through the participation of the whole of the local community, the church would be decked out with a fantastic range of flowers, fruits and crops representing the harvesting that had just been completed. The church appeared so different, full of colour and smells, the smell of ripe apples, bread of many elaborate shapes, sheaves of corn and of course the multitude of flowers gathered from garden and field. The Harvest Festival was celebrated with three services: a morning service followed by a buffet lunch in the church hall; an afternoon service followed by a traditional tea of scones and sandwiches; and an evening service. Each service, although conducted by the resident vicar, had the sermon delivered by guest clergy, with the one with the highest reputation as a preacher presiding at the evening service. Although these occasions guaranteed that the church would be full, it was the evening service that saw the church packed, with the men having completed the milking on the farms having to stand in the aisles and at the back of the church while the women and children were squeezed into the oak pews. My recollection of those evening services is of the candlelit church, the wonderful singing with the tenor and bass voices of the men joining the soprano voices of the women and children, and how different the men looked in their best suits. Indeed the difference was so great that on one occasion I failed to recognise my own father as he arrived at the church.

In many ways the Harvest Festival marked the beginning of winter on the farm, and as the days got shorter and shorter more and more time was spent indoors, undertaking repairs of damaged equipment and servicing other items ready for storage until next spring. During the winter I spent a great deal of time with my mother and aunt, watching their jam making and following the killing of a pig, making faggots and brawn, and salting the meat in large slate troughs ready for it to be hung on the special hooks that were in the kitchen ceiling to complete the curing.

An annual visitor to the house at this time was the clock and watch repairer. Mr Parry was a short, rotund man with long white hair that curled onto his shoulders, who spent most of his time going around the farms and villages servicing clocks and watches. Back in 1880 my grandfather had bought a grandfather clock from J W Hughes, a clockmaker in Llanelly. This clock with its oak case inlaid with rosewood had pride of place in the house and was serviced by Mr Parry every year. Such a service involved the large kitchen table being cleared and covered with newspaper upon which Mr Parry would proceed to take the clock mechanism to pieces. Each piece would be carefully washed in a cleaning fluid, dried and polished and then reassembled. The catgut holding the weights was usually replaced and the clock adjusted for accuracy. All this took the best part of a day, with myself for once sitting at the table fascinated by all that was going on. During his stay Mr Parry would drink endless cups of tea but although offered, I never saw him accept anything to eat.

A more frequent visitor to the farm, especially during the dark winter evenings, was Samuel Morris, known in the locality as Sam. He was a tall, lean man around six feet with receding white hair and a very pale complexion. Sam, who I guess was in his early sixties, was always well dressed in a dark suit and white shirt. He lived in one of two adjoining cottages near the village of Nevern, the adjoining cottage occupied by his spinster sister. Although his background was not well known to the local community, in his numerous discussions with my grandfather and father it transpired that Sam was an Oxford University graduate, had taught and researched at the university and was a fellow of one of the colleges, although he never divulged which one. He had two topics of conversation, which even at my early age I found fascinating to listen to, although not fully able to understand. One was his interest in ancient writings while the other was in pre-Christian religions and the origins of the Bible. Sam viewed the Bible as a product of man, not God. He outlined how the pagan Roman Emperor Constantine the Great had collated the modern Bible in an attempt to calm the religious turmoil that was gripping Rome, with Christians and pagans warring and threatening to destroy Rome. How in 325 AD he unified Rome under a single religion of Christianity. How by fusing pagan symbols, dates and rituals into the growing Christian tradition, he created a hybrid religion that was acceptable to both parties. Examples of this that he often quoted were that while Christianity originally honoured the Jewish Sabbath of Saturday Constantine shifted it to coincide with the pagan's veneration day of the sun god, namely Sunday. Egyptian sun disks became the halos of Christian Saints, while the pre-Christian God Mithras was born on 25 December, died, was buried in a rock tomb, and then resurrected in three days. These fireside discussions naturally resulted in a difference of opinion since my grandfather, who viewed the Bible as having been delivered to man from heaven, could not reconcile himself to the idea that he went to church on Sunday because of some pagan sun god.

In relation to ancient writings and symbolism, Sam was a source of fascinating information, and much of his undoubted expertise he used in trying to interpret the various Celtic writings at St Brynnach Church, in the adjoining churchyard and on the Pilgrim's Cross located on the hillside overlooking Nevern village. On one occasion he accompanied my grandfather and myself to view the marks and scrolls that occurred on the wide stone windowsills inside the church and on one particular stone monument in the churchyard, drawing comparisons between them and early Egyptian markings and those found in South America.

As Christmas drew nearer the farm kitchen became a hive of activity with the making of the Christmas pudding taking priority. The mixing of the Christmas pudding took on a ceremonial status, with all members of the family and servants taking turns at stirring the mixture. My father brought a flagon of ale from the Golden Lion and this was slowly added to the mixture while stirring, while my grandfather contributed the two new sixpence pieces that went into the mixture to be found by some lucky diner on Christmas Day. Once the pudding mix had been deemed right through much tasting, it was placed in the series of pudding basins that had been suitably greased and floured. The top was covered with greaseproof paper and flour and the whole wrapped in a linen bag ready for boiling. Cooking took many hours and when completed the puddings in their linen jackets were allowed to cool and then hung on the kitchen ceiling until enjoyed on Christmas Day and New Year's Day.

In addition to keeping chickens that gave a constant supply of free-range eggs, Deep Well Farm reared around fifty turkeys and twenty geese each year. These were killed, feathered, drawn and trussed the week before Christmas to be collected by a butcher from Swansea three or four days before they would grace the tables of the good people of Swansea. My father in one of the farm's barns undertook the killing of the birds by first rendering them unconscious by a blow to the head and then slitting their throats and allowing all the blood to drain out. Six birds at a time were killed and then taken up to the farmhouse kitchen where my mother, aunt and four women neighbours would undertake the plucking. While the feathers were gathered and bagged, the birds would be prepared on the specially scrubbed kitchen table prepared for the occasion. Although having no previous experience, since arriving on the farm my mother had become highly skilled in preparing birds for the oven and could draw, clean and truss a bird in next to no time. Seventy birds made ready for the oven was a significant task, but a very rewarding one when the Swansea butcher Fred Rowlands turned up in his big black Humber car to collect the birds and hand over the crisp white five-pound notes which were rarely seen on the farm outside the Christmas period.

Once I was old enough to understand about Christmas and told by my mother and father that being good would ensure that a certain Father Christmas would visit and bring me some presents, Christmas Eve was the one night in the year when I wanted to go to bed early. The first Christmas that I can clearly recall was one where I woke up with everything in the bedroom dark. I could hear the steady breathing of my mother and father in the adjoining bed so felt secure in carefully climbing down to the foot of the bed which had replaced the cradle of five years ago, and feeling around until I found the stocking that I had placed on the bed rail the night before and that now was full of interesting objects. On the floor beneath the stocking was a square box, and in trying to open this to find out what it contained, I must have disturbed my father, who upon sitting up in bed struck a match and lit the bedside candle. As the warm glow filled the bedroom I could see on the side of the box the picture of a red railway engine with tender. On opening the box, there was a wooden model of an engine and tender, painted a bright red with the GWR logo on its sides. That day and many days after it never left my side.

Although most meals were served in either the kitchen or living room, Christmas lunch was one of the rare occasions that the dining room at the front of the house was used. The family Bible, that my grandfather read every Sunday, was removed from its pride of place at the head of the long oak table, and the table covered with a white linen cloth with the best cutlery and china brought out from the sideboard and china cabinet. An ornate oil lamp that would be lit as Christmas Day drew to an end would occupy the centre of the table. Christmas dinner on the farm consisted of leek and potato soup, roast goose, followed by Christmas pudding and white sauce. Goose was very traditional for my family with the goose grease that resulted from the roasting collected in an earthenware jar to be used throughout the year for such ailments as tonsillitis and chest colds, and with the wing feathers of the bird making excellent dusters. Dinner was usually over by three o'clock and was followed by the family retiring to the living room to listen to the radio and the then new development of the King's Christmas message.

The next festive event was New Year's Eve, when groups of young people from the various farms formed groups of four to six and visited the farms and houses of the village singing Christmas and traditional songs, and wishing the occupants a happy New Year. Visits normally took place between nine o'clock and midnight, and the householders were expected to invite the singers in for some form of refreshment and to give them some good-luck money known locally as a 'celenig'. Families who had retired for the night usually threw the celenig out of the bedroom window to the singers below, wishing them a good new year.

New Year's Day was a low-key affair with the normal farm routine taking precedence. Young children from adjoining farms would turn up and sing for their celenig and would be made welcome with some sweets or an apple each. In that part of Pembrokeshire adjoining the Preseli Mountains neither Christmas nor the New Year were celebrated, since that community had not adopted the Gregorian calendar and still used the old Linnaeus Calendar with the New Year celebrated on 13 January. Although not having personal experience of these festivities, I heard said that they were a whole day and night affair with family members and friends gathering to celebrate, eat and drink large amounts of the free-flowing home-brewed beer, resulting in many severe headaches the following day.

The period following the Christmas and New Year celebrations and leading into the onset of spring was a relatively quiet time in the farming calendar. Consequently, annual social events took place during this time. One that I recall with much pleasure was the annual Church Social, normally held on or around the first day of March that was, of course, the day that the patron saint of Wales – St David – was celebrated.

The Social, as it was known locally, was held in the village school, normally on a Saturday night. Mothers and children arrived early with baskets laden with sandwiches and cakes, which were laid out on a long table at the end of the schoolroom. While this went on the children played organised games under the guidance and watchful eye of the vicar's wife. When the games were over all us children were given plates of food that we ate alongside our mothers. By this time, farm work had finished for the day, and fathers, husbands, young men and women from the various local farms arrived to take part in the adult part of the evening's entertainment. As I recall, there were games such as musical chairs and spinning the plate, followed by some community singing with the evening drawing to a close with some dancing. This was the time when young men asked the girl that they fancied for a dance, and hopefully, agreement that he could walk her home afterwards. Although on these occasions my mother, aunt and myself walked to the school, my father always organised a taxi to take us home. This to me was the highlight of the evening, since from a very early age I loved cars, and being driven home in a large black 1930 Humber saloon, which was the only taxi in town, was an unforgettable experience.

Growing up in these forever-changing surroundings was, on reflection, an experience that would be the envy of all small boys, with always a constant stream of new and different things happening. Looking back there is little doubt that these experiences that are still as clear today as they were then, had a significant effect on my thinking and reaction to events in later life. Family life in the 1930s was not without its tragic moments, as I was to learn from what I heard my mother and father talk about, and later, from personal experience. One such instance occurred in 1934, and although I was too young to remember, it was a talking point with the family for a very long time.

My aunt Martha who had married a ship's master lived in Newport in a townhouse called Brookfield. In 1934 she became ill and was diagnosed as having breast cancer. Since her husband was away at sea for long periods, his merchant ship making regular voyages between Cardiff and Buenos Aires, Aunt Martha came to stay at the farm. Her illness was of great concern to the family and in particular to my grandfather, who very soon, in consultation with Dr Martin Davies the family doctor, arranged for her to be treated at the Radcliff Infirmary, Oxford. At that time the Radcliff was pioneering radium treatment for breast cancer. This treatment involved placing radioactive radium needles into the breast and leaving them there for varying periods of time. Although this gave my aunt and the family some hope, the treatment proved unsuccessful and Matti, as my aunt Martha was known in the family, returned to the farm with her sister Catherine, who had accompanied her to Oxford. During her stay at Deep Well Farm she shared a bedroom with Catherine, who nursed her and saw to all her needs.

The next occurrence was one of those inexplicable events that go down in family lore. On warm spring evenings, after the evening meal, my grandfather frequently took a walk along the tree-lined driveway that led to the farm. On this particular evening, following a lengthy discussion with the family solicitor who had visited the farm that afternoon, he had not changed out of the clothes that he usually wore when entertaining guests, and still wore a dark suit, white shirt with winged collar and black tie, waistcoat with a fob chain and Hunter watch, while on the small finger of his right hand was a gold ring carrying a square ruby. This ring had been a gift from his brother, John Marsden, who unlike James had left the farming community and after much studying and hard work had become a master mariner. On one of his infrequent visits to the farm, John had presented the ring to my grandfather, saying that he had been given it by a lady friend in some Far-Eastern port as a farewell present, and that now he no longer wanted it. Although my grandfather was not prone to wear rings, he was pleased with his brother's gift, although still feeling that there was more to it than what he had been told. My grandfather had walked as far as the entrance gate to the driveway, and was on the point of retracing his steps when my father, who had ridden to Newport on an errand, returned. On seeing my grandfather he dismounted and leading the horse, both men walked slowly down the driveway towards the farmyard and home. By now dusk had changed to night with the moon just on the point of rising. All of a sudden the horse came to a halt and despite my father pulling on the rains it refused to budge, a strange and sudden darkness enveloped them and neither could see or move. After about a minute, although it may have appeared longer, the darkness lifted, they could see the driveway and overhanging trees again, and the horse moved forward with no compulsion.

On returning to the house where my mother was getting me ready for bed, and Aunt Catherine was upstairs attending to her sister, my grandfather said, 'I've just met a funeral,' and went off to bed. Although it was a topic of conversation at breakfast the following morning, with the incident recalled by both my grandfather and father, very little was said after, except my grandfather muttering to himself, 'I wish I had not been wearing that ring yesterday.'

Six weeks later, on 4 July 1934 my aunt Martha died in her sleep, having been on morphine for many weeks. Hers was a large funeral with the driveway full of horse-drawn traps, a few cars and the hearse. Following a brief service at the house, the funeral procession, with dozens of mourners walking, wound its way through the leafy lanes to St Brynnach Church where, following the traditional church service, my aunt was buried in the family plot alongside her mother and brother Jack.

It was two months later before Captain David James was able to visit his wife's grave, and although the shipping company had advised him of her death a few days after the event, the reality that she was no longer home at Brookfield awaiting his return rendered him heartbroken. He returned to sea almost immediately, and a few weeks later his sister and my family were advised that he had committed suicide and been found in his cabin with a revolver in his hand. He was buried at sea before the whole of the ship's company.

Chapter Three

By August of 1938 my early and carefree days on the farm were about to come to an end, by my mother announcing one morning at the breakfast table that in September, I would be starting school.

The Nevern Primary School was a small school of about thirty pupils. It was housed in a square, stone-built, slate-roofed building surrounded on all sides by a hard-surfaced playground. A large high-arched window, to the right of which was the main entrance to the school, dominated the front of the building that faced the school gates and road. To the left as you entered the playground stood the schoolhouse and residence of the headmaster and his wife, while in the playground at the rear of the school stood the school toilets. These were earth toilets with three allocated to the girls and three to the boys.

On entering the school building, there was a cloaks area with rows of cast-iron numbered hooks to the right, and to the left was the door leading into the main schoolroom. This high-ceilinged room had a raised stage at one end while at the other end was a door leading to a washroom and to the rear of the building. The room was furnished with double-seated cast-iron and oak desks scarred with the initials of hundreds of former pupils, and fitted with a china inkwell in the upper right-hand corner. The desks faced a large open fireplace with a large white-faced clock above. To the right of the fireplace stood the blackboard alongside the headmaster's desk and a large wooden map cupboard containing a selection of large-scale maps of the world and continents. At the rear of the desks was the door leading to the second and junior classroom. This was a much smaller room with a blackboard fixed to the wall, in front of which was the long teacher's table. The remainder of the room was occupied with single-seat desks and two large cupboards containing teaching materials.

The headmaster, Mr Edwards, was a slightly-built man in his forties. His bald head with a fringe of brown hair crowned a kindly face with twinkling brown eyes below black bushy eyebrows. He had trained at Aberystwyth University College and held the degree of Batchelor of Arts. His wife was a small, slim, blonde haired woman who, while keeping the schoolhouse in immaculate order, was rarely seen around the school and did not involve herself with school activities. The assistant teacher was Mrs Rees. She was a short, round, widowed woman in her late forties with a gentle disposition and a warm smile. She was responsible for the juniors, whose ages ranged from the beginners at six years old, to the ten-year-olds who then moved on to the seniors, taught by Mr Edwards. Usually, the junior class had around twelve pupils with the seniors totalling around eighteen.

It was into this new environment that I was taken one September morning.

My mother, who had accompanied me on the two-mile walk from the farm to the school, left me at the school gates, joining three other mothers who had also brought their children on their first day. There being no school uniform, I was dressed in grey shorts and socks, a blue shirt and a brown jacket. On my feet was a pair of black leather wooden-soled clogs. My brown leather satchel contained a pencil box that my grandfather had made, containing some colour pencils and a rubber, and my lunchbox, containing some egg sandwiches and an apple, since meals were not provided at school. Everything looked so large as I entered the playground and made my way past the schoolhouse and through the school entrance. I turned and waved to my mother with tears in both our eyes.

That first morning Mrs Rees, after supervising the hanging of coats in the cloakroom and allocating each one of us with a numbered hook, told us all about the school and what she expected in terms of behaviour, including courtesy, timekeeping, and cleanliness. Whenever the headmaster or any adult visitor entered the room we were required to stand and not sit until told to do so. The school day started at nine o'clock, with a milk break at ten thirty, a lunch break between half past twelve and half past one, with the school day ending at half past three in the afternoon, and we were expected to keep to those times. Before, and following, the lunch break when sandwiches brought from home, would be eaten, we were required to wash our hands in the washroom. There were no exceptions to these rules.

The milk break at ten thirty involved picking up a third of a pint bottle of milk from the crate provided. We were then given some drawing paper from the large cupboard and allowed to draw our favourite object, this in my case was a car, and although looking back it must have been of an unusual construction, I had a 'well done' from Mrs Rees.

My lunch of egg sandwiches and an apple was followed by a session in the playground, where I started making friends with some of my classmates of a similar age. I soon discovered that almost without exception all the juniors came from farms in the area, one of these was Howell, who lived in an adjoining farm and passed our farm gate on his way to school. Howell, I found out, was from a family of twelve children where he was the eleventh, having one younger sister.

The afternoon started with a word recognition session with Mrs Rees holding up a card on which there was a picture of an object and a word, which we were required to recognise. My main problem, as was the case for the majority of my classmates, was that since I had spent the first six years of my life in a Welsh-speaking family environment, being taught through the medium of English presented all of us with some problems, especially with spelling.

The afternoon ended with Mrs Rees reading the class a story, something that I had always enjoyed since my mother's bedtime stories. Grabbing coats from hooks we all ran out into the playground and on this first day, to our waiting mothers. I had a great big hug from my mother and as we walked home I attempted to tell her all about what I had done during the day. The next morning, by arrangement my mother only took me as far as the end of the drive, where Howell, his older brother and two elder sisters were waiting and we all set off for school. The return journey was the same and I felt for the first time that I was no longer tied to my mother's apron strings, and had that independence that the young crave for.

Schooldays passed very quickly, and soon Christmas had come and gone, and we were all looking forward to a new year that marked the end of the 1930s. During 1939 two events occurred, one that changed my world, while the other changed the whole world.

It was on the morning of Saturday, 6 May, while I and the family were having lunch in the living room, that my grandfather, who had declined lunch, suddenly got up from his armchair by the fireside and walked towards the door leading to the front of the house. When asked by my father where he was going he replied, 'I am going into the front room to die.' He entered the dining room and sat in the armchair at the head of the table, placed his right hand on his beloved family Bible and died with the gold ring bearing the large square ruby, glinting in the afternoon sunlight.

The next few days were to me just a blur, with people coming and going and with the work of the farm reduced to a minimum, with only milking a priority. The family doctor who issued the death certificate arrived, together with the local undertaker, and by the following day my grandfather was laid out in his open oak coffin that stood on stands in the front sitting room. Although I was not allowed to see my grandfather, the smell of the wood of the freshly-made coffin was something that I shall always remember. Dozens of family friends and relations visited the farm over the next few days to pay their respects, since my grandfather was very well known, liked and respected in the community. The way in which he had anticipated his death, which many found hard to fully comprehend, was the main topic of conversation.

The day of my grandfather's funeral was warm and sunny, and once again the driveway leading to the farm was crowded with horse and traps, cars and of course the hearse. At my grandfather's request, the hearse was horse-drawn, this task being undertaken by two black shire horses with polished brass-adorned harness. The hearse itself was traditional with ornate roof and glass panelled sides. While my father, mother and Uncle Robert walked behind the hearse as it made its way to St Brynnach Church, I travelled in the following car with my Aunt Catherine and Aunt Elizabeth. It was a large funeral with the church packed with farming families and local dignitaries, with many failing to get a seat and standing at the rear of the church. The eulogy given by the vicar spoke of the many attributes that my grandfather possessed and how he had used them not only in his capacity as a farmer but to the good of the community as a whole.

My grandfather was buried in the family plot alongside his beloved wife Martha and their two children, Jack and Mattie.

Although all the family were familiar with what my grandfather's will contained, his solicitor felt it right and proper to return to the farm after the funeral to read the will in the presence of the whole family. Consequently, after our return to the farm and after we had eaten a few sandwiches and had a cup of tea, we all adjourned to the sitting room where the family solicitor, Morgan Richardson, outlined the will. Since my uncle Robert had received a significant sum of money from my grandfather in helping him set up his own farm thirty years earlier, and since his wife Elizabeth was daughter to the family who owned the Thomas and Radcliff Shipping Company, they had agreed that they would not be beneficiaries. Consequently, my grandfather's estate was to be divided equally between my father and mother, and my aunt Catherine. My grandfather's watch and chain went to my father, with the ruby ring given to me when I reached eighteen years of age. In the meantime it was to be in the safekeeping of Aunt Catherine. The bad news at this time was that the farm had not been run very effectively over the last few years, that economies would have to be made, and spending controlled, if it were to survive as a commercial enterprise.

The second event that not only changed my world, but that of the nation, was the outbreak of the Second World War in September 1939. I recall my father listening to the radio broadcast by Prime Minister Chamberlain advising the country that it was now at war with Germany.

Pembrokeshire, in terms of the immediate effect of the war, was a million miles away from London, and for the first few months nothing really changed. Then came a whole raft of changes, the first being the issuing of gas masks that everyone was required to carry. These came in square cardboard boxes with shoulder straps. The gas mask was a required accessory when attending school, where we were all given instruction on how to put the mask on quickly and correctly. All windows had to have blackouts with no lights shown outside after dark. A requirement of the school at that time was that it had an air raid shelter, and it caused much excitement when a contractor came onto the school's premises to excavate a very large hole behind the toilets. This was subsequently lined and roofed with corrugated sheeting and became our shelter, although thankfully it was never called into use.

The ration book and identity card quickly followed, with a points allocation in respect of the weekly amount of meat, sugar, tea and clothing an individual could purchase. Petrol and fuel oil were rationed and only available to priority users such as doctors, midwives and other essential users. Farms that had tractors were allocated petrol and oil to which had been added a colour that would detect its illegal use in non-farming vehicles.

Demands on farming were ever increasing with special government payments made for the growing of certain crops such as wheat and sugar beat and flax. Milk production was also encouraged by the establishment of a Milk Marketing Board, and for the first time farmers were paid a reasonable price for their product.

Nevern School saw an influx of three eight-year-old boys who had been evacuated from London due to the air raids to stay with families on local farms. They were initially a source of considerable interest, especially in relation to their London accent. Once these communication difficulties were over, however, we all became friends with their understanding and speaking of Welsh increasing very rapidly. As the war dragged on, I became addicted to listening to the BBC News on the radio. Although I was not fully aware of the gravity of those early years, I made notes of the various accounts of air raids and how the British ground forces were placed. My other interest was the collecting of cigarette cards with pictures of all the various war planes currently in action, and since I loved drawing, I made charcoal drawings of these planes, some of which were pinned up on the school notice board as examples of good drawing.

By 1941 and at nine years of age, I was moved from the junior class to join the seniors taught by Mr Edwards. Mr Edwards was a good teacher and kept our interests alive through linking many of his lessons to everyday occurrences. His large supply of maps used in geography lessons pinpointed where the various battles were being fought, and what the terrain and climatic conditions were likely to be. Ration books were used to calculate the amount of food that an individual could be expected to buy over a year, while the costs of commodities were used as examples in basic mathematics. I loved his lessons and at this early age told my mother and father that I wanted to become a teacher when I grew up.

On the farm, the influence of the war was felt by the pressures to increase production. This had been made worse by the financial position following my grandfather's death when it was decided that Ruben be encouraged to seek other employment, which he did by moving to another farm, and by restricting Davy's hours to those times when two men were required for certain tasks. The outcome of this reduction in the farm's labour force was that my mother spent more and more time working on the farm and less and less in the house, with my aunt Catherine taking over most of the domestic tasks, including looking after me. I loved my aunt and she in turn spoiled me. She used to read me endless stories and this greatly assisted both my reading skills, spelling and vocabulary, since she always used to stop and show me difficult words and how they were spelt. This greatly assisted me in the one area were my schoolwork was not what I would have liked it to be.

In the summer of 1943 my mother and aunt went to see Mr Edwards to find out what my chances were of sitting the scholarship to enter Grammar School. Since practically all the pupils at the Nevern Primary School completed their education at the school and then went on to work on their farms or in other aspects of agriculture, the questions posed by my mother and aunt were difficult for Mr Edwards to answer. He was, however, a very honest man, and while he viewed my chances of passing the scholarship as excellent, he was of the opinion that his school was not the best at preparing for such a task, since in his view the teaching that was completely appropriate to the other twenty or so pupils in his class, was not completely appropriate for someone who wanted to enter Grammar School. What did he suggest? was my mother's next question. Mr

Edwards promised he would look into the possibilities and let her know.

So I returned to school in September in the knowledge that my days at Nevern might well be numbered.

Chapter Four

In September 1944, a year after my mother's discussion with Mr Edwards, I entered the Bodowen Private School in Cardigan. This achievement had not been without its problems: firstly my father was of the view that when I completed my studies at Nevern I should come and join him on the farm and learn to become a farmer; secondly, Cardigan was about ten miles from the farm and would necessitate my walking two miles to the bus stop followed by a bus ride of around eight miles each day; and thirdly, it being a private school there were school fees on top of the daily bus fares. These obstacles might have proved insurmountable had my aunt Catherine not stepped in to say that she would meet all the costs from her portion of my grandfather's will. In addition, she promised me a bicycle on my eleventh birthday, thus making the journey from the farm to the bus station quicker and easier.

Bodowen School was owned and run by a Miss Owen. She was a tall, lean woman in her fifties, with thick white hair that was sometimes tied at the back in a bun. She wore horn-rimmed spectacles that had very thick lenses, which sometimes made it difficult to know whether she was looking at you or somewhere else. Her one assistant was Mrs Pattie, a middle-aged lady who undertook individual tuition with pupils who had problems with reading or mathematics, in addition to supervising class work.

The school occupied a single large room off the courtyard of the Black Lion Hotel situated in the main street of Cardigan town. This venue was a source of much ragging by my father, who reckoned that it would at least teach me how to drink. The schoolroom was on the first floor, entrance being via a side door and steep wooden staircase at the top of which was a landing that doubled as a cloak area. The room was dominated by a large arched window overlooking the hotel's courtyard. In days gone by, this yard was the hotel's coaching area with surrounding stables. The teacher's desk, blackboard and piano occupied the area fronting the window. The remainder of the room housed tables of various sizes around which we all sat. News of my impending change of school had spread through the local community and resulted in another family deciding that their son and daughter should also attend Bodowen School. Consequently, Llewellyn, the son of the local vet, and his younger sister Veronica were fellow passengers on the 8.15 a.m. Western Welsh bus that left Newport every morning, returning at five in the evening.

To attend school it was now necessary for me to be up by seven o'clock every morning. Following a quick breakfast, a twenty-minute bike ride on my shiny new bike brought me to the Golden Lion Tavern, where my father had arranged for my bike to be stored safely. At eight o'clock the bus would arrive and Llewellyn, Veronica and myself would climb aboard for the three-quarters-of-an-hour journey to Cardigan. Since it was a public bus the passengers were a varied crowd. There were two office workers, a solicitor, some early shoppers and a few farm workers who got off at various points of the journey. Other passengers who boarded the bus as it approached Cardigan were pupils attending the Cardigan Grammar School, a school that I hoped one day to attend.

The day at the Bodowen School was not dissimilar from that which I had experienced at Nevern Primary. It started with Miss Owen reading a short chapter from the Bible, and there then followed a children's hymn and a short concluding prayer. Lessons, however, were very different and we were grouped according to age and ability. Those pupils that would be attempting their scholarship examinations the following May, and of which I was one, were grouped together and set work by Miss Owen. This work was targeted towards the examination and consisted of endless examples of past questions that we were required to answer. Individual answers were then read out and discussed by the whole group, with Miss Owen highlighting which answers were good and which were not so good. I never heard her condemn any of our answers, always emphasising how they could be improved.

Morning milk was provided at the school, although lunch had either to be brought from home or we could go out into a café in the town. Usually, me and some of the friends that I had made since arriving at the school took the opportunity of walking around the town looking at shops and buying one of the many weekly comics that were on sale. My favourite comics were the *Champion*, *Hotspur* and *Wizard*. On occasions I would buy one of these, two friends would buy the others and after a few days we would exchange so that by the end of the week we had read all three.

The afternoon session at Bodowen followed that of the morning but with the emphasis on a different area of work and concluded with a short prayer read by Miss Owen, followed by the Lord's Prayer and the wish for a safe journey home.

My journey included a walk from the school to the bus station where a Roberts & Sons bus was waiting. This company operated jointly with the Western Welsh to provide a comprehensive service for the area. I usually arrived at Newport by five o'clock, collected my bike from the Golden Lion and was usually home by five thirty:

During the winter months this journey was on occasions difficult, with wind and rain not making the cycle ride very attractive, but I loved school and would brave the worst possible conditions to attend. Spring and summer were a different proposition, with the light nights due to the introduction of 'double-summertime' that was aimed at giving farmers more light hours for their work, making it possible for me to return home from school and spend another five hours out on the farm haymaking before it became dark.

The first six months at Bodowen Private School passed quickly and soon the date of the scholarship examination was known. The days leading up to this were hectic with Miss Owen advising on all aspects of the examination. Sitting the examination entailed attending the Cardigan County School one morning in early May.

The school was situated on the edge of the town on the road between Cardigan and Gwbert-on-Sea. The school was housed in a large, red-brick, single-storey building surrounding two quadrangles. There were two adjoining workshops and a further annex of three classrooms that had been built to accommodate the steady growth in pupil numbers. At the rear of the school were two tennis courts and a large playing field marked out as one hockey pitch and two rugby pitches in winter, and a cricket square and running track in the summer. The front of the school was bordered with lawns and a variety of shrubs, protected from the road by wrought-iron railings and two large wrought-iron gates. It was through these gates that I passed on that morning in May 1945, to sit an examination that was to change my life for ever. Entering the school with its long high corridors, numerous doors and continuous noise was a frightening experience. We were welcomed by a man in academic dress, who ushered us into one of the many classrooms, where we were seated at individual desks. Examination papers were given out; we were told when to start and when the examination would end. Then the scholarship was under way.

We all came out of the examination completely exhausted, but reasonably confident, since Miss Owen's tuition had been on target and all ten of us had been able to attempt all the questions. As we trooped out of the school we were met by Miss Owen, who had taken time off her other duties to ensure that her scholarship pupils, as she called us, were safe and sound. I was happy to see a familiar face. That afternoon Miss Owen, who by some means had obtained a copy of the examination paper, took us through all the questions, giving us further confidence in the outcome of the examination.

The following weeks flew by and the scholarship results were published. Of the ten pupils from Bodowen School, all were successful and would be commencing studies at the Grammar School the following September. Naturally, Miss Owen was delighted with the results and held a tea party for us all to celebrate our success.

When my family heard the news they were of course delighted, with my mother and Aunt Catherine making a great fuss of me. My father was less enthusiastic, again raising the costs involved by my attending grammar school for the next four or six years, although I had the feeling that secretly he was proud of my success.

That year the months of July and August seemed interminable, and although I was involved in the various activities of the farm, the thought of September and my new school was always at the back of my mind.

Work on the farm continued to increase due to the pressures of increased production to provide food for the UK. Rationing was at its hardest, and although living on the farm shielded us from the worst of the shortages, these were becoming more and more evident as the war dragged on… Through my listening to the radio on every conceivable occasion it became clear that the turning point in the war had been reached and passed. This was supported by the fact that there were an increasing number of American servicemen in the locality, while the number of Italian and German prisoners of war working on the farms continued to grow.

At long last September 1945 came, and I was off to my new school. My school uniform had been purchased a few weeks previously, by me, my mother and aunt taking the bus to Cardigan, where one clothes shop, Watts & Son, stocked all the Cardigan County School uniforms consisting, in my case, of a navy cap, a red and navy tie and a navy blazer, grey trousers being optional, as was a navy and red scarf. Although Llewellyn still attended Bodowen School, he had not tried the scholarship, and intended to leave school when fourteen, while his sister Veronica would not be sitting the scholarship until 1946. Their initial companionship on the journeys to and from school was, however, welcomed.

The first day at Cardigan County School is one that I shall never forget since it was so different from any of my previous experiences. The school had around 350 pupils on its roll, these coming from Cardigan itself and from the towns and villages of south Cardiganshire and north Pembrokeshire. Pupils were streamed into three streams according to ability, interests and past record of achievement. These streams that started as Forms 2a, 2b and 2m in the year of entry, went on to Forms 5a, 5b and 5m in the fourth year, when matriculation examinations were sat.

I found myself in Form 2b where the balance of subjects was towards the sciences, while Form 2a was biased towards the arts.

For pupils with no apparent aptitude and with a past record that showed some deficiencies, Form 2m appeared to have been deemed an appropriate starting point, with a balance of subjects that included practical subjects such as woodwork and metalwork.

On arriving at the school we were greeted by the assembly bell that went off at nine o'clock sharp, calling the whole school, both pupils and staff, to the main assembly hall for morning assembly. The assembly hall was a high, vaulted room with a raised stage at one end on which there was a piano, a row of chairs for the teaching staff and in the centre front, a lectern from which the headmaster addressed the assembly. The hall was packed, with the boys standing to the left and girls standing to the right of a central aisle that I later discovered was for the headmaster to make an entrance. At the instruction of the prefects who were senior pupils delegated authority by the headmaster, first-year pupils stood at the front, next to the stage, while the other year groups followed in chronological order. At the back of the hall stood the sixth-form boys and girls.

At five minutes past nine the double doors at the back of the hall were thrown open and in strode the headmaster, Thomas Evans MA. Tom Evans, as he was known locally, was a handsome man in his early fifties, of average height and weight with a fresh complexion. His greying hair was well groomed and topped a stern yet pleasant face with piercing blue eyes. He wore a dark pinstripe suit with an academic gown that hung low from his shoulders. Although this was the first time I had laid eyes on him, it was obvious to me even at that early stage that he was a man of authority with standards that he would not sacrifice.

Following the opening prayer by the headmaster, a familiar hymn was sung, followed by readings from the scriptures by the head boy and girl. The closing prayer by the headmaster was followed by a welcome to all new pupils and general school announcements. These included the results of any sporting activities involving the school, academic successes, and any bad behaviour by any pupils while off the school premises, subsequently reported to the headmaster.

Once assembly was over and the headmaster had departed, the senior master, W R Jones, dismissed the assembly with the exception of us the new entrants. Our names were than called out indicating the form that we had been allocated. Each form was introduced to its form master or mistress, who then conducted us along the long corridors to our respective form rooms. Our form master was a Mr Elvet Davies, and he gave us our weekly timetable of subjects, teachers and rooms. This we had to copy from the blackboard onto a card provided. We were told that the loss of this timetable would not be regarded as an excuse to miss or be late for a class. The rules and regulations of the school were then outlined together with information about who to contact should there be any problems. The form register was then taken. Shortly afterwards, the bell announcing the mid-morning break rang.

The remainder of the morning was spent locating the various classrooms and laboratories where the various specialist subjects would be taught. This was a worthwhile exercise when considering that my past experience was of being taught in one room by one teacher each and every day.

Lunchtime came and we all trouped along a corridor that led past the school kitchen to collect our meals from a serving hatch. The plated meal, consisting of a main course and a sweet, was then carried into the adjoining assembly hall that during lunch-times doubled as a dining hall and where long tables and benches had been set out. Two members of the teaching staff were always on duty to supervise lunchtimes, and ate their lunch at a table on the platform. The majority of pupils ate school meals, the exceptions being those who lived locally and could return home for lunch and those who brought their own sandwiches.

The afternoon saw our subject timetable come into operation, with the afternoon broken down into three forty-minute lessons, concluding with the end of day bell at 3.45 p.m. So, my first day at grammar school came to an end, a day that marked the beginning of a new chapter in my life.

Chapter Five

My days at the Cardigan County School were happy ones highlighted by many events that I will always remember.

I suppose that being essentially a Welsh-speaker living in a predominantly Welsh-speaking community, English had never been my strongest subject, although my aunt's reading of English stories had helped both my spelling and comprehension. My first English grammar teacher was Mr Idwal Jones, who was a middle-aged, grey-haired man with a face like an unmade bed. His one characteristic, in addition to being a good teacher, was his very sarcastic sense of humour. This usually took the form of, 'What's your name young man?'

'Edwin sir.'

'Really? Pity about that,' or 'Where do you come from, girl?'

'Nevern, sir.'

'Oh, I suppose someone must live there.'

His favourite was in relation to asking questions about a previous lesson of a pupil who he knew had been absent on that occasion. When he got the response of, 'I was absent, sir,' his usual comment was, 'No, that is not the answer I was looking for.' Mr Jones did, however, instil in me the basic rules of the language and the use of full stops, commas, brackets, apostrophes, capitals, inverted commas, what constituted a sentence, which word was the noun, pronoun, verb, adjective in a sentence, and how one should string sentences together to form paragraphs.

My first English Literature teacher was Miss Evans, a middle-aged spinster with a soft voice that she used to great effect when reading aloud poems or paragraphs from Shakespeare. Although during the first two years there were no set books or poems to follow, with Miss Evans choosing much of what we studied, forms 4 and 5 saw the introduction works set by the Matriculation Examination Board and which included such work as John Keats' 'Eve of St Agnes', and Shakespeare's *Hamlet*.

Mathematics was not among my favourite subjects until in the third form I came into contact with a new member of staff, a Mr Denzil Booth. It was 1946, the war in Europe had just ended, and some servicemen were making their return to civilian life. Mr Booth had been a pilot in the Fleet Air Arm. He was tall, with blonde hair and stood out among the rest of the staff through being so much younger and almost of a different generation. In a few short months he opened the doors to my understanding of mathematics, algebra and geometry. I grew to love equations, finding the unknown in algebra and calculation dimensions in geometry and trigonometry. At Matriculation I achieved a 98% average pass mark, to which Mr Booths' comment was, 'What happened to those two other marks you should have had?' Despite this I suspected that he was pleased.

Although history was not a subject high on my list of interests, history as taught by Mr Tregonyn was an experience. Mr Tregonyn was a Cornish man probably in his late sixties, with white receding hair, fresh complexion and bright blue eyes. He wore what we all thought was the oldest and most ragged academic gown in the school, which he frequently used to clean the blackboard. This board he used extensively and to good effect in representing events and the sequence of events in pictorial form, with easy to remember headings. Always having been interested in art and drawing, I took pleasure in copying his various maps and diagrams into my history notebook and then adding to them with drawings of Spanish galleons, castles, knights in armour and the like. Mr Tregonyn was always very pleased with my efforts, that were held up to the class, and in his words were examples of best practice.

Although I had little or no previous knowledge of the sciences, these soon became my favourite subjects of study, with biology and chemistry being joint first choice, and physics a close second.

Biology was taught by Miss Rowe, a most attractive Irish-born lady in her early thirties, who all us boys had a crush on. She was petite in stature with shoulder-length black hair, smiling dark brown eyes and a wide, generous mouth. The rumour in school was that the head had appointed her onto the staff just for her looks, although we found out later that Miss Rowe was also a very talented teacher. Again my ability and love of drawing was useful in the study of the structures of animal and plant life, and resulted in Miss Rowe regarding me as one of her best pupils.

Two members of staff undertook the teaching of chemistry. Inorganic chemistry was taught by Mr D J Hill, known to us all as 'DJ', while Organic and Physical chemistry was taught by Mr Bruce, known as 'Bruce'. DJ was a slight man who through ill health had not been called up into the Services. He was rather bird-like in appearance, was very precise in all his work and always wore a brown laboratory coat, which nobody saw him without. DJ never taught in a classroom and rarely left his beloved laboratory, which despite not having any technical assistance, was kept in immaculate order, with all the benches highly polished, the white china sinks clean and all the reagent bottles topped up to the required level. Being taught by DJ was, in addition to chemistry, an exercise in order and logical sequence. Whenever possible lessons had a practical component, with DJ demonstrating how the particular experiment should be carried out, and then allowing the class, working in pairs, to undertake it, observing the results, and then writing these up in our exercise books.

The writing-up of an experiment was, as far as DJ was concerned, a skill in itself, and had to follow a strict format. This format included the heading of the experiment, the apparatus and reagents used, the method, the results and the conclusions. All such headings had to be underlined in red ink with a clear margin on the left-hand side. Although at the time I might not have fully appreciated the reasons for this insistence on structure and sequence, there is little doubt that they served me well in the years that followed.

Bruce's approach to teaching was very different. He was a short, stocky Scotsman in his early sixties with a shock of white hair and a rumpled kind of face, which very occasionally would break into a wide smile. He limited himself to the occasional experiment that frequently did not turn out as expected and usually resorted to board work with the diagram of the carbon ring being ever present.

Physics was taught by a Mr Cecil Thomas who had been discharged from the Royal Navy having suffered a serious leg injury during the early years of the war. Although he was a university honours graduate, and was very knowledgeable of his subject, his ability to convey this to his class was not always successful. His experiments in the physics laboratory inevitably went wrong, at which point he would give the class the result and have us work out how it was achieved. The working out of mathematical problems also tended to end this way, with the result being given and the working out left to the class.

Matriculation in those days required, in addition to English, Mathematics and the subjects of one's choice, a second language, and at the Cardigan County School three languages could be studied, namely French, Latin and Welsh. During my first and second years I was obliged to study all three. The headmaster taught Latin since it was his favourite subject. It turned out, however, not to be my favourite subject, and eventually I ended up hating the subject. Since there were no more Romans around, I viewed it as no great loss, much to the displeasure of the headmaster.

Mr T Jones was the French master, and since we did not know what the 'T' stood for, and because of his short stature, he was known as Tiny Jones. There was little doubt that he was a good teacher, but to me French was the most difficult language to master, and although I could write most of the vocabulary, when it came to speaking French, Mr Jones and I parted company. During one lesson Mr Jones expressed the view that I was to French, what Winston Churchill was to Germany, and that my pronunciation of some French words should be banned. It was all done in a good spirit so I was not unduly upset and accepted the inevitable that French, as a second language, was not for me.

The only remaining alternative was Welsh, and with my existing knowledge it might be said that it was the easy option. In forms 2 and 3 Welsh was taught by a Miss Jones, a recent addition to the staff who originated from Caernarfon in north Wales. Welsh, as spoken in that part of Wales, is very different from the Welsh of south and west Wales, and for months the Welsh class had great difficulty in understanding Miss Jones, and she in turn understanding what we were saying. Gradually, however, the problem resolved itself and I and my fellow classmates became familiar with Welsh grammar with its mutations and change in word endings. As we progressed into forms 4 and 5 Welsh was taught by the deputy headmaster, WR Jones. He was a typical Welshman, stocky, dark hair and a swarthy complexion. WR, as he was usually referred to, was very talented in all matters Welsh, and had won many awards at the Welsh National Eisteddfod for poetry and writings. His jovial approach made him much liked by both pupils and colleagues on the staff, and his teaching always had a touch of typical Welsh humour.

So my academic subjects of study were determined and pursued into forms 4 and 5, and eventual Matriculation examinations.

Another important component of Cardigan County School was its sporting record in the areas of rugby, cricket and athletics. Physical education and games were compulsory subjects of the weekly timetable, with the games period for forms 4 and 5 taking place on Wednesday afternoons. These periods were the breeding ground of future members of the school's first fifteen in rugby, first eleven in cricket and the school's athletic team.

Although I had little or no knowledge of these sports when I entered the school, and my build and stature did not suggest anything special, three years on I had grown into a five foot eleven, twelve-stone rugby wing forward, a useful fast bowler and a commendable athlete specialising in middle-distance running, the mile and half-mile being my favourite distances. A great deal of this development was due to the sports master and my first form master, Mr Elvet Davies. Elvet was a Cambridge blue and had at some time in the past been given a rugby trial for Wales. His knowledge of all three sports that were pursued by the school was extensive. Once I had mastered the basics of the various sports, my enthusiasm was such that I spent hours practising various aspects at home on the farm – much to my father's displeasure, since when I was home I was to him that extra pair of hands.

By the time I was sixteen and in the fifth form, I was a member of the school's rugby first fifteen, and in the following summer played for the school at cricket and represented the school at athletics. This involvement in sporting activities resulted in my being away from the farm most Saturdays, since the school rugby team played such schools as Aberystwyth, Carmarthen, Haverfordwest, Tregaron and Llanelly, with one match being played away and one at home.

Results of all Saturday matches were announced by the headmaster at the following Monday morning's assembly, when he took great delight in drawing the attention of the school to any outstanding performance or any poor performance. There was one occasion when, due to no fault of my own, I missed the bus taking me to the school, consequently missing the game, and although I explained to the headmaster that I had been delayed at the farm due to my having to assist a cow give birth, I was never sure whether he believed me or not. In any case, my absence was announced at assembly, coupled by the fact that my failure to play was due to my being required to be present at a birth. This of course caused much merriment and resulted in my receiving several congratulations on becoming a father. To be fair to the headmaster, however, the occasion when I scored a try in an important match and in so doing received a broken nose, were equally reported upon the following Monday with graphic details of the blood (mine) that had been spilt for the honour of the school.

As I became more and more involved in school activities, so my input to the work on the farm decreased. My father by this time was approaching sixty and was suffering from arthritis in the shoulders and hands that made many physical tasks difficult for him to undertake. A consequence of this was that my mother had to take over more and more of the daily chores of the farm, and although there was never a word of complaint, there was little doubt that she was very tired on occasions. My aunt Catherine, although now in her early seventies, was still very active and carried out all the housework and ensured that all meals were ready and on the table when my mother and father came in from the farm. For my part, the school holidays were the busiest times of the year when I worked on the farm from dawn to dusk. This involvement had its compensations in that I learnt most of the farming skills and could compete with my contemporary friends who had left Nevern School and were now working full-time on farms.

Since my grandfather's death, my father had bought a small grey Ferguson tractor that had replaced the two heavy shire horses previously used for ploughing and harvesting. This purchase had proved a sound investment, and with the various farm equipment modified for use with the tractor, as opposed to horses, my father no longer had to walk behind or alongside the horses and could ride comfortably on the tractor. Driving the tractor was also one of my favourite occupations alongside its general maintenance, which my father was not particularly interested in or good at doing. Milking, feeding and stock welfare was also on my schedule of talents, and although my interests lay elsewhere, I became competent at injecting cattle, assisting in the birth of calves and lambs, and general stock and crop husbandry.

The winter of 1947/8 brought both school and farm to a grinding halt. I had set off for school as usual, despite my father's warning that snow was on its way. Everything was normal at assembly and for the first lesson then it began to snow, not light flurries, but large thick flakes that immediately settled. At ten thirty the assembly bell rang and the headmaster announced that the school was being closed and that we should make our way home as quickly as possible. Those of us who travelled south on the Cardigan to Newport road were told on arrival at the bus station that the service was not operating since buses were either already stranded or unable to negotiate the hills. There were six of us. Veronica, who was now at the County School; John Dalymount, who was in my class; his older sister Margaret and her friend Mona; and another boy called Bryn. We decided that we should try and walk, and although on reflection this could have ended in disaster, off we went on what at the time was a great adventure. The snow had eased a little, but underfoot the going was hard. Nevertheless we covered the first four miles by two o'clock in the afternoon, not having encountered any other walkers or vehicles during that time. Then out of the late afternoon gloom we saw an approaching car that I immediately recognised as the old Humber that my father hired on occasions. Apparently, my father was in Newport, and on finding out that the bus service was no longer running, had decided that either we were still in Cardigan or had decided to walk, in either case he viewed the taxi as the only means of getting us safely home, and consequently had hired the car, instructing the driver to follow the bus route and hopefully locate and pick us up. Although walking through the snow had been great fun, we were all glad to pile into the Humber, that with its great weight and with snow chains made light of the conditions.

It snowed for three days and nights and as the wind got up drifts of up to twelve and fifteen feet were formed. There followed days of hard frost and nothing could move. Deep Well Farm was completely isolated and the roads were blocked for four weeks by frozen snowdrifts so high that one could walk on top of them and touch the telephone wires.

All farm animals had to be housed and fed indoors, with milk, after a few days, poured away since there were no storage facilities.

Although the school opened after two weeks, attendance was low since so many pupils were in a similar situation to myself. I did my fair share of revision and homework and ensured that this disruption would not affect my long-term objective of gaining matriculation and being able to enter the sixth form.

One of the highlights of the school year was the Christmas Dance, held just prior to the Christmas holidays and involving the fifth and sixth forms. This event, held in the school's gymnasium, commenced at seven o'clock, with a formal dinner in the dining hall at eight, followed by dancing until around eleven o'clock. This being my first attendance and since it would be very difficult for me to return home at that time, it was arranged that I would stay overnight with John Dalymount on his farm. John and his sister Margaret also attended, as did Margaret's friend Mona. Since Mona was in a similar situation to myself in being unable to return home at a late hour, she also stayed overnight on the Dalymount farm.

Mona was a very attractive girl with auburn hair, dark brown eyes and a fair complexion, with a figure that belied her years with slim hips and well-developed breasts. She travelled to school on the same bus as myself and I had often longed to ask her out, but had never plucked up enough courage.

One of the rituals of the school dance was that during the pre-dinner session boys found themselves partners to escort into dinner and for the dancing after. I was determined to ask Mona to be my partner as the last pre-dinner dance ended and we waited for the announcement that 'dinner is served'. Our eyes met and I was on the point of making my way to her side, when another girl in the lower sixth named Eira came over and whispered, 'Will you be my partner?' Inexperience and with an element of shyness where girls were involved, prevented me from saying anything except, 'Alright.' I looked over at Mona but she avoided my gaze.

Eira Jones was a pretty girl with jet-black hair, blue eyes and a very white skin. She had a great smile and an equally great sense of humour.

I escorted her into dinner and for the rest of the evening we either danced or sat in the corner of the gymnasium holding hands. Towards the end of the evening Eira suggested that we go for a walk before catching our transport home. Out in the darkness of the school grounds, I vividly recall Eira's warm, inviting lips as she pressed her body against me, whispering that she hoped we could do this again.

That night as a lay in a strange bed, my thoughts were in turmoil. Although I could still feel Eira's lips on mine, and her perfume in my nostrils, all I could think of was Mona being escorted into dinner by another boy, dancing with him all night and now sleeping in the adjoining room.

Chapter Six

In the post-Christmas period my year in the fifth form was characterised by a significant increase in my social life due to continued involvement with Eira, and although Mona never left my thoughts, Eira was good company, fun to be with, and we got on really well. Saturday afternoons saw us at the local picture house known as the Pavilion, where the darkness was highly conducive to some serious necking and petting that Eira was most amenable to. Matinee performances used to end at around seven thirty in the evening, and in keeping with many other young couples, a stroll in the woods adjoining the school playing fields, which could be accessed without entering the school grounds, was the order of the day. It was on these occasions that my church upbringing was tested to the limit. Rugby occupied the remainder of my leisure time, and as spring turned to summer, cricket and athletics. Often, I would cycle the eight-odd miles from home to the school, play a game of cricket or run a half-mile race and cycle home again. Despite these activities and the occasional task on the farm, I never put my studies at risk and used to study for two hours before getting ready for school. My year in the Form 5b culminated with my sitting the Matriculation Examinations of the Welsh Joint Education Committee in English Language, English Literature, Welsh Language, Biology, Chemistry, Physics, Arithmetic, Algebra, and Geometry. All subjects were examined through sitting three-hour theory papers, plus, in the case of Welsh Language, a test relating to spoken Welsh.

In those days, examination results were published in the *Western Mail* on the same day as they were received by the school, and I vividly recall that August morning cycling to the news-agent's in Newport to purchase the paper, and under the heading of the school, checking my results, then cycling back home to tell the family that I had achieved a grade A in all papers with the exception of English Language were I had a grade B. My mother and aunt were crying with happiness and even my father was pleased.

The following day I cycled to the school to meet some classmates and report to the headmaster. Tom Evans was pleased to see me, and stretching out his hand over the large desk that occupied most of his study, said, 'Congratulations, young man, and welcome to the sixth form.' The following September I entered the lower sixth to study botany, chemistry, physics and zoology.

That September also saw Eira, having completed her sixth form studies, leaving for medical school, while Mona left to commence studies at a teacher training college. Many of my colleagues in the school's rugby team had also left to take up studies at college or university, and in many ways things would never be the same again.

Sixth-form study, I discovered, was very different from that I had previously experienced, and involved a much less stressful timetable with periods set aside for private study. Although my initial choice of subjects had been botany, chemistry and zoology, I was persuaded that the inclusion of physics would give me better career options and study at university. Miss Rowe had by now left the school and the post of biology tutor had been taken over by a Miss Price. Miss Price was a somewhat plain lady in her mid-forties, had straight, light brown hair and a serious expression that only occasionally broke into a smile. She was, however, a great teacher and her lessons in both botany and zoology were always well illustrated, explained and presented. Her practical skills in dissecting both plants and animals were outstanding and difficult to match, although she admitted as the year progressed that I was getting close. Inorganic chemistry was taught by Mr Hill, while physical chemistry and organic chemistry were taught by Mr Bruce. Physics continued to be taught by Cecil Thomas.

Due to the high practical content of all four subjects, all pupils were required to wear white laboratory coats, which we frequently kept on while walking around the school, since it gave an air of superiority over those in the sixth form studying history, English or some other subject.

Being in the sixth form also brought its responsibilities, with some of us being appointed prefects. The prefect system that had been introduced into the school by Tom Evans was aimed at promoting leadership qualities in the sixteen to eighteen age group, while at the same time removing some of the routine supervisory tasks from the teaching staff. I was proud when the head announced in assembly that I would be one of the school's prefects, and was invited onto the stage to have a prefect's badge pinned to my lapel.

My next personal highlight was in relation to the school's rugby team, when following the loss of several players, including the captain, a new captain was required, and although this honour went to an upper-sixth player, I was nominated vice captain. This gave me a great uplift and resulted in my doubling my efforts as a player, resulting in my being selected for the Cardiganshire County Team to play Carmarthenshire, and later as a player in the Joint Cardiganshire, Carmarthenshire and Pembrokeshire team, to play east Wales. These matches were the prelude to the Welsh School Boys Trial and eventual Welsh National Team.

Now that Eira and Mona had left the school, my next encounter with the opposite sex came at the Cardigan Fair held annually on 10 November. Although this fair had its origins as a 'Hiring Fair' when farm labours and domestic servants seeking new employment came in the hope of being hired, and farmers offered their stock and produce in readiness for Christmas, the fair was now dominated by a field full of amusements, swings, roundabouts, dodgems and the like. Powered by two huge gleaming steam traction engines, that drove electric dynamos, the fairground with its hundreds of light bulbs resembled fairyland and was a great attraction to all ages.

I met Thelma on the dodgems when we both got into the same car. Thelma was in the fifth form at school and we had often talked, joked and laughed during school time. She was a pretty red-haired girl with blue eyes and a freckled complexion and I had frequently admired her when she was playing netball in the school quadrangle. When the ride ended and I asked her what she would like to do next, to my surprise she said, 'Let's get out of here, I have a boyfriend who is away, and I don't want others to see us together.' We made our way out of the brightly-lit fair-ground down the back streets of the town to the banks of the River Tivey. Although being November there was a chill in the night air, we were soon wrapped in each other's arms with Thelma kissing me with a passion that I am never likely to forget. With my raincoat on the grass and her coat over us, we spent the evening in a cocoon isolated from the world and from reality until it was time for us to catch our respective buses home.

Although I continued to frequent the Pavilion on Saturday nights following a rugby match, it was with my friends on the team, and girls were not involved. Then just before Christmas I met Catherine. She was a friend of one of the girls in the fifth form, but had herself not attempted the scholarship examinations and had not progressed beyond her local school. This I found out later was due to the fact that her mother, who had been left a widow at an early age, was unable to provide the financial support necessary when attending grammar school. Catherine at eighteen was the youngest of three sisters; her eldest sister had recently married, her other sister was a nurse, while she worked as a domestic in a local manor house. Catherine was a short, blonde haired, fair-skinned and well-proportioned girl with a pleasant smile and quiet disposition.

Our first date was a matinee performance at the Pavilion, followed by a stroll along the main road leading from the bus station. At that stage I discovered that not all girls were like Eira and Thelma and that Catherine would not be setting my world alight. We enjoyed each other's company, however, and our relationship continued for around eighteen months, when I left school.

In many ways Catherine's quiet and undemanding nature helped me to concentrate on my studies and to the successful completion of my first year in the sixth form. The demands of my final year at school were ever greater in so far as that in the September, I was privileged to be made the school's head boy and also captain of the rugby team. Both these honours I accepted gladly since they were far in excess of anything that I had ever dreamed of.

One aspect of my sixth-form studies was the compulsory thesis in botany. After choosing the study of ferns as my topic, I spent many hours collecting, pressing, drawing and investigating the internal structure and spore formation of around a dozen species. This kind of study I found most rewarding, and one where I could use my drawing skills to best advantage, and did, I believe, contribute to the desire to undertake original research later in my career.

My dissecting skills were also of great satisfaction to me. Tracing the blood supply to and from the various organs, and tracing the nerves of the central nervous system and autonomic nervous systems, was a learning process that I can recall to this day and probably prompted my thoughts in respect of a career in medicine. Qualitative and quantitative analysis of elements and compounds in inorganic and organic chemistry were a joy to undertake, while experiments in physical chemistry and physics gave me a great deal of satisfaction as well as being an excellent vehicle for learning and understanding.

In the October of my second year in the sixth form, my father was suddenly taken ill and was diagnosed with having pneumonia. Since there were no antibiotics available at that time, his treatment centred round the use of the newly introduced M & B drug. For eight days and nights my father fought for his life, with a high temperature and fever, then on the ninth night his fever broke and the following morning Dr Davies declared that the worse was over, although my father remained bedridden for another month. Throughout this time my aunt Catherine had nursed my father, seeing to all his needs, while my mother had single-handedly ensured that the basics of farm tasks were undertaken. Milking presented her with the biggest problem and on many occasions by starting early I was able to help, and would milk four or five cows before setting out for school. On returning home in late afternoon I would ensure that animal feed was ready for distribution the following morning and would wash down the cowshed, dairy and yard ready for milking the next day. At this time I worried about my mother and the workload she was carrying, and following the slow recovery of my father, which involved him learning to walk, I persuaded them that farm stock had to be reduced and that future crops should be planned and managed to cut down the workload at harvest times.

October also saw my eighteenth birthday when my aunt reminded me of my grandfather's gift of the ruby ring which she had kept safely all this time. She gave the ring to me with the warning, 'Don't you dare lose this. It was special to your grandfather and your Great Uncle John.' It was against this background that I prepared for my advanced levels.

The examinations at Higher Certificate, as it was then known, consisted of four-hour practical examinations and two three-hour theory papers in each subject of study. Questions in both theory and practical covered the whole of the two-year course of study. Practical examinations took place first followed a few weeks later by the theory papers.

In addition to the Higher Certificate examinations there were optional scholarship examinations that could be taken, with the possibility of the results qualifying for a state scholarship. Since these were optional, and I had never considered the possibility of gaining a state scholarship, I did not attempt these examinations.

In the period leading up to the examinations there was the additional task of writing off to the various university colleges requesting details of the courses on offer and seeking application forms. This task I found difficult, since I was torn between a career in teaching biological sciences or in the practise of medicine. In the early 1950s there was only one medical school in Wales based in Cardiff, and since the University College of South Wales and Monmouthshire was also based in Cardiff and had close links with the school of medicine, in addition to providing the relevant biological sciences, I decided that my applications would be restricted to these two institutions. In addition, I had no wish to venture outside Wales, and wanted to be within reasonable travelling distance of home.

My mother, father, Aunt Catherine and myself had visited Cardiff on one occasion back in 1948, to visit Aunt Pattie who was my great-grandfather's youngest daughter and had come to Cardiff to live with her eldest sister, Maria. Pattie had subsequently married a David Jones and lived in Beauchamp Street in Riverside, while he worked at the National Museum of Wales. Aunt Pat, as she was known, was only five years older than my aunt Catherine and they had communicated by weekly letters ever since Pattie left Pembrokeshire. Being very close, the news that Pattie, who by now had been widowed, was in St David's Hospital and probably would not live much longer was very upsetting to my aunt, who immediately decided to hire a car for our journey from Nevern to Cardiff. Following our visit to the hospital, where a very frail, white-haired lady in her seventies was delighted to see her niece, my mother and father and me, we left to have a look around the city. We visited the museum where David had worked as one of the curators, and walked by the castle wall with its range of sculptured animals, and observed the trams that clattered along the rails embedded in the then still cobbled streets. I was so impressed with all I saw that I promised then that one day I would return.

Since the small town of Kenfig Hill was on our return route, it was decided that we would pay a visit to another cousin, Lois Marsden. Lois was the daughter of my grandfather's brother John Marsden, who, following his marriage at St Brynnach Church, Nevern around 1885, left the family home to live in Cardiff and train as a master mariner. He had six children of which Lois was one, the others being George, himself a master mariner who died in active service during the First World War; Andrew, who died when he was seventeen years of age; Eloda, who became a qualified pharmacist and died in 1936; Berti, a qualified marine engineer; and Eddie, yet another master mariner. Cousin Lois was herself a qualified optician and ran a retail pharmacy shop in Kenfig Hill. My first impression of Aunt Lois, as she was known to me, was of a medium build, very smartly-dressed lady with her light-brown hair held in a bun and framing a pleasant face with grey, twinkling eyes that matched her charm and sense of humour. Lois had never married and at the age of forty-six considered herself a born spinster. The visit was generally uneventful, with Lois enquiring as to how we had found Pattie, and expressing her pleasure at my being at grammar school and not following my grandfather and father into farming. Following a traditional late afternoon tea with bread and butter and jam, scones with cream and tea poured from a silver teapot into bone china cups, our visit came to an end and we proceeded on the long journey back to Deep Well Farm.

In early June of that year, I received conditional acceptances from both the Welsh School of Medicine and the University College of South Wales and Monmouthshire, for entry the following October. In keeping with most summer examinations, June and July of that year were sunny and hot, with laboratories and examination rooms hot and clammy. At long last the final examination was over, and I knew that regardless of the results, the next few months would be free of study.

At home, haymaking was almost complete with the hayrick giving off that wonderful smell of maturing hay. Due to the dairy herd having been reduced, the horses having been exchanged for the tractor, and with the calf-rearing enterprise having been disbanded, the amount of winter hay, straw and feed had been greatly reduced. Consequently the demands of the corn harvest were much reduced, as indeed was the income from the crop enterprises.

Come the first week of August and the examination results were published in the *Western Mail* under the names of the various grammar schools. The fact that I had achieved a grade A in all examination papers was beyond my belief and resulted in my cycling to the school that very morning to confirm their accuracy.

When I saw the head he immediately took me to task as to why I had not attempted the optional scholarship papers, since in his opinion and based on my results the school would have had a state scholar. His wrath was, however, short lived, and he warmly congratulated me on my success and wished me well in the future.

Chapter Seven

Having received acceptances from both the School of Medicine and the University College in mid August, together with information relating to student accommodation and detailed study programmes, it was decision time and I decided to accept the University College offer to study biological sciences, including physiology and biochemistry. According to the study programmes, these subjects, for the first two years, were common with those pursued by medical students, and it would appear that transfer between courses was possible at a later stage.

Once my acceptance had been confirmed the next few weeks were fully occupied with seeking financial assistance by means of a student grant from the Local Education Authority, and finding accommodation in Cardiff.

At that time hostel accommodation at any university was either very limited or non-existent. In the case of Cardiff I had been sent details of a hostel for male students run by a religious order known as the Community of the Resurrection. On consulting the vicar of Nevern Church, I decided to make application that the vicar, the Reverend D J Roberts, was kind enough to support with a covering letter. A week later I received an invitation to visit St Teilo's Hall, with a view to being accepted as a resident for three years.

My father, who by now had come to accept the fact I would not be following him into farming, decided to accompany me to Cardiff.

St Teilo's Hall was situated in the Roath area of Cardiff, and consisted of a rambling three-storey building situated at the end of a road known as St Margaret's Crescent, that adjoined the Protestant church of St Margaret's. The hall overlooked one of the many flower parks of Cardiff and the overall setting and appearance was one that my father and I were pleased with.

On arrival we were ushered in to the office of the warden, Father Pearce. Farther Pearce was a man of average build wearing the traditional black cassock and clerical collar of a priest. Three other members of the order formed the management staff, supported by a cook who undertook all the catering, and a number of cleaners. Thirty students could be accommodated at the hall at any one time, ranging from those in their first year to those in their final year of study. Areas of study by students covered the whole spectrum of university work, with arts, engineering, science, and medical students all sharing the accommodation, which consisted of a majority of double-study bedrooms and a few single-study bedrooms, which were usually allocated to the most senior students. Following a brief tour of the premises, that identified the dining hall, common room and table-tennis room, I was asked for my reaction to it all and whether I would be accepting the offer of a place. I was obviously delighted with this offer, which it transpired was triggered by the supporting letter from the vicar of Nevern, together with the fact that I was going to study biological sciences, an area that included Father Pearce's hobby, as amateur entomologist, of collecting bugs.

We returned home with much satisfaction, with my father viewing St Teilo's as a good home while at university.

The next weeks flew by with my mother and aunt busy preparing clothes that I would need to take, and giving instructions as to how they should be washed and generally looked after. There was also the question as to whether I should take my bike with me and so make getting round Cardiff easer and less costly. Having seen the vast numbers of bikes in use in Cardiff, I was convinced that this was the way forward, and decided that my bike would form part of my luggage

By mid September my Local Education Authority had advised me that I had been awarded a full student scholarship covering college and accommodation fees. It was then left to my aunt Catherine to provide a modest expenses allowance, which she had always promised, should I gain university entrance.

The last weeks of September I spent helping on the farm and doing those jobs that were of long standing but had never been done. I also visited school friends, some who had gone into employment and others, like myself, who were about to embark on a programme of college study. It would appear from numerous conversations that I was the only sixth-former from the school who was going to study at Cardiff, the majority going to Aberystwyth, Swansea or Bangor University Colleges or Wrexham Teacher Training College.

During the week prior to my leaving, Catherine invited me to an evening meal at her sister's house in Newport. Her sister Martha had recently married a native of Newport and was busy setting up house. We had a pleasant meal, and after saying my farewells to Martha and her husband, Catherine and I went for a stroll that ended with our embracing, kissing and promising to keep in touch, but with no firm commitment to the future. It was the only time I had seen Catherine show any emotion, and I took my leave with a heavy heart and the feeling that girls were difficult to understand.

The following week saw me boarding a train at Fishguard railway station that would take me to Cardiff. My leaving home for the first time was a traumatic experience for my mother and aunt and we all parted with tears in our eyes and the promise that we would write every week. My father, who had hired a taxi to take me to the station, decided to accompany me and to ensure that the luggage and bike were safely installed in the guard's van.

With a hiss of steam and a bellowing of smoke the train moved slowly out of the station and I was embarking on a life very far removed from that previously experienced on a Pembrokeshire farm.

It was late evening before I arrived at St Teilo's. Parking my bike in the cycle shed at the rear, which I had noted on my previous visit, I reported, suitcase in hand, to Father Pearce, who promptly handed me over to his fellow priest Father Herdson, who escorted me to my room. Father Herdson had apparently been a boxer in a previous career and carried the scars of a broken nose and scarred eyebrows. His appearance seemed at odds with the black priest's cassock, clerical collar and open sandals. My room was a double-study bedroom located on the ground floor adjacent to the rear entrance to the hall. A large Victorian fireplace that housed a small gas fire fed through a coin meter dominated one wall. Two single beds, two desks and two wardrobes completed the furnishings. One bed was positioned below a large double window overlooking the rear yard, while the other occupied the opposite wall. A single light bulb was the only source of illumination while the only vestige of a central-heating system consisted of one large pipe running along one wall at floor level. My roommate, Leslie Bevan, who had arrived a few hours earlier and was busy unpacking, greeted me on arrival. Les, as he came to be known, originated from the town of Brecon in mid Wales and had been accepted to study engineering. He was a tall, thin young man with black spiky hair that stood on end topping a permanently smiling face that sported a pair of very large ears.

Our initial introductions and conversation were cut short by the clanging of the hand bell that summoned all to the evening meal.

The dining hall at St Teilo's was a long room with a top table at one end, flanked on both sides by two long tables that ran the length of the room, terminating in a large serving hatch, behind which was the hall's kitchen. Father Pearce sat at the centre of the top table together with the oldest member of the community – Father Barns, who was approaching ninety years of age – and some of the most senior of the students. Father Herdson sat at the head of one of the side tables with Father Patie on the other.

Father Patie was a rather stout, medium built man in his late fifties. Originally from Ireland, he had twinkling eyes, the Irish wit and sense of humour that endeared him to the majority of students.

When were seated, Father Pearce rose to welcome all students, both new and those returning for their second or third years. This brief welcome was followed by grace that was said in Latin.

The meal was uneventful, and ended with Father Pearce offering thanks for the meal, again in Latin.

I went off to my room to unpack, storing my belongings as tidily as was possible in the limited space available. I had just completed this task when the hand bell sounded for Complin in the hall's chapel. Attendance, as we had been told, was completely voluntary and a matter of personal choice. Both Les and myself decided that we would give it a miss on the first night since we were both somewhat exhausted by the events of the day.

Having had a wash in one of the communal bathrooms I was ready for bed when a knock on the door announced visitors, namely our neighbours in the adjoining rooms. They introduced themselves as David Pryce and David Price, thereafter known as David 1 and David 2. David Pryce was a vicar's son from Somerset studying philosophy and English, while David Price came from the Midlands and was studying Honours French. Although only in the second year at St Teilo's they each had a single-study bedroom.

At this stage I discovered that Les, due to his having been brought down from Brecon by car, had brought with him many useful accessories, which I could not have hoped to carry, and in a few minutes he had water boiling in a coffee pot on a small electric hob, dug out four assorted mugs from his wardrobe, a bottle of Camp coffee and some sugar from his desk drawer, and soon we were all enjoying some black sweet coffee. And so my first day at St Teilo's came to an end, and I could but think of how lucky I had been and how different it would have been if my first day in Cardiff had been spent on my own in lodgings in a private house.

Chapter Eight

The first week of the college session was known as freshers' week. During this week all the various formalities of university entry are completed and first-year students are introduced to the various rules and regulations of the college and to college life in general. My first day started with breakfast and then, in keeping with other first-year students, taking the trolley bus into the city centre. A five-minute walk took me to the main university building in Cathays Park, where the rest of the morning was taken up with formal enrolment. Then back to St Teilo's for lunch. The afternoon I spent in the college library checking the book lists that I had been given and deciding which books I would need to buy, before returning for the evening meal. The following days followed the same pattern with interviews with the various departmental professors and a meeting addressed firstly by the vice chancellor of the college and then by the president of the students' union. Students were then introduced to the various college societies and invited to join. The week ended with the freshers' dance on the Saturday evening when following the evening meal all the freshmen at St Teilo's made their way to the students' union building situated in Cathays Park. I had just arrived at the dance hall when the door opened and in came Eira Jones. Whether she was there by design or accident I never discovered, but we ended up dancing together for most of the evening, and when it was over, we took the trolley bus to her lodgings, which were within half a mile of St Teilo's Hall. We kissed and embraced as we had done in the past, but from my part it was not as it had been, and although as we said goodnight promised that we would keep in touch, this was not to be and I never saw Eira again.

The following week studies began, and my days were occupied by lectures and practical sessions in my various subjects of study. The delivery of information was very different from that experienced at school, while the lecturers were far more distant than the staff at Cardigan County School. Lectures usually involved around thirty students in a lecture theatre, a far cry from the six seated around a table at school. The quality of the lectures was, however, excellent, and some members of staff I shall always remember with affection. Professor James Borough, head of the Zoology Department, was one such member. He was a tall, lean man who had come to Cardiff from the north of England. His receding hairline made him appear older than he really was, while his dress, which was always a rough tweed suit, gave him a countrified look. His teaching was superb and his list of books that he recommended we should buy were the first on my list. Another such member of staff was Professor McLain, head of the Botany Department. He was a tall, white-haired, Scotsman with an international reputation in his subject, and who could make the most boring of topics become interesting. The third member was Dr Bassett, an organic/biochemist who resembled the ultimate university professor in every way. He was a medium built, elderly man sporting long, white hair over a thin, white face dominated by a pair of large spectacles, which if not on his nose, were perched high up on his forehead. His academic gown had traces of acid burns, while his suit was threadbare and had seen better days. He was, however, a great communicator and he fired my enthusiasm for biochemistry.

Practical sessions were usually timetabled for a whole morning or afternoon, and in the case of organic and biochemistry, on Saturday mornings. The younger members of the departmental academic staff and the departmental technicians supervised practical sessions, although the professor usually visited the laboratory, circulating and gradually identifying each and every student.

I loved the practical classes and was able to show off those skills that I had acquired at school. Practical sessions also presented the opportunity of talking to other students, comparing results and solving problems. One such student pursuing the same subjects as myself, although in her second year of study, was Sylvia Elston. Sylvia came from the town of Brecon and was a beautiful, petite girl with long brown hair that she kept in a bun at the nape of her neck, and a figure worthy of a magazine cover. We found that we had similar rural backgrounds, with her widowed father being the reservoir keeper at the Usk Reservoir, where he lived with Sylvia's younger sister. We got on really well and enjoyed each other's company, and although Sylvia told me she had a long-term boyfriend who was now at Cardiff studying engineering, she did nothing to discourage my attentions, and agreed that we could meet some evenings as long as it was in secret.

Sylvia was a resident of Aberdare Hall, the girls' hostel at the university. This was a large, Victorian style, red-brick building in its own grounds adjoining Cathays Park that housed around seventy students. Due to an increase in student enrolments, Aberdare Hall had acquired another two three-storey houses about fifty yards from the main building, and Sylvia had a study bedroom in one of these houses, known as Number Eleven. What transpired was that on designated evenings I would cycle past Number Eleven whistling a few bars of an agreed tune, then Sylvia would slip out and we would spend an hour or so in the adjoining park in each other's arms, wishing that the rest of the world would go away.

As Christmas approached, there were end of term tests in the various subjects, while on the social side there was the annual St Teilo's Christmas Concert. This was held in St Margaret's Church Hall and was the opportunity for the talented residents of St Teilo's to display their skills, either by adapting topical words to well-known songs, producing short humorous sketches, or performing on the piano or other musical instruments. It was also the opportunity for residents to bring along their girlfriends or family members should they wish. Due to my clandestine relationship with Sylvia, I was unable to invite her, but did not feel isolated since the majority of my colleagues did not have regular girlfriends or had girlfriends at home. I was surprised at the hidden talent that existed in St Teilo's and although not personally involved, I thoroughly enjoyed the evening. The following week I was on the train for Fishguard, and Christmas on the farm.

It felt strange sleeping in my old room again, and the familiar furniture now looked old and tired. Although I had written to my mother every week I had been away, and had received letters in return, the next few days were spent answering the endless questions that my mother kept asking about Cardiff, the college, and my new friends, and me trying to catch up with everything that had happened on the farm and whether there were any new problems that I was not aware of.

The post-war period was one that saw agriculture developing rapidly, and through a system of government grants and allowances most farmers were experiencing a rise in their standard of living. Tractors and cars were the order of the day, and although we did not have a car, the overall income from the farm was more than the expenditure, which was a change from the pre-war situation. My father was now sixty-two and suffering a great deal of pain from arthritis that the cold damp winters did not help. My mother, however, remained fit and active and being twenty-five years his junior was able to keep the farm business afloat.

Two days before Christmas the postman delivered a Christmas card from Sylvia, which of course prompted my mother to ask numerous questions as to what she looked like, was she nice and where did she come from? I was able to respond to most of these questions but left out the bit about it being a secret relationship and not likely to develop any further.

Christmas Day was as I had always remembered, with the traditional goose served in the dining room, followed by the family gathering round the radio listening to the Queen's Christmas Message.

Soon the holiday was over, and I was once more on board the train taking me back to Cardiff. In my luggage was my rugby kit, since I had been approached by the captain of Cardiff Medical School's rugby team, who was a fourth-year medical student at St Teilo's, with an invitation to have a run-out with the team if I was interested. Also tucked away safely in my hand luggage was my grandfather's ruby ring.

The next major event in the St Teilo's calendar was the annual dinner and dance. Traditionally this was held in late February at the Angel Hotel, Cardiff, and was a full evening dress and partner event. Once again I found myself wondering what to do about inviting a partner. I viewed the chances of Sylvia accepting as remote, but felt I had to ask her. My delight was unbounded when she said yes, subject to my agreeing that as far as her boyfriend Brian was concerned, she would tell him that the invitation was a purely platonic arrangement due to my having a girlfriend back home who was unable to attend. I agreed, and set about preparing for the big night. I bought an evening dress shirt and bow tie, and in keeping with most of my colleagues, hired my dress suit from Moss Bros. I ordered a white camellia for Sylvia and arranged for a taxi to collect us from Aberdare Hall to take us to the Angel Hotel. For the first time since leaving home I wore my grandfather's ruby ring.

Sylvia, in a strapless, off-the-shoulder pale blue gown with silver shoes, gloves and clutch bag, looked absolutely stunning and our entrance was the centre of much attention and comment. Father Pearce appeared most impressed with my partner, while Father Patie whispered the words of the song of 'Who is Sylvia, What is she?' Following the dinner, we had our photographs taken by the resident photographer and then danced to a live band until five minutes to midnight when the festivities came to an end. Sylvia and I made an early exit from the ballroom and on walking down the stairs to the reception hall in search of a taxi a memorable night came to an end. In the hall was Brian, complete with taxi driver, to take his girlfriend home. I looked at Sylvia and her eyes said it all. I bid her goodnight and walked out into the dark of Westgate Street.

Since we had been the first to leave, the episode in the reception area had not been observed by any of the others, and was never mentioned. The walk back to St Teilo's was long and lonely and I promised myself that I would never again become involved in such a situation that would always end in grief.

The next day, being Saturday, saw me in the biochemistry laboratory engrossed in practical work. Around eleven o'clock one of the technicians came to tell me that I was wanted outside. In the long, arched corridor outside the laboratory was a red-eyed, pale-faced Sylvia. Coming to me with tears in her eyes, she expressed her sadness and guilt at how the previous evening had ended, how she had no idea that Brian would come and collect her, and how my walking out had made her realise how much I had become part of her life.

I could only hold and comfort her by saying that I was sure it would all work out if destined to do so. Little did I know that over twenty years would pass before I held Sylvia in my arms again.

The rest of the term I devoted to my studies and to playing the occasional game of rugby for Cardiff Medicals.

Easter came and once more I was home on the farm. On Easter Saturday I discovered that there was to be a dance at the Memorial Hall at Newport, and since this was a new innovation, decided to attend. On entering the hall, the very first person I saw was Mona. For a moment I thought that my eyes were playing tricks on me, and could hardly believe she was there. I immediately went over and asked her for a dance. She appeared pleased to see me and for the rest of the evening we danced and talked. Apparently, Mona had completed her two-year Teachers' Certificate at Wrexham, had obtained a teaching post at a primary school in Harrow on the Hill, and was now enjoying a few days' holiday with her married sister Loma, who lived in Newport. She, in turn, wanted to know how university life was treating me, and the evening ended with my walking her home to her sister's house and for the first time taking her in my arms and kissing her as I had wanted to all those years before.

During the following week I saw Mona on numerous occasions and on the following Saturday we took the bus to Cardigan and went to see the film showing at the Pavilion. We did not see much of the film, but the warmth of Mona's kisses and the thrill of being close together I shall always remember.

All too soon the Easter vacation was over, with Mona returning to her school in Harrow, and me to Cardiff. True to her promise Mona wrote on a weekly basis and I responded.

Two events dominated the summer term at Cardiff. One was the annual Rag Week when lectures were cancelled and the student population were engaged in activities designed to raise money for a specific charity, and which ended with the Rag Ball at the City Hall. The other was the field trip organised by the college for those students studying biological sciences and which this particular year was based at Aberfeldy, a small village just north of Loch Tay and south of Pitlochry in Scotland.

As soon as I had details of the Rag Ball that was always held on the Saturday of Rag Week, I wrote to Mona inviting her to Cardiff for the weekend. She immediately wrote back saying that she would love to come.

I booked a room for Mona at one of the many private hotels in Newport Road, and then set about hiring an evening suit, ordering an orchid for her to wear on the evening, and ensuring that a taxi was booked to take us to and from City Hall. The fact that I had a partner coming from London to Rag Ball caused much speculation at St Teilo's and there were many questions as to what happened to Sylvia, to which I was diplomatic in my response.

Saturday saw me on Cardiff Central Station awaiting the early train from London. Would she be on the train, would everything be all right?

The Paddington to Cardiff express arrived on time and there was Mona, smiling as usual, running to greet me. We took a trolley bus to Newport Road and the hotel, and after Mona had unpacked and ensured her evening dress was in order, we went for a walk round Waterloo Park that adjoined St Teilo's, when I was able to point out the various features of where I lived while in Cardiff.

The City Hall, with its marble hallway leading to the ground-floor bar area, and its curved marble staircases leading to the first-floor marble columned reception hall and vaulted ball room with its polished dance floor and revolving lights, greatly impressed Mona, since she had never been to Cardiff before. Mona, for her part, looked stunning in a black strapless top and a dark plum coloured full-length skirt. We danced to the Joe Loss orchestra, and in keeping with others, stood at the front of the rostrum when vocalists performed. We had the occasional drink at the downstairs bar and at the end of the evening Mona declared that it had been a wonderful night and one that she would always remember. Our taxi took us back to the hotel and we spent a further twenty minutes saying our goodnights.

I walked the short distance to St Teilo's, undressed, washed, slipped off my ruby ring and went to sleep, dreaming of Mona and the future but with a shadow in the background, that I recalled but could not understand when I woke the following morning.

The next day being a Sunday, I collected Mona from the hotel and after a stroll around the deserted and closed shops of the city centre, we had lunch at a small restaurant and then it was time to return to the station. We both wished that the weekend could have gone on for ever, and our embrace and kisses, as the train pulled out, were reflective of our feelings for each other.

The weeks following Rag Week and leading up to the first year final examinations rushed by. My approach to revision for examinations had always involved two hours' work every morning before breakfast, and this same approach I followed on this occasion as well. Theoretical and practical examinations in three subjects based on the year's work came and went, and by the last week of June the pass lists were posted on the various departmental notice boards. I had survived my first year at university with marks well above the cut-off red line that appeared on all pass lists.

That night I celebrated with colleagues with a pint of black and tan at the Royal Oak Tavern. Returning to St Teilo's, I telephoned the adjoining farm in Nevern requesting that they pass on the good news to my family, and wrote a short note to Mona to tell her my good news.

The next day I was packing, getting ready for the field trip to Scotland, which was leaving Cardiff that evening.

At eight o'clock that evening the party of twenty-five students and four members of the college staff boarded the night train to Glasgow.

I was sharing the compartment with five other male colleagues, and as soon as we pulled out of Cardiff a suitcase was placed between the seats and we started playing pontoon for penny stakes.

We played until dawn when the train eventually steamed into Glasgow. A coach awaited our arrival and then followed the long journey north through wild, heather-clad hills and places such as the Bridge of Allan until we eventually arrived at Aberfeldy to be greeted by two departmental technicians who had driven up in a university van, bringing with them all the equipment necessary to carry out the various surveys of the region's fauna and flora.

We were housed in what could best be described as a stately home that had been donated at some time to the university as a field centre. In keeping with many such buildings it occupied high ground overlooking the River Tay that wound its way between the hills before entering Loch Tay a few miles south. The views from its windows and lawns were breathtaking and reflective of the grandeur of the highlands. The accommodation consisted of bunk-bedded dormitories, a recreation room and a dining hall, a large sitting room and a small laboratory-style room, where the various field equipment could be stored and any microscope work carried out.

The next few days were a blur of activity, lead by Professor McLain, Dr Percival, Dr Catherine Benson-Evans, and two research students from the department. Quadrants and transects of the native flora were taken at different altitudes and the frequency of the different species charted, while the fauna and flora of Loch Tay was investigated using dredging equipment and the hire of a small motorboat. Any unusual specimens were brought back to the laboratory for further investigation. With Professor McLain leading we climbed Ben Lawers, the second highest mountain in Great Britain at 1214 feet, and visited the woollen town of Pitlochry, famous for the production of the various tartans of Scotland. Since Aberfeldy was within walking distance of the field centre, the occasional evening visit to the one local tavern was the only source of relaxation. Aberfeldy boasted several unique features, which although difficult to verify were obvious tourist attractions. One was a plaque on the wall of an old stone cottage claiming that Pontius Pilot was born there during the Roman occupation of Great Britain, while in the churchyard a yew tree was deemed to be the oldest tree in Great Britain.

Soon it was time to pack for the return journey to Cardiff and the summer vacation back home on the farm.

On returning home, there was a letter from Mona letting me know that she was home from Harrow and would be staying with her sister the following week. On the farm everything was the same as always; my aunt, although approaching eighty years of age, was still active and full of energy and kept the house in good shape. In addition to her domestic duties she regularly visited Nevern Church on Sundays for the morning service, and on occasions during a weekday visited the family graves to ensure that they were neat and tidy. There were many occasions when I joined her in this task, assisting with the weeding and the cleaning of the headstones, while flowers would be placed on all four graves at Christmas and Easter.

My mother and father as usual were deeply involved with the everyday activities of the farm with the summertime being one of the busiest periods. I assisted whenever possible and especially with any heavy tasks but made sure that these were finished by early evening when I cycled to Newport to meet Mona. On these occasions we went for walks in the countryside or along the seashore of Newport Sands. On Saturdays we made the occasional visit to the Pavilion at Cardigan that usually ended up with her sister inviting me in for coffee.

So the summer of '52 drew to a close and it was time once again for us to say our goodbyes until the next college and school holiday.

Chapter Nine

On returning to St Teilo's I discovered that Les and I had been allocated a new study bedroom on the top floor overlooking Waterloo Gardens. Although the three flights of stairs were good exercise, means of escape in the event of a fire was somewhat hazardous, involving a friction pulley, rope and harness, located on the outside of the rear window, which would, in theory, gradually lower you to the ground. Thankfully, it was not required during our stay. A feature of the previous room that I did not miss, however, was the constant stream of colleagues who failing to return before the main door was locked at ten thirty, used to gain entry by knocking on the window directly over my bed, and then proceeding to crawl over my bed regardless of whether it was occupied or not. We soon settled into our new accommodation and to the second year of our degree course.

Since second year finals consisted of studies in two subjects only, I was able to discontinue studies in organic/biochemistry, concentrating on the two major biological sciences, including my favourite subject of physiology.

Sylvia, having completed her second-year finals was now in the Honours year; consequently, the opportunity of sharing practical sessions did not exist, and although we occasionally met over mid-morning coffee, I was careful not to encourage further involvement. She had, however, noted Mona's presence at the Rag Ball and complemented me on my choice of partner, and the beautiful orchid that she had been wearing.

Another highlight in the college year was the Aberdare Hall annual Dinner Dance. This was the occasion when the girl residents had the opportunity of inviting partners of their choice to attend, be introduced to the warden, Miss Parry, and enjoy a highly rated evening. In my finals class was a petite, black-haired very pretty girl called Mary Rees. She was a resident of Aberdare Hall, and on this occasion, without showing, as far as I was concerned, any previous interest, she invited me to be her partner. Caught slightly off guard and to some extent flattered, I said yes, and so my brief interlude with Mary began.

I decided that since this was a one-off occasion, I would not let Mona know since I had no wish to upset our relationship in any way. The news of my being invited to attend the Aberdare Hall dinner dance soon circulated round St Teilo's and the usual questions of, 'How did you manage that?', 'What about Sylvia?', 'What will Mona say?' were soon coming my way. A few days later I met Sylvia over coffee. Her response to the news was to let me know that due to Brian being away from university on a works placement, she had hoped to reciprocate to my inviting her to the St Teilo's dinner dance, by inviting me to Aberdare Hall, and was sorry that she had not asked me sooner.

The Aberdare Hall dinner dance was a very formal affair. Those invited presented their invitation card to the duty porter upon arrival and congregated in the reception area, ready to be escorted into the main oak-panelled dining room and be formally received by Miss Parry, who was in full academic dress. A seating plan for the dinner was posted in the reception hall, and supported by place names resting on the long, white linen-clad tables. Vases of fresh flowers completed the table decorations. Miss Parry and her personal guests sat at the top table, while Mary and I occupied seats on one of the five 'spurs' arising from top table. Following the usual words of welcome, a four-course meal was served, accompanied by copious amounts of soft drinks. At the conclusion of the meal a selected representative from among the male guests extended formal thanks to Miss Parry, her staff and the girls who had invited us. Dancing followed and after a few dances, Mary suggested we go outside into the gardens for some fresh air. We sat on one of the many bench seats, Mary snuggled up to me, and we kissed. I told Mary that I had a steady girlfriend, and she in turn admitted that she also had a boyfriend back in her hometown, but that he would not fit into the kind of evening we had just experienced. These admissions cleared the air and I felt much more at ease, and enjoyed the rest of the evening.

Following the evening at Aberdare Hall, I saw Mary on a few occasions outside classes when we went rowing on Roath Park

Lake or visited one of the many cinemas in Cardiff, but the relationship did not progress and we soon decided that it had been a mistake.

Lectures and practical work in the biological sciences took place at the Newport Road site of the University College, and were held in temporary wooden huts that had been built behind the original building facing Newport Road. Prior to becoming the main campus of the college, the site had housed the Cardiff Infirmary that was subsequently moved to the newly-built Cardiff Royal Infirmary located at the junction of Newport Road and City Road. In addition to housing the biological sciences the site also accommodated the Engineering Department and the Anatomy and Physiology Departments of the Welsh School of Medicine. By not continuing studies in biochemistry beyond the first year there was no longer a need for me to visit the main college campus in Cathays Park that housed all aspects of chemistry.

My days leading up to the Christmas vacation and beyond involved cycling from St Teilo's to Newport Road, attending lectures and practical sessions, returning to St Teilo's for meals, revision and sleep.

The Christmas vacation came and went with my going home, and meeting up with Mona on a few occasions since at Christmas time she always stayed with her mother and father on their farm, as opposed to staying with her sister in Newport. Mona had never invited me to her home and neither had I invited her to meet my mother and father. So in that respect there appeared to be no commitment on either side. Although my mother had seen Mona on one occasion in Newport and had commented that she looked a very nice girl and when was I bringing her home, I never did.

The spring term rushed by, and the examination timetable for the final examinations soon appeared on the departmental notice boards. Revision lectures and practical sessions were held in the four weeks between Easter and Whitsunday, with the week following Whitsunday devoted to private revision. To avoid any disruption to my revision schedule covering two years' work, I remained at St Teilo's over Whitsunday and the following week, writing to my mother and Mona in between time. My final examinations turned out better than I had anticipated and when they were over I was quietly confident of the results.

The end of the finals course was marked by a zoological field study investigation of the marine fauna off the coast of Port Erin in the Isle of Man, and would take place immediately after the final results were published.

Came the day of the results, and once more we all gathered around the notice boards to see whether our names were above or below the red line that divided pass from fail. Being third and fourth from the top of the pass list gave me a great thrill, and on returning to St Teilo's, I immediately wrote to my mother and Mona with the good news that I could place Batchelor of Science after my name.

The following day, in keeping with tradition, those students who had successfully completed their finals examinations were required to see the professor of the department in which they hoped they would be accepted to complete their honours year of study.

I was one of the first to report to Professor James Borough's office the following morning. He appeared in good spirits, shook my hand and congratulated me on my results and in his usual abrupt way enquired as to what I wanted to study in my honours year. I emphasised my long time interest in physiology, and my view that linking physiological function with histological structure was an acceptable programme of study for an honours year. Professor Borough agreed and I went back to St Teilo's confident that my next year at university would be the best year yet.

Three days later I received a letter from Mona that brought all my plans for the future crashing down. She and a colleague at the school where she worked were going abroad to work over the summer holidays, and consequently she would not be coming home and would not be able to see me during July and August and probably not for the remainder of the summer vacation. Although there was no mention of a break-up, reading between the lines it was obvious to me that she wanted more from life than school, home and me. Being busy packing for the field visit in two days' time coupled with saying farewell to many colleagues who would not be returning to St Teilo's next session, I did not write back, feeling that a few weeks' delay would do no harm.

Fourteen students together with Professor Borough, Dr Edith Shepard and the honours tutor Dr W A L Evans, known as 'Wally', boarded the night train to Liverpool. As per usual those interested in playing cards gathered in one compartment, and we spent the night playing pontoon until at around seven o'clock we pulled into Liverpool. From the station it was a brisk walk to the docks and the ferry to the Isle of Man. The crossing was un-eventful and we soon arrived at Douglas, the main port and capital of the island. From there a chartered coach took us to Port Erin, a medium size town located at the southern tip of the island and where the Marine Interpretation Centre was housed.

Our accommodation while at the centre was in one of Port Erin's many seafront hotels. The rooms were three-bedded with the majority overlooking the sea. In addition to the Cardiff party of seventeen, there was a similar group from Southampton University. Once checking-in had been completed we had a stroll along the seafront, and in so doing ascertained where the nearest hostelry was located. The evening meal at the hotel was most acceptable and the evening was rounded off by a visit to a seafront bar where we sampled the island's brew. The following morning we attended the marine centre and commenced the study programme that was outlined by Professor Borough.

The centre consisted of three fully-equipped laboratories with adjoining stores for shore and deep-sea investigations. On the walls of the main laboratory hung the coats of arms of the various university colleges that used the centre for their studies. The exception to this was University College Cardiff, and it was unanimously decide that this omission should be rectified. Dr Shepard immediately suggested that I should undertake the work, being in her opinion the best artist among the students she had taught. This was greeted with much cheering and so I was landed with a task that took up most of my evenings.

On the third day of my stay I received a telegram from my mother letting me know that my uncle Robert had passed away. Uncle Robert had been in farming all his life, and following his marriage at the age of eighteen to Elizabeth, had farmed for himself on a farm known as Wild Woods near the village of Velindre in Pembrokeshire. I was very fond of the only uncle I had ever known, and from the age of twelve had visited him on numerous Saturdays when he would take me trout fishing in the River Nevern which ran through his land. I still recall my very first catch when, due to my eagerness to land the fish, it ended up in a tree with the line tangled in the branches. Uncle Robert never let me forget that incident since he claimed it was the first flying fish he had ever seen. After fifty years' farming, and in failing health, my uncle decided to retire to a small house in Newport, were after eight years of happy retirement he passed away at the age of seventy-six. Although my mother had mentioned the day of the funeral there was no chance of my attending, and all I could do was to write a few words of sympathy to my aunt Elizabeth, promising that I would visit her as soon as I arrived home.

Although news of my uncle's death took some of the gloss off my studies, the schedule of work kept all of us busy until late in the evening, and following dinner and further work on the coat of arms there was little time for social activities. I finished the coat of arms two days before we were due to leave. It was then taken to a local shop that undertook picture framing, where it was framed ready for its installation in the Marine Centre alongside all the other coats of arms. I was very proud of the finished article, which received unanimous acclaim.

On our last day at Port Erin work finished early, and following an early dinner all adjourned to the local bar, and there I met Cynthia.

Cynthia Chambers was a finals student at Southampton University where, like myself, she was studying biological sciences. She was a very attractive, slim girl of average height with beautiful auburn hair plaited and forming a bun at the nape of her neck. She had fair skin with catching blue eyes that completed her model-like appearance. We started talking and I found her to be a very attractive and well-mannered girl with a good sense of humour. I bought her a drink and at closing time we walked back to the hotel together, stopping on more than one occasion when Cynthia drew me into a doorway and we held each other and kissed.

On returning to the hotel, the rest of the party were gathered around the piano singing a mixture of songs, some respectable and others rather racy. Cynthia whispered to me that she was tired and suggested we call it a day. I escorted her to her room, which unlike the one I shared with two of my fellow students, was a single one. I was on the point of kissing her goodnight at the door when she suggested I come in, and soon we were on the bed in each other's arms with Cynthia telling me that this was the very first time she had ever been alone with a boy indoors, let alone in a bedroom. I asked her why me, and she responded by saying that although we had just met, she trusted me. We then proceeded to tell each other of our backgrounds, her, of being the only child, of what I guessed was a fairly wealthy middle-class family living in the Wimbledon area of London, of her schooling that had been in a girls' private school and of her two years at Southampton University; and me of my farming background and my hard-working but relatively poor family.

Cynthia appeared thrilled with my account of life on a farm and proceeded to tell me that she knew that I was different the moment we met. This gave my ego a boost and I ventured to stroke her hair, shoulders and gradually her small breasts, which were firm and peaked in a round, hard nipple. I commented on her hair and asked how long it was and why not let it down. Cynthia said that she had never done this before but would to please me.

Sitting in front of the dressing table mirror she slowly let down her thick, auburn tresses that reached her waist, and at that moment in that setting, I guess she was the most beautiful girl I had ever seen. Getting up from the bed and standing behind her I cupped her breasts in my hands while brushing my lips against her hair, promising that I would always be there for her.

We both knew that come the morning we would be leaving Port Erin, Cynthia to catch the early boat back to Liverpool and my group to catch the later afternoon boat and the overnight train back to Cardiff. We exchanged home and college addresses and promised that we would both write as soon as we arrived home. After deciding that we would not see each other before leaving in the morning, we returned to the bed where we embraced and kissed until the first light of dawn filtered through the hotel window.

I made my way back to my room, careful not to wake my companions. On slipping into bed I discovered that it was full of shoes, some books and other odds and ends that my thoughtful colleagues had placed there. Shifting them to one side I put my head on the pillow and fell asleep dreaming of the beautiful red-haired girl I had just left and vowing that I would see her again.

Chapter Ten

On arrival at Cardiff, I collected my personal belongings and bicycle from St Teilo's and boarded the train for home, and the three months' summer vacation. My very first task was to visit my aunt Elizabeth and console her on losing her dear Robert, and although she appreciated my being away, I felt that she could not understand why her only nephew was not at the funeral. There then followed the visit to my uncle's grave at Nevern churchyard, where even when I was a small boy, the silence was something you could almost feel. I placed some wild flowers on the raised earth and said my goodbyes.

Upon my arrival home, my mother, father and aunt had hugged and kissed me and congratulated me on achieving my finals and a BSc, pass degree. They were also very happy with my news that I had been accepted onto the honours year to study animal and human physiology and histology, although what these studies involved was probably beyond their understanding.

Some significant changes had been initiated on the farm during the past twelve months. The sheep flock had been sold and the dairy herd reduced to five milking cows, while a considerable proportion of the land had been rented out to adjoining farms for grazing purposes. These changes were the result of my mother losing some of her vitality, and at the age of thirty-nine looking tired and pale. She had visited Dr Davies, the family doctor, who had prescribed iron tablets to treat her anaemia, and a less stressful life style.

A consequence of these changes was that many of the once familiar seasonal farming activities no longer occurred on Deep Well Farm. The limited amount of hay required by the much reduced herd resulted in haymaking occupying one or two days only, with only one hayrick in the yard, and only an aging Davy Jones coming to assist with the work. My father had decided that cereal crops were no longer an economic proposition so harvesting and threshing were events of the past. My mother had, however, decided that the poultry enterprise should remain, so the chickens and young turkey chicks were still in evidence, together with two geese destined for the Christmas table.

A further consequence was that there was not a great deal of work for me to do while home, and when a cousin of my aunt let it be known that she could do with some paid help on her farm, I decided that a few days' paid employment would help my failing budget and avoid my asking my aunt Catherine for further financial assistance. The farm, known as Hendre, was located on the coast a few miles south of Newport, and following the death of her auctioneer husband a few years earlier, was run by a Mrs Vaughan and her unmarried daughter Margaret who was a graduate of an agricultural college.

Mrs Vaughan, who was now almost eighty years old, was a very remarkable woman and although my aunt Catherine referred to her as a cousin, I never discovered which of my grandfather's two sisters her mother was. She had apparently married very late in life to an auctioneer, and given birth to three children when she was approaching fifty years of age. Her eldest son had become the chief executive of Lloyds Bank in London; her second son was Bishop of Belize; while her daughter Margaret, who had graduated in agriculture, now ran the family farm. Despite her age, Mrs Vaughan still ran and kept the farmhouse in perfect order and was always aware of all aspects of farm activity. I was made very welcome when I turned up on my first day, and for the following weeks I enjoyed her company at meal times, when she recalled details of her sons' careers and her hopes for their futures. Margaret was a most pleasant lady who I guessed had just turned thirty. She was an excellent boss and she and I got on well and I learnt some aspects of farming that I had not previously considered.

Another activity that occupied my summer of '53 was cricket. I had always played cricket while at Cardigan County School, although not achieving first team membership, and when the local cricket captain heard that I was home he requested that I come and join the team since they were short on bowlers. This venture resulted in most Wednesday evenings and Saturdays being taken up with cricket. This I enjoyed very much and in addition to the actual matches spent a lot of time practising my bowling in the field adjoining the farmhouse.

True to her word, Cynthia wrote every few weeks and I responded in like manner. Cynthia's letters were lengthy and passionate, recalling our brief time together and how she would always remember every single minute of her last night at Port Erin. She always concluded with the hope that we would soon meet again. It was true to say that her letters were very different from those I had from Mona, and although I had not heard from her since she went abroad, I felt sure that she would eventually get in touch.

So the summer passed and soon it was time to return to Cardiff to complete studies that I hoped would result in a good honours degree.

My third year at St Teilo's saw my being granted a study bedroom of my own. This was situated on the ground floor and while being most comfortable did have the disadvantage of my being required to pass through another study bedroom in order to gain access to mine.

The honours group consisted of five students, two males and three females. We had all previously studied together and knew each other quite well. The honours year had two main tutors, Dr Wally Evans, who conducted lectures and practical sessions in physiology, and Dr Bernard John, who was the specialist in histology. The only other input to the year was by Professor Borough, who ran a series of lectures on specialist topics such as 'The history of science' and 'Neoteny & recapitulation'.

The honours programme I enjoyed very much, with practical sessions involving such experiments as the effect of chemicals and drugs on muscle contraction using the muscle from a frog's leg, or on the rate of heartbeat using a rabbit's heart, which I will always recall. Histology, involving the fixation of animal tissue using chemical fixatives, embedding a piece of the fixed tissue in wax, cutting it into thin sections, staining the sections with various dyes, and then investigating the detailed structure under a microscope, was equally rewarding. The learning process that such practical sessions stimulated was outstanding since they generated a fundamental understanding without the need to memorise.

By this time, I had become a regular member of the medical school's rugby team and played most Saturdays. My position of blind-side wing forward was demanding of fitness and I cycled almost everywhere. During Rag Week of '54 a charity rugby match between the medical school and Cardiff Old Players was arranged at the home of the Cardiff Rugby Club – the Arms Park. This was a great event with past Welsh International players such as Dr Jack Mathews and Bleddyn Williams making guest appearances. I can to this day recall the tackle that Dr Jack made on me that day. He was a small man but immensely strong and at the peak of his career was regarded as the best crash-tackler in the world. When his arms encircled me it was as if two steel bands had gripped me and I was lifted and thrown backwards.

As Christmas approached, I had a letter from Mona. In it she explained how she had been trying to broaden her curriculum vitae with experience outside primary school work in the hope that one day she could find a job back in Wales. She hoped I understood and was sorry that she had sprung her going abroad on me, and hoped we could continue to be friends.

Cynthia continued to write and we exchanged progress reports on how our honours years were progressing. By this time we had also exchanged photographs, with Cynthia showing mine to her parents, and reporting favourable comment. She was returning to Wimbledon for Christmas and suggested that if I gave her a telephone number she would ring me on Christmas Eve.

Returning home a week before Christmas I was once again involved with the killing of the turkeys and their preparation for collection by Fred Rowlands. Exceptions to this collection were the two geese that were scheduled for the family table at Christmas and the New Year.

Having given Cynthia the number of my school friend's farm and a time to call, Christmas Eve saw me waiting by the telephone. True to her word the call came through and we wished each other a good Christmas and the hope that the year to come would see us together again.

The term leading up to Easter was a busy one, with studies and rugby dominating my time. As the term drew to a close I was approached by a fellow student at St Teilo's with a proposal that I join the University Athletic Club, since it had been rumoured that I was a reasonable middle-distance runner, and the club were desperately short of half-mile and mile competitors. I pointed out that my honours examinations were scheduled for May and that my time would be limited but would give it a try. Shortly after this conversation I was informed that the Inter-University Athletics Competition would be held on the weekend prior to the Whitsun holiday, the venue being Southampton University.

I immediately wrote to Cynthia, letting her know that I would be arriving in Southampton by the morning train on the Saturday of the athletics competition.

I did not return home for the Easter vacation, choosing to stay at St Teilo's and undertake some serious revision that was not always possible when home on the farm. I wrote to my mother explaining the situation as I saw it and hoped that she was not disappointed.

So Easter came and went and by the time the summer term commenced, I was reasonably happy with my preparation for the honours examinations. The following weeks involved further practical work and the writing-up of a scientific paper based on work that I had undertaken jointly with Dr Wally Evans and which he considered worthy of publication in the respected scientific magazine *Nature*. The project related to the enzymes produced by the larvae of the blowfly *Lucilia*, responsible for the condition known as 'sheep strike'. In simple terms, a female blowfly lays her eggs on the skin of the sheep and when these eggs hatch the larvae produce enzymes that enable them to digest away the skin and underlying flesh causing the condition known as 'sheep strike'. The resulting wounds can lead to secondary infections if not treated, while the wounds result in holes in the skins, and a non-marketable product. I was delighted when the paper appeared in *Nature* as it was the first time I had seen my name in a scientific journal.

The Athletic Team of Cardiff University College consisted of thirty athletes covering the major track and field events. I had been selected to run in the half-mile, a race that I was very familiar with, having recorded a number of successes over the years. We steamed into Southampton at around eleven thirty and there on the platform was Cynthia, looking as if she had just stepped out of *Vogue* magazine. With her glistening auburn hair gathered in a bun, her flawless complexion and a black, tight-fitting dress that showed off her slim figure, she looked stunning, and when she ran towards me and threw her arms around my neck, my colleagues were completely dumbfounded, since no one knew of our previous association. Their disbelief was furthered when upon leaving the station Cynthia whisked me off in a taxi for lunch at a nearby restaurant.

Following a lovely meal that I insisted had to be light, as my race was scheduled for four o'clock; Cynthia walked me to the hotel where she had booked me in for the weekend. There then followed a further taxi ride to the stadium and the athletics meeting. We arrived just in time for my race and I had to rush to change and be on the track in ten minutes. Cynthia joined some of her girl friends who were at the stadium, while I had a quick warm-up. My Cardiff colleagues wanted to know who this stunning girl was, how had I met her, and would she be joining the post-competition celebrations? I responded with a no comment, and proceeded to run one of my fastest half-miles, coming second to an English International runner. A quick shower, and I was back with Cynthia who, having introduced me to her various girl friends, made her excuses saying that we had a prior engagement.

After a brisk walk I discovered that the prior engagement was at the hall of residence where Cynthia had a single-study bed-room, and where boyfriends were admitted on Saturdays between the hours of twelve noon and nine o'clock in the evening. The hours leading up to nine o'clock we spent recreating the experi-ences of Port Erin and enjoying each other's company... Following the bell that announced that guests should leave, we walked to my hotel, and spent a further hour saying our good-night, and outlining plans for Sunday. I drifted off to sleep well pleased with the day. On the bedside table was my wristwatch and the ruby ring that Cynthia had slipped on her finger at Port Erin and again a few hours ago.

I was up early and after a full English breakfast, I sat in the lounge reading one of the many Sunday papers available for guests. Promptly at ten Cynthia arrived and off we went for a sightseeing walking tour of Southampton. Although the athletics team were scheduled to leave at noon to return to Cardiff, Cynthia had persuaded me to stay until Monday, and since the rail ticket allowed this, I did not object and was in fact delighted with her suggestion.

We spent the best part of the morning strolling around the parkland adjoining the hotel. Following a snack lunch we went back to my hotel room where we spent the rest of the day enjoying each other's company and wishing that the day would last for ever. As was the case when we left Port Erin, we decided to say our goodbyes that night and not the following morning, so it was with reluctance that we parted at the door of the hall of residence late that evening.

The next morning saw me on the early train to Cardiff.

News of my being met by a fabulous looking girl at Southampton station had already filtered back to St Teilo's, and when I had not returned with the team on Sunday stories of my having been kidnapped by this Eastern Princess were circulating. I wrote to Cynthia thanking her for a wonderful weekend, and then it was time to concentrate on my honours examinations.

The results posted on the departmental notice board were beyond my wildest dreams. I had achieved a First Class Honours Degree of the University of Wales. I went to see Professor Borough, who in congratulating me on an excellent result went on to suggest that I apply for a University of Wales Research Fellowship should I wish to continue study for a higher degree. It was decision time, and although I had not given the issue previous thought, I immediately accepted his suggestion.

The next day, after saying my farewells to colleagues at St Teilo's, I was on the train home. My mother, father and aunt were delighted with my news and all decided that they would travel to Cardiff for the graduation ceremony in July. News of my success filtered through the local community and Mr Edwards, my old primary school headmaster, placed a congratulatory letter in the local weekly newspaper. A few days later I received a letter from Tom Evans, the headmaster of Cardigan County School, recording his warmest congratulations and inviting me to join the staff until the end of the term, as he was short-staffed due to Miss Price being on sick leave.

I accepted his offer and so obtained my first experience of teaching.

The graduation ceremony was held at city hall in mid July. My father had hired a car, and following a very early start, we arrived in good time for the ceremony. After acquiring the hired academic robes from Ede & Ravenscroft, I joined my fellow graduates and family in the grand ballroom on the first floor. One by one our names were called out together with details of the degree being awarded, and I felt considerable pride when my name was called and I mounted the rostrum where the vice chancellor of the University of Wales and the vice chancellor of the University College Cardiff presented me with my degree scroll.

Following a snack in a nearby restaurant, we drove to Kenfig Hill where my aunt Lois was expecting us for afternoon tea. She was delighted with my achievement and proceeded to give me a present of fifty pounds and an open invitation to come and see her at any time in the future. We then left for the long journey home to Nevern.

The events of the last five weeks had left me with little time to become involved in any farm work or social activities, but on returning from Cardiff it was time to discuss the future with my mother, father and aunt. The topic had already been raised in conversation as to what I was going to do now that I had completed my degree course, and would not be receiving further funding from the local Education Authority.

I explained that I had been offered a University of Wales Post-Graduate Fellowship to conduct research towards a higher degree, and that subject to finding a suitable research topic I had decided to accept this offer. Although at the time I was not aware of the exact amount of money the Fellowship would provide, it would be significantly more than the Local Authority award. For once my father was most supportive, as having read my joint research paper on sheep strike viewed that kind of research as useful with applications in the real world. My mother and aunt were as always happy to go along with my decision, with Aunt Catherine promising to support me financially as and when the need arose and to the best of her ability.

I returned to Cardiff in early September to formalise my application for post-graduate funding, discuss possible research projects, and arrange if possible a further stay at St Teilo's.

Application for fellowship funding was fairly straightforward when supported by the department, and that was the case with Professor Borough. In relation to the research topic, he dispatched me to see his colleague in the Department of Pharmacology at the Welsh School of Medicine, who he believed was looking for someone with my field of interest.

The Pharmacology Department was housed in the parade that was around the corner from the university college buildings. It occupied the first and top floors above the Public Health Laboratories, as well as the basement below the laboratories. Upon reporting to the departmental secretary, a Miss Owen, I was shown into Professor Landgrebe's office.

Professor Landgrebe was a slightly built man in his early fifties with a very informal and relaxed approach. We started talking and I immediately knew that we could work together. After a very large mug of coffee I was shown around the department, given an indication as to where I would be working and then we returned to his office to discuss the research programme.

At that time the Pharmacology Department ran the only pregnancy testing centre in England and Wales. Tests, which were still in their infancy, used the South African clawed toad (*Xenopus laevis*) as the vehicle for diagnosis. Consequently the department housed and bred in excess of 500 female toads to undertake its work. Although it was known that a urine sample from a pregnant woman, would, if injected into a female toad, cause that toad to lay eggs within twenty-four hours, very little else was known about the animal. Professor Landgrebe was of the view that the physiology and histology of *Xenopus* should be investigated with a view to possible other applications. I viewed the proposals with much enthusiasm and we decided there and then that I should embark on a three-year programme of research, leading to the degree of Doctor of Philosophy that Professor Landgrebe would commend to the Post-Graduate Fellowship Committee.

My only remaining task was to seek Father Pearce's approval to continue my stay at St Teilo's. Father Pearce was delighted when I told him I was returning as a post-graduate fellow, but could only offer one further year of residence. This I was delighted to accept and returned home well pleased with my achievements.

Chapter Eleven

Being a postgraduate research student is very different from being an undergraduate. There is no set timetable and one comes and goes as one likes, the only restrictions being one's own. My first day at the Pharmacology Department commenced with an introduction to the staff and an insight into the working of the department and its students.

In addition to Professor Landgrebe there were three other members of the academic staff. Dr Mitchell, or 'Mitch' as he was known, was a short, stocky Scotsman with a fresh complexion and a wicked sense of humour. He was the medically qualified senior lecturer. His colleague Dr George Graham was another Scotsman with a rather gruff and abrupt manner and deeply involved in drug research, while the junior member of staff was Dr Bob Tonks, an Englishman in his late twenties undertaking original research into a number of pharmacological topics.

Bob Hilliard provided the technical support within the department. He was a tall, lean, white-haired man in his early sixties who I discovered later was a highly skilled craftsman. Mrs Willis, an elderly lady, undertook all the cleaning, together with tea-and coffee-making duties for the whole department. Dr Graham had his own personal technician called Thelma, while the room housing the 500-odd toads, was managed by Jean Curry, a pretty blonde teenage girl. The remaining staff consisted of two male technicians who looked after the animal house on the top floor.

Bob Hilliard was based in a workshop that had the appearance of an engineering workshop and it was only afterwards that I came to understand the reasons why this was so.

Professor Landgrebe was one of those rare individuals with qualifications at PhD and D.Sc. level in two areas of study, namely engineering and pharmacology. He was a graduate of St Andrew's University in Scotland and having qualified and undertaken research in engineering, switched to pharmacology eventually through research, obtaining Doctor of Science status. A consequence of this was that being a very practical man, he designed and made much of the apparatus required for research, resulting in the metal turning lathe and drilling machines being the dominant equipment in the departmental workshop.

Another of his interests was motorcars, owning a black Rover 14 which he used daily, a 1938 V12 Lagonda, and a 1951 2.5 Lagonda drop-head coupe. These he kept in a large garage adjoining the house that he had designed and built with direct labour on a plot of land at the village called Miskin located about six miles outside Cardiff. The Landgrebe family consisted of wife Margo, teenage daughter Pat and young son Peter. The family often visited the department for morning coffee or a sandwich at lunchtime, and over a period of time I got to know them all quite well. Within a few days I had settled into the family atmosphere of the department, and felt that I belonged.

My workstation occupied a small corner of the large main laboratory, where I had been provided with a microscope and other basic equipment. In addition, I had use of other equipment within the department as and when required, and the use of the darkroom that was situated in the basement for my photographic requirements. So my first year of research into the histology and pharmacological properties of the skin of *Xenopus levies* commenced.

Term time was now rapidly approaching and although my first two weeks at St Teilo's had been very quiet with hardly anyone to talk to, very soon the place was buzzing with previous residents returning and first-year students making their first appearance. I still had my study bedroom on the ground floor, although the occupants of the adjoining room had changed.

It was during the quiet period that I had written to Cynthia letting her know of my research project and of my being granted a University Fellowship. She was of course delighted and hoped that soon she could come to Cardiff for a weekend to see me. Following her gaining an honours degree, she had decided to return to Southampton to pursue a Post-Graduate Teachers Certificate, since she had decided that teaching was what she would like to do. I had also written a short note to Mona letting her know what I was doing and hoping that she was having success with applying for a teaching appointment back in Wales.

One of the essential pieces of equipment that I soon discovered I required was a high-resolution microscope capable of producing images of a much better quality than that of the normal student microscope.

On researching the availability of such an instrument I discovered that there was only one in the entire college, but as luck would have it, it was located in the Microbiology Department adjoining the Biological Sciences Departments. Professor Landgrebe contacted Dr Ted Hill, the head of department, and arranged a time when I could visit the department and discuss my research needs with Dr Hill. The outcome of our discussions was that I was given a set number of hours per week access to the microscope with all its photographic attachments that, up until that time, had only been used by Dr Hill. Needless to say I was delighted and could see real progress being made early on in my research.

The other aspect of my research was the need for me to obtain a Home Office Licence for work I would be undertaking with animals such as toads. Being within the school of medicine this was easily obtained, whereas a different location might have presented major problems. The final plus was the offer by Dr Graham that I could use any of his animals for physiological purposes once he had completed his drug trials on them.

Friday afternoons in the department were normally devoted to the professor and Bob Hilliard stripping down or rebuilding some component of one of the professor's cars. Carburettors were stripped down, cleaned and refurbished; valves were ground into cylinder heads; new piston rings were fitted to old pistons; and a whole range of mechanical and electrical components were refurbished to a very high standard. These components were then installed in the car during the Saturday and Sunday. Very soon I was involved in this Friday activity and so began my life-long interest in cars, and more importantly at that time, the ability to undertake those repairs that older cars frequently require.

On returning home for Christmas I realised that my mother was not well. Although she still undertook her daily farm tasks she looked pale and tired. The course of iron tablets that she'd had prescribed did not appear to have had any effect, and her new doctor, Dr Evans, who had taken over the practice following the retirement of Dr Davies, had requested that she have a blood test. I accompanied my mother when she visited Dr Evans a few days before Christmas, when he was able to tell us that the blood test had revealed a low red cell count, which was expected, but more worrying was the low levels of the white blood cells that in their various forms protect the body against infections. At that stage he suggested a bone marrow test would be advisable. While agreeing to the test my mother was not happy with the prospect of hospitalisation for a few days.

The Christmas of '54 was a quiet affair with my mother putting on a brave face despite worrying about the forthcoming tests. The New Year came and went and having seen that tasks that my father could no longer undertake were taken care of, I returned to Cardiff and my research, despite wishing that I could stay until my mother had returned from hospital.

St Teilo's dinner dance loomed, and since it would be my last opportunity to attend, I decided to invite Cynthia as my partner. She was delighted and I set about making plans for her stay in Cardiff. Once again I chose a private hotel near St Teilo's, arranged for the hire of an evening suit, ordered some flowers and was on the platform waiting as the Southampton train steamed into Cardiff Central Station.

Cynthia looked as immaculate as always, wearing her favourite black outfit that showed off her pale complexion and auburn hair. Once she had checked in at the hotel we spent the rest of the afternoon having a look around the city centre.

All eyes were on Cynthia when she entered the function room at the Angel Hotel. Her black strapless evening gown was all revealing and her hair, arranged in a coil, set off her heart-shaped face and startling blue eyes to best effect. As the most senior student at St Teilo's I was required to toast the guests and this I did with much pleasure, and in the case of Cynthia, much pride.

On returning to the hotel we spent the next few hours saying our goodnights, with Cynthia not wanting me to leave, and with me finding it more and more difficult to stay, and still behave as a gentleman.

The following day being Sunday was spent showing Cynthia around the Civic Centre and university campus and following lunch it was time for her to catch the train back to Southampton where she had lectures first thing on Monday morning. I returned to Teilo's well pleased with the way the weekend had gone.

A week later I had a letter from my mother letting me know that at long last she had a date for her hospital tests and that she would only be away from home for two nights, which she considered as not being too bad. She also promised that as soon as she had any results she would let me know. Over coffee the following morning I mentioned to Professor Landgrebe the health problems that my mother was experiencing and enquired as to his views of the situation. He was cautious in his response but told me not to worry and to update him when the results were known. This helped me a lot and I came to realise how fortunate I was to have had the opportunity of belonging to this most friendly and caring group of people.

Work progressed at a pace, and soon I had histological material of sufficient quality to photograph and draw. Within the hours allocated to me I visited the microbiology department and with the initial assistance of Ted Hill and his then technician Constance, or Connie as she was known, I was soon able to take high quality photographs of skin structure and the three different glands that secreted a white mucous-type fluid, the active ingredients of which I was still to discover.

Connie, who I had seen occasionally during my undergraduate days, was a petite, very attractive, auburn-haired, green-eyed girl now in her early twenties. She had a most pleasant personality and working together was great fun since we both had the same sense of humour.

After a few weeks of working together, I plucked up the courage and asked her to come to the cinema with me. She agreed and our working relationship soon developed into a personal one, although Connie made it clear that there was no commitment on her part, since at that time she, being the only child of aging parents, was committed to caring for them to the best of her ability. Mindful of the situation that might well apply to myself in the not too distant future, I admired Connie for her caring attitude towards her parents.

Although we continued to see each other several times a week it was always in a work situation, and although I invited Connie out to the cinema on several occasions, she usually refused, claiming a family commitment, or cancelled at the last moment.

My mother's next letter informed me that she'd had the bone marrow tests at Haverfordwest Hospital and was now awaiting the results. She also said that during her stay they had checked her blood results and decided to give her two pints by transfusion and that now she felt fine. I discussed what my mother had told me with Professor Landgrebe and Dr Mitchell and they were of the view that she might be in the early stages of leukaemia. This was shattering news as far as I was concerned, and reading up about the condition in the various medical books readily available in the medical school's library did nothing to ease my concerns.

Professor Landgrebe and his wife Margo were most supportive and their kindness I shall never forget.

The Easter vacation of '55 I spent on the farm. My mother looked much better but told me that she would probably need to return to the hospital for another transfusion within the next few months. The fact that she looked better, felt stronger, and was more cheerful, was a great comfort to me although the future looked bleak.

Returning to Cardiff I set about my work with renewed urgency, mindful of the problems that might occur in the future and the time off from college that I might require. One morning as I cycled along Newport Road to college, a girl running to catch the trolley bus as it was moving off the stop, dropped some papers which scattered on the road in front of me. To avoid running over them I stopped and offered to help pick them up and that is how I met Judith.

Judith was a petite, dark-haired, blue-eyed girl with a pale complexion. Her dark brown, shoulder-length hair was straight with a hint of a curl at the ends. She wore a wine-coloured raincoat with black collar and belt and high-heeled, wine-coloured shoes. She appeared most appreciative of my assistance and when I said, 'We must do this more often,' she smiled but did not say anything.

Although following this incident I saw Judith on many occasions as I cycled to college in the mornings, our greetings were restricted to just a wave and a smile. The next time I talked to her was at one of the Saturday night dances at Sophia Gardens Pavilion. I rarely frequented this venue and had only gone along with a colleague from St Teilo's, when following a hard week's work, we both decided we needed a break and he was not keen to go alone. We talked, had a few dances, and I then asked her could I walk her home, to which she agreed.

Judith lived in a tree-lined road consisting of large three-storey terraced houses. The road, known as Connaught Road, had long been a favourite location of large professional families, since the houses boasted eleven good-sized rooms. In conversation I discovered that she lived with her widowed mother and twin sister Ann, in three rooms plus kitchen in a house owned by her father's married sister Nan, her husband Horace and her divorced sister Dorothy. Apparently her father, who was an engineer, had died suddenly of a heart attack, and not having sufficient money to retain the family home near Oxford, her mother, herself and her twin sister were forced to move to Cardiff when they were fourteen, and where they rented a living room, kitchen and two bedrooms from their mother's sister-in-law and her husband. Following two years at commercial college, Judith took up employment with an insurance company while her sister Ann worked for a large construction company.

Judith was quite different from girls that I had previously met, being rather shy and possibly lacking in confidence. I recognised this as one of my characteristics when I was eighteen. I enquired whether she would come out with me again and having fixed a time and date, I kissed her goodnight and walked the half-mile or so back to St Teilo's.

I saw a lot of Judith in the following weeks, picking her up from work and walking her home, visiting the cinema once a week and walking around Roath Park Lake at the weekend. Soon the summer vacation was upon us and I left for home, having outlined to Judith why this was necessary but not mentioning my mother's health problem since I felt that this was best kept to myself. When I arrived home I decided that I would take out a provisional driving licence and find somebody who would give me some top-up lessons, since although only having driven a tractor I was very familiar with all aspects of the motorcar and had driven Professor Landgrebe's Rover on a few occasions. My old school friend Howell came to the rescue and three weeks later we decided that I was ready to take my driving test. The nearest test centre was Cardigan, and despite getting the question on the colour sequence of traffic lights wrong, I obtained my driver's licence at the first attempt.

My mother appeared to be in reasonable health, with the warm, sunny weather of the summer of '55 bringing some of the colour back to her cheeks. She tired easily, however, and her boundless energy of the old days was missing.

During the last six months my letters to Cynthia had got fewer and fewer and hers to me tended to get shorter with less news as to how her Teachers' Certificate Course was progressing. She often recalled her visit to the St Teilo's dinner dance and her weekend in Cardiff. Whether she hoped for a further invitation I will never know, since although I missed writing and seeing her, I knew that her upbringing and family background and my world were very different and I could not see Cynthia accepting anything less than what she had experienced all her life.

I returned to Cardiff, since my first task was to find accommodation, having said farewell to my friends and colleagues at St Teilo's when I left in July. Father Pearce expressed his sadness at my leaving, but was mindful of the fact that normally students stayed at St Teilo's for a maximum of three years, I considered myself lucky. The other fathers gathered to wish me well in the future.

After a few days' searching I came across suitable accommodation in Partridge Road. This was a pleasant tree-lined road off Newport Road and within easy walking distance of the college.

The two-storey house was owned by a Mrs Redman, a widowed lady in her early sixties. My room on the first floor was fitted with a bed, desk, wardrobe, chest of drawers, and two armchairs. Heating was provided by a gas fire on a meter while in the corner was a small hand basin. Across the landing was the shared bathroom and toilet. Also provided was a small electric hob suitable for boiling a kettle or warming up milk. The rental was modest and much less than what I had been paying at St Teilo's, although food was not included.

On my return to Cardiff, Judith invited me home for an evening meal and to meet her family. Although the twin sisters were very alike in looks they differed in personality, with Ann being more sociable and outgoing. She was engaged to John, a young man who was at the time undertaking his National Service in the Royal Air Force. He was based at Hereford and only returned to Cardiff at weekends. Their mother, Gwyneth Llewellyn, was a slight, grey-haired woman who had brought up her daughters in a strict, old-fashioned way. She was born in the Rhondda of Welsh parents, and in her teens had immigrated to Canada with her brother, where she had embarked on a semi-professional career as a singer. On her return to Wales she had married Harry Llewellyn, a plant engineer, and taken up residence outside Oxford where the twins had been born.

The evening turned out to be a very pleasant occasion, and following the meal I was introduced to the other members of the family – Horace, his wife Nan and her sister Dorothy.

My research continued apace with everybody in the department being very helpful, always asking about my mother's health, and generally making sure I was looked after. Mrs Willis tended to mother me with a constant supply of coffee and the odd sandwich, while Jean, who looked after the toads, ensured that I had an adequate supply for my work. I still met Connie when working in the microbiology department, and despite not being an item, the bond of two people understanding each other, which we had established early on, remained.

In October I had a telegram informing me that my mother was in hospital again and the following weekend I returned home to see how things were. The hospital being thirty-five miles away from the farm without a car and no local bus service, my family were entirely dependant on the kindness of friends who had cars and were prepared to take them to Haverfordwest.

After a few days in hospital and a further blood transfusion my mother was allowed home, much to our delight and that of her collie dog who latterly was her constant companion, and on her return home refused to leave my mother's bedroom, where she curled up a the foot of the bed.

I returned to Cardiff in the knowledge that my journeys home would become more frequent and that in the longer term, I would need to consider the future and work outside the university.

I discussed these issues with Professor Landgrebe, and he considered my assessment as being correct. His constructive suggestions included the purchase of a small, cheap-to-run car that would make travelling between Cardiff and Pembrokeshire more cost effective; that I consider modifying my initial three-year research programme to a two-year one aiming at a Master of Science degree; and finally, that I consider seeking a teaching appointment at a grammar school, thereby qualifying for exemption from compulsory National Service.

By the next morning, I had decided to take up his suggestions.

Although the Post-Graduate Scholarship of the University of Wales was fairly modest, I had managed to save a little money during my first year, while the major part of the second year's award was still in my bank account.

Mindful of the professor's emphasis on cheap and economical, I spent many hours sourcing a suitable vehicle. At a small dealership off City Road, which at that time was the Mecca for car sales, I came across a 1934 Austin 10 in apparent good order and with an asking price of £28. After a ride and an inspection, when I used all the knowledge I had acquired as a result of Friday afternoons in the department, I satisfied myself that this was the car I wanted. I explained to the dealer the reason for my wanting a car, my mother's illness, and my lack of money due to being a student, and eventually we agreed on a price of £25. Since the car had a valid road tax disc, and I had paid in cash, the only outstanding task was to obtain insurance cover, and here the dealer was most helpful in obtaining for me a cover note for thirty days.

That evening I drove around to Connaught Road to show Judith my new possession. The following Friday afternoon I drove the Austin into the yard behind the department, where Professor Landgrebe gave it the once over and instructed me as to what checks I should make before embarking on the journey to Pembrokeshire.

Curtailing my research programme by one year meant that all the work that I had undertaken, involving photographs, histological drawings of various structures, and the results and conclusions of physiological experiments, now had to be written up, typed and bound as a piece of original research leading to an MSc degree.

The week before Christmas I set out for home in the Austin, which I had cleaned, polished and serviced for the occasion. It ran sweetly and soon I was passing through those townships one does not see in a train: Cowbridge, Bridgend, Port Talbot, Neath, Morriston, Pontardawe, Carmarthen, Newcastle Emlyn, Cardigan and finally Nevern. My arrival was a surprise and when I drove up the driveway and parked in the yard, my father could hardly believe his eyes, while my mother hugged and kissed me. My aunt was also delighted with my arrival and enquired when was I going to take her for a ride.

The Christmas of '55 was different, since in the days leading up to Christmas Day I was able to take the family out to Cardigan shopping and then to visit various relatives and friends that my mother and aunt had not seen for months. I rang Judith on Christmas Eve, wishing her and the family a merry Christmas and the hope of seeing them early in the New Year. New Year's Day came and went and I was on my way back to Cardiff. I drove straight to Connaught Road where Judith gave me a warm welcome, saying that she had missed me. We then went out for a ride in the car that ended up on the bed in my room at Partridge Road with Judith being more demonstrative than I had experienced to date.

The next few weeks were busy with my reading the *Times Education Supplement* from cover to cover in search of suitable teaching appointments. Eventually, I narrowed my search to three possible appointments. All were at head of department level, one being at the College School Loughborough, one at Jesus College School Oxford, and one at the Grammar School for Boys, Cowbridge. After carefully constructing my curriculum vitae, and seeking the approval of my three referees, these being my headmaster at Cardigan County School, Professor Borough, my initial degree tutor, and Professor Landgrebe, my research tutor, I posted off my applications.

All three appointments had the same closing date by which applications should be received. Following initial acknowledgement of my applications, I received invitations for interview within a further three weeks from all three schools.

The first interview date was at the Loughborough College School, and although I did not rate it as my first choice, I decided I must attend. Starting off from Cardiff in my Austin 10 that by now had been christened Susie, I headed for Leicester, staying overnight at a hotel in Leicester and completing the journey to Loughborough the following morning. Upon arrival I was greeted at the school by the headmaster, a short, bearded man in his fifties, who showed me around the department and introduced me to the chairman of the school's governors, a grey-haired country gentleman who appeared very interested in my farming background and why I had left farming. Much to my surprise, it appeared that the other applicants had been interviewed the previous day, and I was the only remaining candidate. On returning to the headmaster study I was offered the post. I then explained that since I had two further interviews pending, and in fairness to all concerned, I would not be able to give a definite answer until the following week. I could see that the headmaster was disappointed but hid his feelings, while the chairman expressed his hope that I would consider their offer favourably.

It was a long journey back to Cardiff and it was approaching midnight by the time I rolled into bed, tired but well satisfied with my very first job interview.

Two days later saw Susie and me on the familiar A48 road to Cowbridge. Although I had passed through Cowbridge on many occasions, I had never seen, or thought about its well-known boys' grammar school.

In the mid-fifties the main A48 road joining Cardiff with Swansea and West Wales passed through the centre of Cowbridge and constituted its main street and shopping area. Like many other market towns, Cowbridge's main street had a plentiful supply of hostelries dating back to coaching times, with the Duke of Wellington and the Bear Hotel being the most prominent. Turning off the main street at the Duke of Wellington Hotel led me to the grammar school.

The main school buildings nestled between the parish church and the stone-arched south gate of what had originally been part of the wall surrounding the town. The building, erected between 1847 and 1852 on the site of an earlier building, was typical of that period, with arched stone doorways and windows, stained-glass leaded lights and numerous tall, grey stone chimneys. I was shown into a small reception room adjoining the headmaster's study. On this occasion I was not the only applicant, the other being a middle-aged man who I discovered was already teaching at Swansea Grammar School and was in search of promotion.

I was ushered into the headmaster's study by a young man who was obviously acting as clerk to the appointments' panel. The panel consisted of two persons: the headmaster Mr Idwal Rees and Councillor Percy Smith, chairman of the school governors. Councillor Smith was a small, white-haired, pleasant-looking man with a welcoming smile. Idwal Rees was a tall, lean man in his late forties. Although I had no knowledge of his background at the time, I subsequently discovered that he was a distinguished classics scholar and an outstanding athlete, being a Rugby International representing Wales on fourteen occasions and captaining the team in 1938. He had graduated from the University College Swansea, gaining an honours degree in Greek and Latin, and then gone up to St John's College Cambridge where he took his MA degree in the Classical Tripos.

The background to the appointment was then explained to me. Biological sciences were being introduced into the sixth form provision to ensure that pupils wishing to go on to medical school would no longer be required to move to another school to gain their entry qualifications. At the present time the new laboratory and adjoining rooms were in the process of construction, while the equipping of the unit would be the responsibility of the person appointed. There then followed various questions, including whether I would be prepared to undertake a few hours' teaching science in lower school, and how I felt about assisting with games periods and in particular rugby. I felt that my short period of teaching at my old school at Cardigan, my captaining the school at rugby and my continued involvement with rugby and athletics while at University College and the Welsh School of Medicine were looked on very favourably by the headmaster, and both he and the chairman were smiling when the interview concluded.

Ten minutes later I was called back into the study and offered the appointment. In those ten minutes I had decided that although I had one further interview pending, I would, if offered, accept the post. This I did, much to the delight of the headmaster, who in our subsequent conversation mentioned that he had received a personal telephone call from Tom Evans singing my praises, a factor the committee could not ignore. Thus my career in teaching had begun.

I drove back to Cardiff on cloud nine, immediately wrote to my mother with the good news, sent a rejection letter to Loughborough and cancelled my pending interview at Oxford.

That evening I celebrated with Judith with a visit to the Royal Oak public house followed by some fish and chips in newspaper.

Chapter Twelve

The next few weeks were a blur of activity mixed with a sense of achievement. I had bought a car; I was well on the way to completing my Masters Degree; and most important of all had a wonderful job waiting for me in September. Professor Landgrebe and all the departmental staff were thrilled with the news of my appointment, with the professor admitting that he had secretly wished that I would get the job, since he hoped that in a year's time his son Peter would be a pupil at the school, and my being on the staff would be an added bonus.

I reported to Professor Borough with the news and he was equally pleased, while I wrote a special letter of thanks to Tom Evans.

Easter was fast approaching, and I decided to ask Judith to accompany me home to Pembrokeshire. She was delighted, but her mother was somewhat reluctant and only agreed after I had assured her that her daughter would be safe and would come to no harm. Once she had given her approval, I wrote to my mother letting her know that I was would be home on the Thursday before Good Friday and that I would be accompanied by a girlfriend.

All my family came out to welcome us as we drove into the farmyard. My mother gave us both a big hug and immediately put Judith at ease with her usual smile. My Aunt Catherine was equally welcoming and even my father was enthusiastic with my success and warmly welcomed Judith to Deep Well Farm.

Judith had been given my old bedroom while I had been moved to the spare room across the landing. My mother and father now occupied what used to be my grandfather's bedroom, while Aunt Catherine occupied the other front facing room.

Following an evening meal, Judith and I went for a short walk around the various farm buildings, most of which were now empty and dilapidated, with the only building in use being the cowshed and dairy. The workshop where my grandfather used to make farm gates and styles was locked and probably had not been used for many a year, while the stables only had one occupant – my father's horse, which he still used to visit Newport and his favourite Golden Lion Hotel.

As we walked down the driveway that was once kept in a good state of repair by Davy Jones, and was now being invaded by grass and bramble, I realised that I was seeing the end of an era, since with my mother's very uncertain health; the spirit had gone from the place.

As usual the family retired early and Judith and I were the last to ascend the stairs. Having had a quick wash, I undressed and then crossed to Judith's room to say goodnight. She was sitting up in bed reading a book, but when I came in she blew out the bedside candle and drew back the covers, inviting me to come to her bed. That night we made love for the first time, on the bed and in the room where I had been born twenty-four years earlier.

That Easter weekend was one that I will always remember since in many ways it marked the beginning of another phase in my life.

On the Wednesday following the Easter weekend we said our goodbyes with my mother and aunt crying and my father hoping that we would return soon. Little did he know how soon that would be. Returning to the department I was soon steeped in paper, photographs and drawings, with Miss Owen, Professor Landgrebe's secretary, typing out page after page of the text that would form the basis of my research thesis.

About a week later, I had a dream, and although not prone to dreaming, this particular dream I shall always remember. I was entering a long hospital ward of about a dozen beds, one shrouded by curtains. On passing through the curtains I saw my mother looking pale, with her greying hair bathed in sweat. She held out her hand to me and whispered through dry lips, 'goodbye, dear son,' then drew her last breath. I woke with a start feeling that I had been granted a snapshot of the future.

Two days later a telephone call to the department informed me that my mother was back in hospital having suffered a haemorrhage.

Within two hours I was on my way home, arriving as dusk was falling.

The next few weeks saw me taking my father and aunt back and forth to the hospital at Withybush Haverfordwest on an almost daily basis. The hospital being around thirty-five miles from the farm, this journey, together with the two-hour visiting time, took up the best part of the day. Local friends and relatives calling to enquire as to my mother's condition occupied the evenings.

When I first entered the ward I got a shock, since it was exactly as I had seen in my dream, although by mother occupied a bed halfway down the room. My mother was now suffering from infections which appeared as swellings on her face, arms and other parts of the body, and despite blood transfusions, that previously had made her feel much better, their effect was now less obvious.

I had numerous discussions with the consultant and although he was still not absolutely sure, he agreed that leukaemia would appear to be the most likely diagnosis.

On the morning of 28 May 1956 the hospital telephoned to let us know that my mother was very poorly. Accompanied by my father and aunt I drove as quickly as possible to the hospital. The ward sister met us and suggested that we should see my mother one at a time so as not to disturb her. My father and aunt made me go first, and as I entered the ward and saw the curtained bed next to the door, I realised that this was my dream coming true.

The change in my mother's appearance in twenty-four hours was hardly creditable. I clasped her hand and as she opened her eyes there was a flash of recognition and maybe the slightest of smiles, then she drew her last breath. In that moment and looking back, I felt, and could swear that I saw her spirit or soul leaving her body and my mother was no more.

Going outside I did not have to tell my father and aunt what had happened since the look on my face told them all.

Funeral arrangements were put in the hands of the local undertaker, with instructions that he was to bring my mother's body direct from the hospital to Nevern Church on the day of the funeral, stopping for a few moments at the end of the driveway to Deep Well Farm since that had always been her wish. I hired a car to follow the hearse from the hospital to Nevern and then back to the farm.

What no one had realised was the affection that the local community had for my mother, with dozens of letters and cards from those who knew her coupled with numerous visits from those who lived near. The local newspaper printed two poems in her memory, one in English that read:

> She never failed to do her best,
> Her heart was true and tender,
> She laboured hard for those she loved
> And left us to remember.

The one in Welsh, written by a local man – William Owen read:

> Pam oedd gwanwyn mewn gogoniant,
> Canai'r adarn yn y coed,
> Alice annwyl tithau'n marw
> Pan oad taiur a deugain oed.
>
> Nid oes iaith all dreathu'r golled
> Calon pur gymeriad hardd,
> Oedd o hyd ar bawb yn gwenu
> Fel blodeuyn yn yr ardd.
>
> Mae'th gyfeillion lu yn wylo
> A'u calonau heddyw'n glwy,
> Pan yn meddwl na chant yma
> Weld dy wyneb siriol mwy.
>
> Cest dy symud yn y gwanwyn
> Ni chest fwyniant tymor haf,
> Ond enillaist yn dy fywyd
> Enw a chymeriad da.
>
> Gwag yw'r aelwyd yn y cartref
> Nid oes angea gofyn pam,
> Collodd Marsden ei hoff briod
> Collodd John ei annwul fam.

Anawyl deulu cymrwch gysur
Y mae Alice eto'n fyw,
Rhodio mae yng nghwmni'r engyl
A'r hyd aur heolydd Duw.

Fe gewch eto gyd-gyfarfod
Yn un dyrfa fawr di-ri,
A chewch dreulio tragwydd
Yn ei chwmni annwyl hi.

The day of the funeral arrived and for the last time we visited the hospital to bring my dear mother to her resting place. As she had requested, the hearse drove very slowly past the gates to the driveway of the farm, and there waiting at the gate was her collie dog, just as she had been on the other occasions when my mother was returning from hospital.

My mother's funeral was one of the largest that Nevern Church had ever seen, with people from far and wide attending and paying their respects. Many were not known to my father, aunt or myself but had one thing in common; namely, they wanted to be present to say goodbye to someone special.

My mother was buried in the family plot alongside my grandfather, grandmother, and Aunt Martha.

The next few days were taken up with my discussing with my father and aunt what was best for the future. My aunt, who was eighty years of age on 25 May, and my father, who would be sixty-six years of age in August, were in no position to carry on with the farm, so the decision was made to sell the farm and auction all surplus effects. Then there was the question as to where they should live. One possibility was that they acquire a small townhouse in Newport. The other option was that I acquire a property in or near Cowbridge and my work, and that they come to live with me. Their immediate response to these two possibilities was to choose the latter, and so started my house-hunting experience.

I went with my father to see the family solicitor who had arranged the initial purchase and subsequent mortgage on the farm, and instructed him to negotiate a sale as soon as possible.

The next day I returned to Cardiff, calling in on my aunt Lois at Kenfig Hill.

She was very sad at the passing of my mother, but delighted with my obtaining a post at such a school as Cowbridge Grammar. She wanted to know what the future was for my father and aunt, and was pleased when I told her they were going to live with me and that I was going to look at properties in or around Cowbridge.

Aunt Lois was a very kind and generous lady, and when she heard of my plans she immediately offered her help financially with the deposit on any property that I decided to buy. This was a great weight off my mind, since although I had agreed to have my father and aunt coming to live with me, there had not been any time to consider the short-term financial implications. I gave my aunt a big hug and left her feeling more confident than I had upon arrival.

It was dusk before I arrived in Cardiff and Connaught Road where Judith and her family were pleased to see me, while at the same time recording their sadness at the passing of my mother.

After recording the events of the last ten days, I was exhausted and made my excuses for an early night.

Professor Landgrebe, his family and all the departmental staff expressed their sympathy and support, with Jean Curry showing true emotion and hugging me with tears in her eyes. On reflection, the support and kindness of Professor Landgrebe and his colleagues over the last eighteen months had been outstanding, and I was eternally grateful to Professor Borough for directing me towards the Pharmacology Department initially.

It was a week later that realisation of the significance of the events of the last few months hit me. My mother, who had always been my strongest ally and friend, was no more; arrangements for the sale of the farm, its stock and implements were pending; I had a new job that I had little experience of; I had committed myself to buying a house, and to providing a home for my father and aunt, and of course completing my degree. Perhaps I needed an understanding shoulder to cry on, but it was not Judith I turned to but Jean. One day she asked me whether I would like to come over to her house for supper and meet her parents. Normally I would have said no, but in my state of mind I said yes. Jean's parents were a nice Roman Catholic couple who made me most welcome since it appeared that Jean had told them all about my mother passing on and the resulting problems that I was faced with. The very relaxed atmosphere probably contributed to my talking more than usual and about my thoughts and feelings, and I left, after kissing Jean goodnight, feeling considerably more at peace with myself. I felt guilty about making an excuse to Judith regarding my non-appearance on the evening in question, but promised myself that I would make it up to her.

The following week my degree submission was finished to the satisfaction of both Professor Landgrebe and Professor Borough, and three copies were dispatched for professional binding.

I then turned my attention to finding a suitable property in Cowbridge. Professor Landgrebe had advised me to seek the advice of a solicitor before embarking on any negotiations with an estate agent. This advice I had taken, and had arranged an appointment with a partner in the firm Dolman & Son in Cardiff. My solicitor, who later became my long-term mentor and friend, was Strad Jones. He was a delightful character, with snowy white hair and a reddish complexion, bright blue eyes and a welcoming smile. His only piece of advice to me was, 'Do not go over the figure you had in mind when buying a property, and when buying always consider how easy it would be to sell.'

Cowbridge, being a relatively small market town, had a limited supply of properties for sale and since there was only one estate agent in the town, the search for what was available on the market was relatively simple. One was priced well over what I could afford, while the other faced the main A48 as it ran through the town towards East Gate. The property had at one time been a shop of some kind, but now the ground floor consisted of two good sized rooms, one with a large bay window, a kitchen and a small washroom. The first floor consisted of three bedrooms and a bathroom. At the rear of the property was a small courtyard with double doors leading on to a side street, and a small vegetable garden. The asking price was within my budget, but before committing myself, I called in on my aunt Lois, who immediately came with me to have a second look at the property. We both decided it fitted my needs and a deposit was paid with a completion date fixed for the last week in August. My aunt Lois proved a tower of strength at a time when I needed it most, and on that very day on returning to Kenfig Hill wrote me out a cheque for £800. That evening I returned to Cardiff in high spirits and in the knowledge that come September I would have a job and a home in Cowbridge.

I called round on Judith to tell her what had been achieved, and she and her family were very pleased for me. My next task was to return to Pembrokeshire and finalise arrangements for the auction of the farm, stock, implements and household furniture that would be surplus to requirements at our new home at Cowbridge. Although my father had stood up well to my mother's death, the longer-term effects of not having her by his side were now beginning to show and in some ways he was a broken man and just wanted to leave the place which held so many memories. My aunt Catherine, however, remained unchanged, and went about her housework, attended church on Sunday mornings, attended the family graves midweek and went shopping in Newport every Friday. I gave a full account of what their new home was like, pointing out all the advantages such as my aunt being able to walk to the shops and my father being able to walk to at least five different hostelries.

A letter was received from the solicitor informing us that the farm had been sold with a completion date of the first of September. My father and I then approached the auctioneer regarding a suitable date for the auction, which was fixed for the second week in August.

While in Cardigan arranging the auction details I met Thelma. She had read of my mother's passing in the local newspaper and expressed her regret at not having met my mother since the obituary obviously reflected a rather special person. Thelma, although now in her early twenties, looked just the same as on that night of Cardigan Fair, and proceeded to tell me that she had parted from her long-term boyfriend, and would I like to visit her at home for tea the following week, since, as she told me, she had often spoken of me to her mother, who had many times expressed a wish to meet me.

I was flattered, and against my better judgement said yes.

Thelma lived in a bungalow in a small village about six miles outside Cardigan called Llechryd. I arrived at the appointed time, and after being introduced to her mother, the three of us sat down to tea in the living room. Thelma's mother was an older version of her daughter, with her once red hair now streaked with grey and an appearance that made her look older than she really was. Thelma's father was out, and from what I could gather was rarely at home. She made me feel most welcome and congratulated me on my degree and my new job that Thelma had told her about. After tea she ushered us into the lounge saying that young people should be together and not with oldies.

Thelma was very loving, with kisses that became more ardent as the evening wore on. She said she wanted me more than ever before and wished we'd had continued the brief relationship we had five years earlier. For my part, all the stresses and worries of the last months faded into the background, and all I could think of was that I was with a beautiful girl who wanted me to make love to her. For the next hour or so we were in our own magical world of two people as one, not caring about the past or the future, only the present.

It was dark by the time I drove away, since after saying goodbye to her mother, Thelma and I spent almost an hour sitting talking in the car outside the bungalow. Although we both knew that I would shortly be leaving the area and taking my family with me, and that a very special effort would be needed if our relationship was to continue, we both promised that we would write and keep in touch as much as possible.

The auction involved animals being numbered and then sold individually by the auctioneer. Animals were paraded in a ring that had been roped off in the farmyard, and where they could be viewed by potential bidders. Farm machinery, equipment and household effects were grouped in lots in the field adjoining the house, with the auctioneer and potential bidders moving from lot to lot as the sale progressed. The sale was over in around two hours, with buyers reporting to the house, where the auctioneer's clerk took cash or cheques and issued receipts for the items sold. It was a sad day for me, but I felt for my father as he wandered around seeing familiar items being carried away by strangers. I believe that the biggest wrench of all was to see his one remaining horse, named Kit, being led away by her new owner.

The following day I returned to Cardiff to ascertain progress on the purchase of 51 East Gate. Strad Jones was his usual cheerful self and assured me that everything was on track for a completion during the last week in August. That evening I went around to see Judith, and spent several hours recalling the events of the last weeks, the sale of the farm and the auction, the buying of the house in Cowbridge and the completion of my degree. Having met my father and aunt, she was of the opinion that the change of environment from a farm in Pembrokeshire to a townhouse in Cowbridge would be quite a culture shock and would probably need careful handling. We then returned to my room in Partridge Road where we made love before I walked her home.

The next morning I called in at the Pharmacology Department. Being August none of the academic staff were in and the technical staff consisted of Jean and Mrs Willis. After the compulsory cup of coffee Mrs Willis went off to do some work, leaving Jean and me on our own. She was disappointed I had not been in touch before, and wanted to know how my arrangements were progressing. I outlined briefly the situation, pointing out that due to all the pressures I would be under for the next few months she should forget all about me and get on with her life. I could see that she was upset and longed to comfort her, but knew that any relationship with Jean would be from her point of view a serious commitment, which right then I could not handle.

True to his word Strad Jones arranged the completion date for the purchase of 51 East Gate for 28 August. He had arranged a mortgage for me with a Mutual Friendly Society, and with the deposit paid, on the morning of the 28th I was handed the keys. 28 August also happened to be Judith's birthday, so we celebrated both events that evening with a glass of wine and a session of love-making at Partridge Road. The next day I drove down to Pembrokeshire, stopping at Cowbridge to view my new property. On 31 August the furniture van with my father on board, followed by my aunt and my mother's collie dog, Juno, in the back of my car, left Deep Well Farm for the very last time. It was truly the end of an era.

Chapter Thirteen

The Free School, as it was originally named, at Cowbridge, was founded by two members of the Stradling family of St Donat's Castle, late in the first decade of the seventeenth century. The school was therefore the oldest in the county of Glamorgan. There was also a myth, which many regarded as true; that the foundation by the Stradlings was a latter-day adventure, for the school was in some sense a direct descendant or continuation of the old College of St Illtyd, believed to have been at Llantwit Major. Established in the Age of the Saints, with St Illtyd as founder, St Patrick as an early master, and St David as a pupil, the school at Cowbridge was not only the oldest educational establishment in the Western World, but a direct and most hallowed survivor from the culture of Celtic Christianity.

Sir Edward Stradling of St Donat's Castle was a figure of the English Renaissance. He came of an ancient and noble line and founded the school in 1608–09. The earliest known master was a Rev. Walter Stradling, a poor relation of the founder who became master in 1618. Sir John Stradling, great nephew of Sir Edward, was a scholar and poet; he had graduated with a Bachelor of Arts degree from Magdalene Hall, Oxford, and was instrumental in ensuring the development and success of the school in its early years.

There was little doubt that the school was constituted by Sir John as a charity, which was later transferred to Sir Leoline Jenkins in 1684. At that time the master was given the use of the schoolhouse, with an annual salary of twenty pounds. Sir Leoline subsequently bequeathed the school to Jesus College in his will, and got the college to agree to accept its control, with the master of the school appointed by the principal of Jesus College.

Many famous masters were appointed by this means, including Daniel Durel; Thomas Williams; John Walters, succeeded by his brother Daniel Walters; William Williams, who served as master for sixty years; Hugo Daniel Harper, who achieved a distinction fit to rank with that of Dr Arnold; W Holt Beever; the second Thomas Williams; Rev. James Colin Morson; Rev. Morris Price Williams; Rev. W F Evans; and Richard Williams, MC, MA, who was master for twenty years and was the last master to be appointed by the principal of Jesus College. Following the appointment of Richard Williams in 1919 control of the school passed from the hands of the principal of Jesus College to those of a new governing body in such a way as to make the school an assisted school maintained by the Glamorgan County Council. It was this governing body, consisting of ten members – six appointed by the County Council and four by Jesus College – that in 1938 appointed J Idwal Rees MA, as the fourteenth master.

Cowbridge Grammar School was apparently the first home of Rugby Football in Wales. The Rugby Football Union was formed in 1871 and three years later Cowbridge Grammar School was well enough known as a nursery of the game to become the scene of the newly-formed Cardiff RFC's first away fixture played at Cowbridge on 21 November 1874. The Cardiff team apparently journeyed to Cowbridge in a coach and four, everyone having enjoyed the outing, especially the coachman, as on the return journey he was unable to keep his seat on the box, and one of the players took the reins and brought the party safely home, although they smashed the turn-pike gate which stood at Ely, in consequence of the gatekeeper's endeavouring to stop them as they were driving through, in the belief that they were going to evade payment. The only other collision was with a lamppost in front of the Cardiff Town Hall in St Mary Street.

On the morning of the second Monday of September 1956, I stepped through the main entrance – under the School Motto, '*Vigiliis et Virtute*' taken from the coat of arms adopted by Sir Leoline Jenkins and since his time prominently displayed on the walls of Jesus College and on the school badge – into a historic school steeped in tradition and long-established practice, and housed in what I can only describe as not an unattractive Victorian Tudor block of buildings, commemorated by an inscription on the outer wall in Gothic lettering that read: '*In honorem Dei et Ecclesiae hancce Scholam novis aedificiis amplificatam restituit munificentia*

125

Collegii Jesu Oxon. Anno Domini MDCCCLXVII'. (To the honour of God and of the Church, this school was enlarged with new buildings and restored by the generosity of Jesus College, Oxford, AD 1874). Upon entering the headmaster's study I was warmly welcomed, with Idwal Rees expressing his pleasure that I was now a member of staff and also a Cowbridge resident. In giving me my teaching timetable, he explained that I was to be form master to a first-year form and would be expected to teach them two hours of science per week. I was allocated a further two hours per week tuition of boys in the fifth form wishing to pursue biological sciences in the sixth form, while the remainder of my timetable was devoted to those boys in the lower sixth wishing to pursue medicine or related careers. Wednesday afternoons were devoted to upper school games and Idwal hoped that I would participate. He then invited me to accompany him to morning assembly in the main hall where I was introduced to the assembled school as the new master with responsibility for the biological sciences.

Morning assembly at Cowbridge Grammar School was very similar to that which I had experienced at Cardigan County School, although in this instance the headmaster occasionally lapsed into Latin. The boys stood in rows with the lower forms at the front and middle and upper school at the rear of the hall. The teaching staff, in academic dress, stood along one side of the hall, while the master addressed the assembly from the stage at the front of the hall. At that time there were around 300 boys attending the school, of which ninety were boarders, with the remainder being known as day boys.

The school buildings were spread over three sites. The main building housed the master's study and private accommodation, the assembly hall, the dormitories of the boarders, kitchens and a selection of classrooms that faced onto the master's lawn that led up to the French windows of the master's study. This Victorian Tudor building stood next to the great stone arched South Gate of the town and occupied the site of the original Free School. Crossing Church Street from the main building gained entry to Old Hall. This building, which overlooked the main street of the town, had at one time been the home of Archdeacon Edmondes, founder president of the school's Old Boys Association, and was leased to the school in 1931. Old Hall, with its beautiful grounds and oak-panelled rooms, housed the staff room, physics laboratory, a selection of classrooms and Mr Penny, the school caretaker's, private accommodation. Adjacent to the grounds but separated from them by a stone wall with entrance arch, was a single-storey building that had been converted into a woodwork shop. The third site occupied by the school was outside the South Gate and consisted of relatively new purpose-built accommodation, including a gymnasium, the dayboys' dining room and kitchen, the chemistry laboratory, a selection of classrooms used by middle school, and the new biological science accommodation completed a few weeks before my arrival. Across the road from this site was a small white-washed cottage that housed the school handyman and porter, Tom Carter, and his wife.

During the course of my first few days at the school, I was introduced to the eighteen members of staff, the majority of whom had been at the school for many years. The oldest of these was the deputy headmaster and chemistry master J D Owen, known by both boys and staff as 'JD'. A tall, well-built, white-haired, jovial man in his early sixties, JD had taken over as acting master during the Second World War when Idwal Rees was on active service. Upon Idwal's return JD continued as the master's right-hand man. The assistant chemistry master was Maurice Vaughan, a resident of Cowbridge who had spent all his teaching life at the school and was an example of a dedicated teacher. The senior English master was Arthur Codling, a tall, aristocratic Englishman with a dry sense of humour. His teaching ability was highly regarded among the boys and by his junior English colleague, Andrew Davies. Mathematics was taught by Darwin Adams, a tall, lean, white-haired man in his late fifties who had two sons at the school, both of whom, as I discovered later, were anxious to pursue a career in medicine. Darwin was an outstanding mathematician and in addition to his teaching undertook some consultative work for the manufacturer of 'one-arm bandits' gaming machines.

Welsh language and literature was taught by Tudor Hughes. Tudor originated from North Wales but over the years had lost much of his North Wales accent. Among his many talents I discovered later was that he was an outstanding cricketer and batsman. The senior French master was Bryn Edwards, a medium-built man with dark hair and black horn-rimmed glasses who shared the teaching with the junior French master Andrew Davies – a short, stocky man in his early forties. Bryn had twin sons who also attended the school and again both were interested in a career in medicine. Morley Davies was the geography master. He was a most pleasant of persons and had spent most of the war years as an aircraft navigator in the Royal Air Force. Another war veteran was Sid Harris, who had served in the Eighth Army under General Montgomery. Sid shared the teaching of Latin with the headmaster, and in addition to being an excellent teacher was, like the master, a good rugby football player. Sid's one weakness was driving; having only driven a tank while in the army, his approach to driving a family car on the road had distinct similarities, and his very first driving lesson, when I foolishly agreed to be his tutor, was an experience I shall never forget.

The senior history master was Jim White, a Cornishman who lived on his own and travelled to and from school on a Vincent Black Shadow motorbike. This bike was the topic of much conversation and attention, and Jim giving fellow members of staff a ride on the pillion was a favourite lunchtime activity. Physics was taught by the senior physics master Tommy Evans and his assistant master Ken Helyar. Tommy was a short, stocky man who was known for a somewhat short fuse and quick temper. He travelled to and from school on a small moped made to look even smaller when Tommy's not inconsiderable bulk was seated on it. He originated from a small village in the Rhondda Valley, where he still lived sharing a small terraced house with his widowed mother. Ken Helyar had arrived at the school the previous term and next to myself was the youngest member of staff. Ken was of medium build with receding red hair and a cheerful disposition and he and I soon became good friends. As I discovered later, Ken was an exceptionally talented spin bowler and was the star of the Boys v Masters annual cricket match.

Woodwork was in some ways a surprising element of the school's curriculum, but it was popular with those boys who desired to work with their hands as well as their heads. The woodwork master was Reg Whittle, an ex-Royal Air Force man, who had come to the school upon leaving the service in the late 1940s. He was an exceptionally talented craftsman who was much liked and admired by the boys and popular with colleagues since he instructed many, including myself, to turn pieces of wood into exquisite fruit bowls and the like.

Being a school with a classics reputation the classics were taught jointly by the master, Iolo Davies and Peter Cobb. While Iolo only taught the Greek and Latin, Peter also taught religious knowledge. Iolo and Peter were, in addition to being subject tutors, the resident masters with private accommodation in the main school building, and who together with the headmaster's wife, had responsibility for the ninety boy boarders at the school. At a school with the sporting traditions of Cowbridge Grammar, games and physical education rated highly in the overall provision, and required a master with a broad range of sporting interests, ability and talent. Such a man was Donald Pugh, a science graduate who had pursued post-graduate studies in sport education following his initial degree. Don was a lean, athletic man who when he was not teaching, sending the junior boys on country runs, or coaching the school's rugby team, frequented the Duke of Wellington Hotel, which was, according to him, his place to relax.

The female contingent of the staff consisted of Miss Mary Davies, a middle-aged lady who taught art on a part-time basis, and Miss Eira Williams, the school's secretary. In her early fifties, Eira, although crippled with arthritis, still managed to deal with the headmaster's secretarial work, the ordering system for the school, and the occasional demands of the teaching staff when typed material was required.

The wearing of school uniform was compulsory for all boys. This consisted of grey flannels, black shoes, a grey or white shirt and a black blazer with the school badge on the breast pocket. This badge, in the form of a shield, was white with three red cocks over the school motto – *Vigiliis et Virtute*. The shield was similar to the arms of Judge David Jenkins of Hensol, who appeared to have been a patron of the young Sir Leoline Jenkins.

Originally it appeared boys were placed in school houses according to the district that they lived in or came from. These district names were in 1933 abolished in favour of houses named after persons who had contributed in some way to the development of the school. When I arrived in 1956, there were four houses – Durel House, Seys House, Leoline House and Stradling House, each captained by a school prefect. Although the main revelry was on the sports field, this competition extended to many of the social activities of the school.

So it was that my career in teaching began, surrounded by buildings shrouded in history and tradition, colleagues who were as individual as you were ever likely to come across, and boys of all shapes and sizes all eager to learn and live up to the proud traditions of their school.

I have always regarded the teaching of science as essentially practical based, and my teaching of it to Form 2 at Cowbridge was no exception. Through the cooperation of the headmaster, all my teaching during my first year at the school was in the new biological science laboratory, which for me was the ideal situation. Since I had a free hand with the curriculum I started with everyday objects that all the boys were familiar with and then developed scientific principles around such objects. A common weed or garden plant provided the basis for identifying structure followed by simple experiments illustrating the function of the parts so identified. Chemical crystals and how they are formed was a basis for great competition among the boys as to who could grow the largest crystal. Spectacle lenses were the basis for light rays and how they can be bent or concentrate light, while a study of the dozen toads – *Xenopus laevis* – which I had brought with me from Cardiff formed the basis of animal behaviour. The one that proved most popular with the second-formers was my turning water into wine, illustrating the effects of acids and alkalis on indicators.

My teaching of biology to the fifth form required more structure since all the boys were attempting their ordinary level examinations at the end of one year's tuition, although the syllabus normally stretched ever two. Again my emphasis was on learning through seeing or doing with numerous practical demonstrations, or when possible the boys undertaking their own practical work. Demonstrations of dissections and muscle physiology experiments were very popular and indicative of a good lower-sixth next year.

My first year six who had no previous knowledge of biological sciences, consisted of five boys: William Adams, the eldest son of Darwin Adams, the mathematics master; Victor Harris, the only son of a miner's widow living in Talbot Green; Michael Morgan, the son of a consultant surgeon at a nearby Bridgend hospital; Francis Taylor, the son of a civil servant; and David Green, the son of an RAF Officer based at the local Airbase of St Athan. These were young men only five or six years younger than myself, so I had to adopt a different approach to the teaching of both botany and zoology. Basically my approach was to highlight the main features of the topic under discussion, indicating the textbook or reference book that would provide the detail. Once such background knowledge had been identified, practical work in the form of investigations, dissections or experimentation I would demonstrate, and then this would be undertaken by the boys, working individually or in two groups. This approach proved popular with all my students and provided what I believed was good experience to later studies at university.

My demands for equipment and consumables to undertake the necessary practical work proved a culture shock to the headmaster, since his experience of student requirements started and ended with the supply of appropriate textbooks. He was, however, very sympathetic and had allocated, upon the advice of HM Inspectors, a generous budget, although he was somewhat less happy when I told him these demands would be made annually, and would increase as pupil numbers studying at sixth-form level increased.

My other contribution to school activity at this time was to referee and coach the various rugby football teams during the Wednesday afternoon games periods. This proved to be great fun, with Don Pugh and myself often playing for opposing teams, much to the delight of the boys. Playing and refereeing at the same time was a skill and often one was accused of bias regarding a forward pass or late tackle although it was always very good natured, with the boys enjoying the informal relations with staff. Saturday matches against outside opposition were however, very different and the highest standards of refereeing were expected.

Chapter Fourteen

My father and Aunt Catherine had survived the move from Pembrokeshire to Cowbridge with no ill effects, and had settled down in their new home with surprising ease. My aunt, although now in her eighty-first year could walk to the shops, while my father was busy investigating the numerous hotels and hostelries that Cowbridge supported.

For the first weekend in our new home, I invited Judith for a meal and to acquaint her with all the news relating to my first week in my new job. Judith appeared to like the house and the way the furniture from the farm had fitted in, with the only new items being two single beds for my father and aunt and a double for me. I drove Judith back to Cardiff that evening and made arrangements to meet her later the following week. My next invitation was to Aunt Lois, who arrived the following Monday just as I was returning home from school. She was naturally delighted that everything had gone so well and that her nearest cousins were settled down and happy. Her parting comment to me, however, was that all it now required was for me to find a nice girl and get married.

The next morning I received a letter from Thelma addressed to the school, since when we parted I did not know for sure what my home address would be. She wanted to know how the new house and new job were turning out and when was I coming down to Cardigan next. She recalled the time we had together, and how since that time she had missed me a great deal. I had always thought a great deal of Thelma and liked her very much, so that evening I wrote back listing all that had happened but omitting any reference to seeing her again since I did not want to mislead her in any way.

On Friday afternoon I drove directly from school to Cardiff, picked up Judith from her place of work and we went for tea at the Dutch. The Dutch was one of Cardiff's older restaurants that still served traditional teas, and was much frequented by those wishing to start the weekend as soon as possible after leaving work.

After tea, and since the evening was still quite warm, we went for a stroll through the flower park adjoining the civic centre, and there I asked Judith how she would feel about getting married and living in Cowbridge with my family.

Looking back I can honestly say that it had not been my intention to ask her that evening, but having known her for quite a time, having enjoyed our lovemaking and getting on well as far as everyday issues were concerned, it appeared the natural thing to do. To my surprise Judith said yes, and we returned to Connaught Road to break the news to her family. Judith's mother, sister, aunts and uncle were delighted with the news, although her mother expressed the view that starting married life within a family situation could present problems. She did, however, agree that it was our decision, and gave us her blessing.

By the time I returned home my father and aunt had retired for the night so it was the following morning when I broke the news to them. Both were happy for me, although my father hoped that Judith could put up with him being around the house. I explained that she would still be working full-time in Cardiff and that the only days that she would be home would be at weekends, when I would also be home. That evening I drove to Kenfig Hill to acquaint my aunt Lois of the news. She was very pleased but urged caution not to rush things since I had been through a lot of changes recently which, as she put it, might affect one's judgement. Her cousin, Glyn Marsden, who with his wife Olive ran the pharmacy for my aunt, also congratulated me and wished me well in the future. The wedding was arranged for the Saturday before the school's half-term holiday, and following a visit to St Margaret's Church in Cardiff, which was Judith's parish church, it was agreed that the bands would be read out on the following three Sundays leading up to the wedding. A visit to the Angel Hotel in Cardiff ensured that a wedding breakfast would follow the wedding service and provide guests with suitable refreshments. The guest list was relatively easy to construct since we both had small families and relatively few friends. On Judith's side of the family there was her mother; Ann, her twin sister, and her fiancé; her three aunts and two uncles; and three girl friends. On my side there were just my father; Aunt Catherine and Aunt Lois, since I had chosen not to invite any of my college friends or friends from Pembrokeshire. In the absence of such friends I had invited Judith's uncle Horace to be my best man, a function he readily agreed to carry out.

A few days before the wedding I developed a very bad cold, and when on the morning of the wedding Aunt Lois came to collect us in her car, I did not feel well with a high temperature, and wished I could have stayed in bed. It was a quiet wedding with Judith looking every inch a bride in white and her twin sister acting as bridesmaid in pale blue. Following the reception, where Uncle Horace spoke of the pleasure my becoming part of the family had given him and how he hoped my family would be happy at their new home, we travelled back to Cowbridge where Aunt Lois dropped us off.

Judith and I then got into Susie and drove off on our weekend honeymoon. I had reserved a room with dinner, bed and breakfast at the Langland Bay Hotel on the Gower Coast for the Saturday and Sunday nights. The Langland Bay Hotel was a medium-size establishment perched on rocks overlooking the curved, sandy Langland Bay. It was a family-run hotel with no liquor licence, but had the advantage of a small public house within walking distance. The Saturday night was a disaster, with my high temperature, much perspiring and no desire to eat or drink. Despite these problems, however, we walked along the beach to the pub where I downed a few whiskeys and Judith had a gin and tonic. The whiskey made me feel somewhat better, but resulted in my perspiring even more and dropping off to sleep on returning to the hotel. The only consolation was Judith's comment the following morning of, 'Bad beginning, good ending.'

Sunday was a better day and following lunch we toured the Gower coastline with its winding country roads and little hamlets tucked away between land and sea. That night after dinner we made love and went to sleep in each other's arms.

Returning to Cowbridge on the Monday, we decided that while Judith had to report for work the following day, the rest of my half-term holiday should be devoted to decorating our bedroom and the adjoining stairs and hallway. Travelling to and from Cardiff was relatively easy, with a good coach service provided by the N & C Coaches, and although the travelling added a few hours to Judith's working day an acceptable pattern was soon established. On the Friday morning of what had been an eventful half-term holiday. I received a letter from the University of Wales letting me know that I had been awarded a Master of Science degree.

On returning to school, news of my marriage and of my obtaining a Master's degree spread like wildfire and both my colleagues in the staff room and the boys were most generous in their congratulations, with the headmaster and his wife extending an invitation for us to come round for drinks and an evening meal the following week.

So began another phase of my life, a phase not without minor problems but one that I could not have imagined a few years previously. My only deep regret was that my dear mother was not there to see it happen and share in my joy.

The school year at Cowbridge was punctuated by a series of traditional events. 11 November saw the parade to the school's war memorial in the adjoining parish church, when the head read out the names of boys fallen in the two World Wars before the two minutes' silence. Leading up to Christmas there was the annual carol service at the church, with the boys reading the lessons and the master reading the last lesson. Following the service both boarders and dayboys were served Christmas dinner in their respective dining halls. In terms of sporting events, the highlight of the rugby year was the match with Jesus College Oxford, and the matches with Christ College Brecon and Llandovery College. Over the years heroes were long remembered by the boys with their achievements usually grossly exaggerated. The highlights of the cricket season were again the matches with the old rivals of Brecon and Llandovery, and the traditional Boys v Masters match, which was the topic of conversation for many weeks leading up to and following the actual event. An event open to all boys with a sporting disposition was the annual cross country run, which started and finished at the

South Gate and covered approximately four miles of winding Vale of Glamorgan minor roads and pathways. This event, organised by Don Pugh, demanded considerable organisation and supervision, with members of staff and prefects dotted around the course to ensure that none of the junior boys got lost or that in the event of a twisted ankle or blistered foot aid was at hand. The annual sports day held in July after the end-of-year examinations, was the culmination of the school's sporting year, with field and track events watched by proud parents, teaching staff and their wives, and members of the local community.

Another highlight of the school year was the school play. Produced and directed by Peter Cobb, this event took place at the Cowbridge Town Hall and usually, by popular demand, ran for four nights, culminating in the Saturday night finale. Although some of the productions would not be my personal choice, the performance of some middle-and upper-school boys playing female rolls in such plays as *The Importance of being Ernest*, was outstanding and on occasions they were rated by fellow pupils as better than the 'real thing'.

As far as my personal contribution to the school was concerned, my method of teaching in the lower and middle school appeared to go down well with the boys, while in the sixth form the group of five boys had bonded as a team and with only minimal guidance from myself were developing into budding scientists, eager to learn and slowly but surely developing the practical skills that their subjects demanded. News of my marriage and my being awarded a Master's degree prompted them to purchase a congratulatory card which they all signed and which I believed was symptomatic of our pupil–teacher relationship. This gesture was very much appreciated by both Judith and me.

Just before the school closed for the Christmas holidays there was a letter that was less congratulatory from Thelma. News of my marriage had by some means filtered down to Cardigan and to Thelma, and although there had been no commitment on my part, she had viewed our last encounter in a more serious way and in the context of a possible long-term relationship. Her letter made me very sad, and although I knew that to write back would only prolong the situation, the feelings that she had penned in what would be her last letter to me were to remain in my thoughts for a very long time. The cold winter months of January, February and March saw the school covered in the occasional dustings of snow, with night frosts resulting in the school yard adjoining the main building becoming an ice rink. Although the newer parts of the school buildings had central heating, all the classrooms and the staff rooms in Old Hall and in Main School had open fires, which were tendered by Mr Penny and Tom Carter. These gave off a significant amount of localised heat and on damp days boys were known to steam while sitting in the front desks. One of the casualties of the cold weather was my old Austin 10 that had served me so well in travelling between Cardiff and Pembrokeshire. A combination of a spent battery and faulty wiring caused major starting difficulties. Coupled with worn tyres and an engine that had covered an estimated 60,000 miles, it was decided that I would look for an alternative vehicle. A few weeks later I saw an advert offering a Lanchester 10 for sale. A telephone call directed me to the location, which was a small garage located in Eweny, a small hamlet between Bridgend and Ogmore-by-Sea. The garage owner, who also had an adjoining smallholding, obviously collected and had a passion for old cars, since in sheds adjoining the small garage workshop were a range of other old cars including a BSA Sport, a Daimler 18 and two Austin 7s. The Lanchester was a 1934 model with black coachwork with a fixed fabric roof, brown leather interior, and an overhead camshaft engine and a fluid flywheel transmission. The owner explained that he had fitted new tyres, and had initially thought of using the car as everyday transport, but had now decided in favour of the Daimler 18. We went for a test drive with the owner pointing out the advantages of the fluid transmission, which was as near as one could get to an automatic transmission in 1934. The car performed faultlessly and appeared in good order, although the owner commented that if he were keeping the car, a cylinder head removal and valve reseating would not go amiss. I then asked would he be interested in buying my Austin and again after a short test drive where Susie behaved well, it was decided that a part-exchange would be possible. The following evening, armed with £30, I set off for Eweny, returning with a new car and leaving Susie to the tender mercy of her new owner.

Parked in the yard at the back of 51, the Lanchester was given a full valet with the leather seats cleaned and treated with leather feed, the carpets cleaned and vacuumed and the coach work both inside and out given a good coat of wax polish. At the end of several evenings of hard work the car looked as good as new and both Judith and I were pleased with the result. The following day I drove the car to the school, parking just outside the laboratory. The appearance of Sir in a gleaming black Lanchester was the source of much interest by staff and boys alike, and I spent the best part of my lunch break showing off its various attributes, commenting that the only outstanding work necessary was the removal of the cylinder head and the resurfacing of the valves.

At this stage I was reminded of my Friday afternoons with Professor Landgrebe, and my introduction to the workings of the motorcar. With this in mind, I enquired of my sixth-form boys whether anyone would be interested in helping me carry out some work on the engine of the car. All five declared an interest, and with the headmaster's blessing what became known as the 'Cowbridge Car Club' was born.

To give some theoretical background to the work to be undertaken I decided on giving those interested some information about the origins of the Lanchester Motor Company, which was one of Britain's oldest manufacturers dating back to 1894, and how it was taken over by the Daimler Company in 1930.

The acquisition of the Lanchester name had several advantages for Daimler, including obtaining the services of George Lanchester, brother of Frederick and again a brilliant engineer. Another area of interest was that in the manufacture of its early cars Frederick Lanchester had devised a system of jigs and limit gauges that guaranteed complete interchangeability in production, an idea later developed by Henry Ford in his early assembly-line production.

The Lanchester engines of the early 1930s were technically among the most advanced of their day, with pressed-in dry cylinder liners and a full-pressure lubrication system designed to keep the oil clean, with not only gauze filters on suction and delivery sides of the oil pump, but also a magnet inside the delivery filter to take out metallic particles from the oil. Another clever feature was a carefully gas-flowed multi-branch exhaust system which added some 8 per cent to the power output.

With this background information and many of the boys re-searching further information from public libraries, we set about removing the inlet and exhaust manifolds, carburettor, and cylinder head. These were then transferred to the preparation room behind the biological sciences laboratory, were further dismantling and cleaning took place. Since this work could only be undertaken during lunch breaks or free periods, progress was slow but rewarding, with the boys learning how to grind in the valves by hand to make a gas-sealed combustion chamber, honing the tappet surfaces to remove any indentations caused through wear, and measuring with a micrometer the wear in the rocker shaft, valve guides and valve stems.

As work progressed, the far end of the preparation room became a popular port of call for many middle-school boys as well as the sixth-formers and the more mechanically minded members of staff.

Although by working on my own I could have completed the work in a quarter of the time, the involvement of the boys resulted in many spin-offs, including me getting to know a great number of boys who dropped in to see what the 'Car Club' was all about, and who I would otherwise not have met. A few boys became very interested and decided that motor engineering was a possible future career.

When work on the cylinder head was completed, attention became focused on the main engine block, which was still in the car. It was decided that the rubber hoses of the cooling system should be replaced and the block and radiator cleaned with a suitable flushing agent. This part of the work proved to be less popular with the boys since struggling with a ceases clamp in a most inaccessible location led to grazed knuckles and sore fingers. The final work on the block was to ensure that all traces of the old cylinder-head gasket were removed, the head of the block was clean, and that the new gasket was a perfect fit.

The big day came when the engine was reassembled, the cyl-inder head tightened down to the recommended torque figure in foot/pounds, the tappet clearances set using the micrometer gauge, the radiator filled with water, and it was time to see whether the engine would start and all the hard work had been worthwhile.

The engine fired first time to much cheering by the assembled crowd of boys. The Lanchester moved off the school premises on to the road and back into service to the familiar whine of the fluid flywheel transmission.

Easter came and went with most of my time spent decorating the rest of the house and repairing those little things that make the house more comfortable. By this time my father and aunt were well settled, with my aunt making daily visits to the shops where she would chat to the friendly staff and my father visiting the Duke of Wellington and Bear hotels and getting to know all the locals. Judith continued to travel daily to her work, while at the weekends we visited her mother and sister at Connaught Road.

The summer term at Cowbridge was relatively short, with the period following Whitsun being devoted to examinations. The upper sixth were involved with advanced and scholarship examinations, together with entry examinations for Oxford or Cambridge, while the lower sixth, which included the group that were studying the biological sciences, sat internal theory and practical examinations that determined their progression to the second year. My fifth formers sat the ordinary school certificate in biology set by the Welsh Joint Education Committee. The period between the end of the examinations and the end of term was devoted to sport, with the Boys v Masters cricket match being the highlight. Held on a sunny afternoon in July and watched by a large crowd of boys, parents, friends and members of the local sporting community, my first experience of this match proved most memorable in that I was requested to open the bowling with my colleague Ken Helyar bowling from the other end. In the first three overs, I took two wickets while Ken, showing great skill as a medium spin bowler, took a further wicket leaving the boys at twenty for three. Ken and I were then replaced by Sid Harris and Don Pugh, since the headmaster, who captained the masters' side, was of the view that everybody should be involved at some stage.

The boys' innings ended at eighty-six all out. Then it was the masters' turn to bat with the innings opened by Tudor Hughes and Sid Harris, both extremely competent batsmen despite the fact that Tudor was in his early sixties. Sid was out when the total was thirty to be followed by Jim White and the head who together with Tudor remained until the winning hit.

The following day marked the end of term with boarders being collected by parents, many of whom had been at the cricket match, and day boys saying their goodbyes to friends and staff. By five o'clock that evening the school fell silent marking the end of my first year at Cowbridge Grammar School.

Chapter Fifteen

My summer vacation was spent doing a variety of odd jobs that being a house owner entails, punctuated by short day trips in the car when Judith had her two weeks' leave during August. These trips, involving my father and Aunt Catherine, included a day at Kenfig Hill where we were entertained by Aunt Lois, a day at Ogmore-by-Sea, and one to Ogmore Vale where I met, for the first time, Sam Marsden, a cousin of my father and Aunt Catherine. Sam was the son of my grandfather's brother David, and lived with his sister and her family. Sam had never married and had spent the best part of his life as a miner in the Ogmore valley. He was a short, stocky, white-haired man in his sixties with a great sense of fun and he, my father and Aunt Catherine had a memorable afternoon talking of the old days and of the family in general. Accompanied by Sam's niece, Judith and I went exploring the narrow streets of small terraced houses built at the turn of the century and where in the 1950s miners still lived and worked until overtaken by lung disease caused by the dust of the mines.

A few days before school was due to restart, I received a visit from the secretary of the Cowbridge Rugby Club, who had been told that there was a rugby-playing master at the school, who having played for his school, county and Cardiff Medical School, might be persuaded to play for the town. After discussing the offer with Judith, I contacted the secretary and turned up at the ground the following Saturday. Although I had not expected to play on my first visit, a few injuries had resulted in a shortage of forwards and so I played the first of many games as wing forward. Although somewhat rusty, not having played in the last eighteen months, I had a good game returning home pleased but very sore.

Returning to school, the main topic of conversation was the examination results, and although I was not involved with the upper sixth's results, it was pleasing to hear the headmaster relate at the first morning assembly the outstanding achievements of the school in obtaining six scholarships to Oxford and Cambridge, and one hundred per cent acceptance of sixth formers at other universities.

In relation to the Ordinary Certificate of Education, all the boys who had studied biology on the one-year course passed with A grades, which, mindful of the fact that this course normally took two years, was quite an achievement. All the boys in last year's lower sixth who had sat internally set theory and practical examinations in Botany and Zoology had passed with distinction and were now looking forward to their final year.

So my second year at Cowbridge Grammar School commenced with five boys in my upper sixth; eight in the lower sixth, including William Adams' younger brother David; and a further ten fifth-formers studying biology at Ordinary Certificate level. Despite this increase in sixth-form teaching, the headmaster had still requested that I continue teaching science to the lower school, since, as he put it, he had received good reports from the boys.

Although the Car Club had been a short-term project it had caused several boys to look for other interests outside their studies, and the upper sixth were always asking whether another project was on the cards. This set me thinking, and recalling the photography experience I gained while pursuing my research at the Pharmacology Department, I approached the head with a request that the school acquire some photographic equipment including a developing tank, printing trays, an enlarger, developing and fixing agents, a camera and cine camera. This equipment would be housed in the preparation area of the biological sciences laboratory, which could double up as a dark room, and would be used under supervision by middle-and upper-school boys in association with their studies or as a leisure pursuit. Bemoaning the fact that the biological sciences department was the most costly of all the school's departments, but acknowledging that my idea was a good one, the head was persuaded, and agreed to my plan. Shortly after half term the equipment arrived and the Camera Club that was to prove to be one of the school's most successful ventures got underway.

By acquiring, on loan, a microscope camera attachment from Professor Landgrebe's department, upper-sixth students were soon able to take photographs of microscopic slides that they had prepared, then develop, enlarge and print the results, while middle-school boys, under six formers' supervision, were able to develop and print their own family films.

My second year at the school appeared to pass even quicker than my first, with the occasional Wednesday afternoon and Saturday morning being devoted to refereeing inter-school rugby matches, and most Saturday afternoons playing for Cowbridge Town.

In April of my second year at Cowbridge, Judith announced that she was pregnant, and although we had not really planned this to happen with Judith relying on me for birth control, we were both happy with the news and started planning for the happy event which would be in the following January.

Judith's family doctor lived in Cardiff and although now living in Cowbridge she had not been happy to change. Consequently there were many visits to Cardiff to visit Dr Nick, as he was known to all of Judith's family. Dr David Nicklas was one of the old breed of GPs. White-haired with twinkling blue eyes and a great bedside manner, he was also a great believer in safety first, and after a few visits to the surgery he advised Judith that the baby should be born in a nursing home where specialist care was available. His recommendation was the Romilly Nursing Home in Romilly Road, Cardiff. Having visited the home, viewed the facilities and obtained details of the costs involved, since the Romilly was a privately run home, we were happy to accept his recommendation.

Judith's family were delighted with the news, as were my father, Aunt Catherine and Aunt Lois. Judith's sister, Ann, who was due to get married in July following John completing his National Service, was thrilled with the news and hugged her sister and me saying that she wanted to be the godmother when he or she was baptised.

The period following the Easter vacation and leading up to the examinations period in June was one of the most demanding that I had ever experienced, with preparing my upper sixth for their

Advanced Certificate and scholarship examinations being number one priority. Michael Morgan and Francis Taylor had also been entered for the Cambridge Scholarship Examinations in Life Sciences.

At that time both the subjects of Botany and Zoology were examined through two three-hour theory papers, and one four-hour practical paper, all based on the two years of the course. In addition, the subject of Botany required that entrants submit a dissertation of around 3,000 words on an area of study of their choice.

All the examinations went without a hitch with all the boys reasonably confident that they had done well, thanks to some question-spotting that I had indulged in during the weeks leading up to the examinations. Michael Morgan was particularly pleased with his day at Cambridge and felt that he stood a good chance of admission in October.

The year ended in the traditional manner with the Boys v. Masters cricket match and the collection of boarders the following day.

Judith had her annual leave towards the end of July and we spent a few days touring west Wales in the Lanchester, being well aware that this might well be the last holiday that we would have with just the two of us.

On our return, and Judith's return to work, I spent two weeks at Kenfig Hill decorating some rooms for Aunt Lois, since I was always mindful of the assistance she had given me when I needed it most. The remainder of my vacation I spent taking my aunt Catherine and my father on day trips around the beautiful countryside of the Vale of Glamorgan, since I was conscious that things would soon change with the advent of an addition to the family.

The first week of September saw Judith's sister getting married at St Margaret's Church in Cardiff. This brought back many memories not only of my own wedding but of my time at nearby St Teilo's Hall. It also marked the first occasion of Judith letting me know that although she was happy living at Cowbridge, she would still prefer Cardiff and hoped that one day we would return to live there.

Chapter Sixteen

On returning to school I discovered that my upper sixth had excelled themselves in the previous year's Advanced Certificate examinations, all obtaining 'A' grades in all their subjects of study, while Michael Morgan had obtained a distinction in his Cambridge University examinations. All ten boys studying biology in the fifth form had also passed their Ordinary Level Certificate and were now eager to enter the lower sixth. Needless to say the headmaster was very pleased with these results and recorded the fact that the biological science department was now an established and highly successful part of the school's curriculum, at the first assembly of the 1958–59 academic year.

1958–59 also marked the 350th anniversary of the founding of the school in 1608–09, with a special Service of Commemoration held at the Cowbridge Parish Church and attended by the whole school, the school governors, representatives of the Glamorgan Education Authority, old boys of the school and local dignitaries. While the service was held during the autumn term of 1958, another celebration in the form of a black tie formal dinner was held at the Duke of Wellington Hotel in the spring term of '59. This was a grand affair with the guest speaker being the vice chancellor of Jesus College Oxford, and attended by many old boys who had achieved positions of eminence in their chosen careers and on the rugby field. One of the new boys entering the school that September was Peter Landgrebe, who following discussions with his father, the headmaster had seen fit to place in the form in lower school where I would be his form master.

Peter, at the age of twelve, was a quiet, slim, fair-skinned, blonde-haired, blue-eyed boy, who I guessed felt somewhat dominated by his clever parents. Being a day boy, he was now experiencing the rough and tumble of travelling daily from Miskin to Cowbridge on the school bus, and the not unheard of boisterous behaviour of some of his form mates. The first few months at the school were consequently punctuated with incidents when Peter was missing from class only to be found at the bus stop waiting for a service bus to take him home or on the road out of Cowbridge having decided to walk the six miles home. I had little or no experience of this kind of behaviour and consequently had to rely on common sense and the belief that it would be a short-term problem. To avoid him being seen as one of my favourites with his classmates, I sought the help of two of my upper-sixth boys who travelled on the Cowbridge to Miskin school bus, requesting that they keep an eye on Peter, and if necessary, encourage him to stand up for himself should there be any hint of bullying. This tactic appeared to work and by half term Peter had settled down, appeared to enjoy his studies, and had become a popular member of his form. I was particularly pleased with this outcome since I felt that I owed so much to his father in making what I had now possible.

Judith gave up working shortly after half term, since the travelling and walking to and from work was proving too much for her. There then followed two months when Judith felt that living in Cowbridge with my working every day and only my family as company was proving to be rather lonely, despite the fact that I took her up to Cardiff most weekends to visit her mother. Following both her daughters getting married and leaving home, Gwyneth had decided to move out of Connaught Road and was now sharing a two-bedroom flat with a widowed school friend in Pearce field Place in Cardiff. Since her friend was spending Christmas with her family, Judith invited her mother to spend Christmas at Cowbridge. Christmas was a quiet affair and in the New Year Judith decided that she would like to spend the last few weeks of her pregnancy in Cardiff with her mother. This would make transfer to the Romilly Nursing Home much easier and she would also be nearer her twin sister, Ann.

January 1959 was a dark, dismal, and very wet month, with the boys struggling into school with wet clothes and steaming gently as they warmed themselves before the open fires of old school, or up against the radiators of the laboratory. As the month drew to its close I was very much on edge, constantly waiting for the telephone call that would tell me that Judith was in the nursing home. At noon on 28 January the call came to the school, and following the longest afternoon I had ever experienced, I set off for Cardiff.

Judith's confinement was long and difficult, and when I arrived at the Romilly Nursing Home at around seven o'clock that evening she was still in labour, with Dr Nick in attendance. Shortly after nine o'clock, and with the aid of forceps, David Lawrence was born, weighing in at eight pounds.

My first task, after briefly seeing Judith and the new arrival, was to drive to Ann's house with the news. That night Cardiff was shrouded in a dense fog and driving was almost impossible, and it was only after several stops to check street names that I eventually arrived at Bwlch Road in the Fairwater area of Cardiff. Ann was, as expected, delighted with the news and said that she would be visiting her sister the following day. I then had to call on Gwyneth to inform her that she was now a grandmother, a role I felt she was very happy and proud to assume, although she was concerned at the long period of labour that Judith had experienced and wanted reassurance that all was well.

News of my becoming a father soon spread around the school and I was the recipient of many congratulations, and observations that my life would never be the same again. These views did indeed prove to be true since although initially David Lawrence would be sharing our bedroom, this would be a short-term solution and the need for an additional bedroom would soon become of paramount importance. There was also Judith's wish to return to live in Cardiff.

Towards the end of the spring term tragedy struck the school with the untimely death of Tommy Evans, the senior physics master. One morning while on his way to school on his trusty moped, Tommy was involved in a minor accident and was thrown off his bike suffering a minor cut to his forehead and a skin graze to one hand. Although he arrived at school apparently none the worse for his experience, and came over to my laboratory for some first aid which involved cleaning the cut to the forehead and applying a plaster, he refused to accept colleague's advice to visit the local GP and my advice to have a precautionary X-ray. Over the next few days his behaviour was noted as being strange, with his writing a dozen letters to his insurance company regarding his accident, and culminating in his eating his sweet before his main course at lunch, much to the concern of his fellow diners. Two days later he was found dead at his home in Gilfach Goch, a home that he had always shared with his widowed mother.

Houses in Gilfach Goch were typical of those found throughout the Rhondda Valley: terraced with two rooms and a kitchen on the ground floor and two bedrooms upstairs. The entrance hallway was a long, narrow affair partly occupied by the staircase to the bedrooms with narrow doors leading off to the front room, as it was known and back living room. In keeping with tradition of the time, the dead were kept at home with the open coffin occupying centre stage in the front room and where visitors would come in their droves to pay their last respects. The problem with this arrangement arose when it was time for the coffin to be taken out, and this usually entailed removing the lower sash of the front window and carefully handling it through the space provided. It was by this means that Tommy made his final exit under the watchful eyes of numerous female neighbours standing on their doorsteps in aprons and the compulsory headscarf. The school was represented at the funeral by the headmaster and five members of staff including myself and Ken Helyar, who had worked with Tommy over the last three years.

Easter came and went and soon the examinations timetable was in operation once again. The vacancy of Head of the Physics Department due to Tommy Evans' death was advertised, and despite Ken Helyar having high hopes of being appointed, it was not to be, with an outside applicant, Adrian Trotman, being appointed for the following September.

By this time Judith was a familiar figure pushing David Lawrence around the town in his pram, going shopping or catching the N & C Coach to Cardiff, where she would spend an afternoon and evening with her mother or sister before being collected after I had finished work.

On a Sunday afternoon in early June, when he was six months old, David Lawrence was baptised at St Margaret's Church, with his aunt Ann and her husband John being the godparents. My father, Aunt Catherine and Aunt Lois, together with Judith's mother, aunts and uncles, attended the service which was followed by afternoon tea at the godparents' house.

As I started my fourth year at Cowbridge Grammar School I was mindful of the changes that were occurring both at the school and in my domestic situation. The cloud of Comprehensive Education loomed over all grammar schools in Wales and Cowbridge was no exception, since having come under the financial control of the Glamorgan Education Authority, its policies were becoming more evident in their effect on the school, its catchments area, its selection policy and its areas of study. Although the majority of the teaching staff at Cowbridge who had taught at the school for very many years were confident that such changes would not occur in their lifetime, Ken Helyar and myself were less sure, and we were of the opinion that the traditions, academic standards and sporting excellence of the school were features that would soon be under threat in the pursuance of political dogma. On the domestic front I was deeply aware that the house at East Gate was too small for our needs and that this, together with Judith's declared wish to return to live in Cardiff, was a pressing problem that required action in the not too distant future.

For the second year running the Advanced Certificate Examinations resulted in a 100 per cent pass rate in the biological sciences, with 80 per cent of the boys gaining 'A' grades, while in the Ordinary Level Examinations all the boys were successful, giving a 100 per cent pass rate.

Towards the end of the autumn term I made an appointment to see my solicitor and now friend, Strad Jones. Following an exchange of the usual pleasantries with Strad wanting to know how I was getting on in my chosen career and how the family were settling down, I sought his advice on property prices and availability in Cardiff, and in particular the larger type house capable of accommodating two or more families. Strad immediately set about telephoning an estate agent friend who he said could be trusted, and within the hour I was at the offices of Hern and Crabtree in Westgate Street. Having explained my requirements and the price that I would be prepared to pay, Mr Crabtree, an elderly white-haired man not unlike Strad Jones, informed me that he thought he had the very house I was looking for and that he would arrange with the owner, a Harry Bents, for me to see the property the following Saturday. I returned to Cowbridge well pleased with the progress made but made no mention of it to Judith, my father or aunt since I had no desire to raise Judith's hopes or unsettle my father and aunt with the prospect of another move.

The following Saturday on the pretext that I was refereeing an away rugby match with the school, I set off for Cardiff. Harry Bents was a middle-aged Londoner who had established himself as an antiques trader and now owned a thriving business in Albany Road, Cardiff. He made me feel welcome with a cup of coffee in his office behind the shop, which was brim full of beautiful antique furniture, china, glassware and gold jewellery. Antique gold jewellery would appear to be Harry Bents' speciality since he had immediately spotted the ruby ring given to me by my grandfather all those years ago, and wanted to know its origins, which he guessed were Caribbean, and should I ever wish to sell it, to let him know. Although his house was only a hundred yards away in Claude Road, he insisted that he take me there in his British racing green Mark 2 Jaguar that was parked outside the shop.

The moment that I stepped through the front door of 107 Claude Road, I knew that it was the house for me. In many ways it resembled the house that Judith had lived in at Connaught Road, and knowing how much she had liked that house I was confident that my choice would receive her full approval. Two of the three ground-floor rooms were stacked to the ceiling with antique furniture and boxes of various sizes, while the third was the family dining room with adjoining fully-fitted kitchen and cloakroom. The first floor consisted of a large front room overlooking Claude Road, which the family used as a living room, while the remaining two rooms were used as double bedrooms. A large modern bathroom with separate WC completed the first floor accommodation. The top floor was made up of two double bedrooms and a single together with a storage attic. The house had a warm, welcoming feel, added to by the charming Mrs Bents who insisted that I be shown every nook and cranny, including the old basement coal cellar which now accommodated more antiques, and a rear garden that had been landscaped with various statues and classical urns, which regrettably were not included in the sale price. Following another cup of tea that Mrs Bents insisted I must have, I returned to the offices of Hern and Crabtree and made my offer, which was immediately accepted, since it would appear that Harry Bents had already bought a property in Lake Road West and was anxious to sell. I returned to Strad Jones and instructed him to find me a mortgage provider and proceed with the purchase.

Returning to Cowbridge I surprised the family by announcing that we were all going to live in Cardiff. Judith was delighted, especially when I described the house and its location, while my father's and aunt's response was that if that is what we wanted it was all right with them. The following day I approached the local estate agent and placed 51 East Gate on the market.

News soon got around the school that we were moving, and although it was appreciated that the family required more space, many of the staff and pupils living in the town recorded their sadness at our leaving, although it was accepted that like two other members of staff, Morley Davies and Sid Harris, my commuting from Cardiff on a daily basis did not present a problem.

The house was sold just before Christmas, with Strad Jones in his usual efficient manner conducting the conveyance of both properties, although the completion date was some time in the future.

Knowing that it was to be the last Christmas spent in Cowbridge cast a shadow over the festive season, and I found it difficult to settle down, always thinking of the months ahead and all the upheaval of moving house. It was David Lawrence's first Christmas and everybody made a big fuss of him with numerous presents and stories of Father Christmas, although it was doubtful if he understood all that was going on. My father and Aunt Catherine had taken to the little lad and would spend hours entertaining him while his mother carried out housework and more recently packing in readiness for the impending move.

We moved on Saturday 1 April 1960, and although the date was not of my choice, Strad Jones was of the opinion that in terms of income tax relief on mortgage payments, it was an appropriate date. Although Judith had seen the house from the outside on several occasions, it was the first time that she had viewed the fitted kitchen, bathroom and garden area, and luckily for me she was delighted with what she saw. Initially, the plan was for Judith, David and me to occupy the ground floor, with our bedroom being at the front of the house, David's bedroom being the middle room, while the back room would be our living room with adjoining kitchen, cloakroom and access to the garden. My father and Aunt Catherine would then occupy the first floor with their living room overlooking Claude Road and their bedrooms each side of the shared family bathroom and WC. The single bedroom on the top floor that already had a water supply laid on became their kitchen, leaving the two remaining bedrooms empty. Despite my private concerns, all were pleased with the arrangements, especially my father who viewed sitting in the bay window observing all the comings and goings of Claude Road as something to look forward to.

The following Monday morning I drove off to work in the knowledge that our accommodation problem had been solved, and Judith's wish to return to live in Cardiff had been granted.

The Easter vacation was a God send in that it allowed me to do all the decorating work necessary and install all the necessary facilities in the top-floor kitchen.

Throughout the selling and buying process I had kept Aunt Lois informed, but due to making a modest profit on the house in Cowbridge and acquiring a 90 per cent mortgage on the house in Claude Road I had no need to ask her for financial assistance. She had, however, expressed a wish to see my new house in Cardiff, and a week into the Easter vacation I drove down to Kenfig Hill to collect her so that she could spend the day at Claude Road. As we pulled up outside the house and Aunt Lois got out she was visibly shaken, since without her or my knowing, I had bought the very same house that her father and mother, John and

Margaret Marsden, had lived in following their move from Pembrokeshire in 1889, and where she, as their youngest daughter, had been born 1902. This remarkable occurrence was the main topic of conversation that day, with Aunt Catherine recalling the time her uncle John Marsden had visited the farm in Pembrokeshire to see his brother. As I drove Aunt Lois back to Kenfig Hill that evening, she remarked that she felt as if she had been transported back in time, and that there must have been a guiding hand that had made this possible.

The weekend before school was due to open following the Easter vacation, another development took place that was to change my life.

Being in education, I often purchased the *Times Education Supplement*, published every Friday. On this particular occasion, having read the various educational articles, I turned to the further and higher education appointments pages where I saw an advertisement for a lecturer responsible for biological sciences at the Llandaff Technical College, Cardiff. Although I knew nothing about technical education, the salary on offer was almost double my present one, and following the house move and solicitors' bills such an opportunity appeared most attractive.

A week later I submitted my application using Professor Landgrebe and Idwal Rees, my headmaster, as referees. When I approached the head with my request for a reference he recorded the fact that he was devastated by the possibility of the school losing my services, and enquired if there was any way he could tempt me to stay. I explained that while I loved working at Cowbridge Grammar School and could not envisage working in any other school, the possibility of the school changing in the foreseeable future due to the introduction of Comprehensive Education could not be ignored, and I wanted to find out what technical education had to offer while at the same time enjoying a significant increase in salary. Professor Landgrebe was equally reluctant to see me leaving Cowbridge, although he fully supported my desire to broaden my career in education.

On 28 May, the anniversary of my dear mother's death, I was called for interview at the City Hall in Cardiff. As I climbed the white marble staircase to the committee rooms on the first floor, I recalled previous occasions when I had visited this great building: the occasion of Rag Ball, when I was accompanied by Mona, and the day when I showed Cynthia around the Cardiff Civic Centre, it was truly a return to the past. The five short-listed applicants including myself were interviewed by a panel of three, made up of Alderman George Turnbull – chairman of the college board of governors and managing director of a steel making company, Councillor Iorworth Jones, a politician representing the Local Education Authority, and Joseph Cottrell, an engineer and principal of the Llandaff Technical College. On reflection, I believe I gave a good interview, being able to balance my academic achievements and teaching record with my other interests, and how I had developed these during my three and a half years of teaching at Cowbridge. After a brief wait I was called back in and offered the appointment, which I was delighted to accept. There then followed some informal discussions, during which Iorworth Jones indicated that I had given an impressive interview, while Principal Cottrell invited me to the college that afternoon to meet colleagues and view the facilities.

Llandaff Technical College, situated on Western Avenue, Cardiff, had been officially opened by His Royal Highness the Duke of Edinburgh in December 1954, the first students having entered the college in September of that year. The foreword to the college prospectus, written by the principal, read as follows:

Llandaff Technical College is a college in its own right, recognised by the Ministry of Education as an institution for further education. Its aim is twofold, to produce both skill and social leadership. It is necessary that workers should be skilled to meet the highly specialised demands of industry in a scientific age. Thus the college is staffed with teachers who are familiar with current industrial methods and equipped with modern machinery and apparatus. In addition to possessing technical and scientific knowledge, workers must also have an understanding of everyday human relationships, for industry today is a large-scale social organisation, and success in it depends upon qualities of personality no less than upon acquired knowledge. To a much greater degree than in the past, it is necessary to foster a corporate life in our college. To this end it is hoped that a self-governing and responsible students' union will be established aimed at developing the corporate life of the college. In so doing the students, through assuming the responsibilities of such a society, will extend their range of interest and their social powers and learn to become better citizens. To help in the development of this corporate life, the college is equipped with playing fields, and in the next phase of the building programme, students' union rooms and a hall are envisaged which should further the success of indoor activities. Finally, as this is the first session of the college, there is a challenge to all who are associated with it to think and act so as to create a vital, distinctive, and independent college tradition of which students of the future will be proud.

At two o'clock that afternoon I walked into Llandaff Technical College to be met by my predecessor, Jack Goldsmith, a short, grey-haired man of Jewish decent who having been responsible for the biological sciences since the college opened, had now been appointed to a similar post at a teachers' training college. Jack introduced me to Dr Donald Lewis, the head of the Chemistry and Biology Department who had apparently only been in the post since the previous Christmas, and as we walked around, to various other members of the departmental staff. Our last port of call was the large biological sciences laboratory situated on the first floor, which at the time was filled with between twenty and thirty white-coated students of various ages, colour and nationalities, all earnestly looking down microscopes. Then I saw Margaret threading her way between the benches towards me with a welcoming smile and outstretched hand. Margaret Prethero had been an honours student at university, working alongside Sylvia when she and I had a relationship going, and although I sensed at the time that she did not approve of this relationship due to Sylvia already being in a long-term relationship, she had often passed on messages to Sylvia when I called by and she was not there. Clad in a spotless white laboratory coat and with her curly auburn hair glinting in the sunlight that streamed through the laboratory windows, Margaret looked a picture and once again within a few hours, I felt I was going back in time.

The following morning I informed the headmaster that I had been offered and accepted the appointment at Llandaff Technical College and handed in my letter of resignation. Idwal was most distressed at the prospect of my leaving Cowbridge, so much so that I promised him that I would investigate the possibility of finding a suitable applicant from the University of South Wales and Monmouthshire, who might be interested in a teaching career. For my part I was, in many ways, sad at leaving what I considered a unique school with a reputation second to none, yet apprehensive of the next thirty-six years, were I to stay.

Chapter Seventeen

News of my leaving spread like wildfire through the school, since no member of staff, apart from those retiring or dying, had left the school over the past forty years. Although my upper sixth knew I would see them through their final examinations, the lower sixth were very apprehensive and wanted to know what the prospect was of having a new tutor by September. Fifth formers were more relaxed about the situation and one member, Duncan Marsden, who was a nephew of Aunt Lois and consequently a distant relative of mine, informed me and his fellow students that he was going to study his 'A' levels at Llandaff Technical College, a promise that he later carried out with some success but much to my embarrassment.

Following the family move to Cardiff and the arrangement between Sid Harris, Morley Davies and myself that we should share transport costs by using one car by rotation on a weekly basis, I was discovering that while the Lanchester was fine for single trips and leisure motoring, travelling to and from Cowbridge to a strict timetable with three adults on board was taking its toll on the twenty-six-year-old car. When I started work at Cowbridge I had transferred the Lloyds Bank account that I had used while at university, from Cardiff to the Cowbridge branch, the branch manager at that time being Kerry Davies who was a Cardigan boy who had known both my grandfather and father when a bank trainee at their local branch of Lloyds. When I initially transferred my account, he had been most helpful with advice and guidance and had informed me that if he could be of any assistance in the future to please contact him. When I now approached Kerry with my problem of requiring a newer car, and although he knew that I was now living in Cardiff and would be leaving the school at the end of August, he regarded my having what he referred to as a 'modern' car as essential to someone in my position, and suggested a loan of around £300 would be appropriate.

The following weekend I trawled the car showrooms of City Road, which at that time was the Mecca for second-hand cars. I spotted MOH 306 in the showroom of a small corner premises run by a Mr Williams and his son. MOH was a gleaming black, low slung, front-wheel-drive 1952 Citroen Light Fifteen, with a red leather interior and fitted with a sunroof. The two-litre overhead cam engine appeared in good order, and following a trial run accompanied by Mr Williams Junior, during which I learned to master the rather strange dashboard-located gear change, I decided that this was the car for me. Having paid the £295 asking price I returned to Claude Road well pleased with my purchase, which impressed both Judith and my father and drew complementary comments from some of the neighbours and passers-by since at that time the detective series Meagre was on the television, with the car used by Inspector Meagre, played by the pipe-smoking actor Rupert Davies, being a black Citroen of the same era. Kerry Davies was also well pleased with my purchase when I called in at the bank the following week to show off my purchase – or as I put it 'his purchase', since it was the bank's money that had made it possible.

The problem of disposing of the Lanchester was easily solved thanks to one of the boys in my upper sixth persuading his father that a car to take him to and from university the following year would be a good idea, and at the asking price of £20 could be an investment.

The last term at Cowbridge Grammar School was a blur of activity with practical examinations to be organised, theory papers for the lower sixth to be set and marked, and extensive revision exercises for the upper sixth and fifth form, since I was determined that the boys would not be affected in any way as a consequence of my impending move.

That last term also saw the Camera Club make its mark by producing two short films using its 18 mm movie camera. The first was one of the school annual run, while the second was that of the Masters v. Boys cricket match. Planning the sequence of shots and the best angles and locations that these should be taken was a lengthy and time-consuming process, but the end results were highly acclaimed when the films were shown in main hall on the last day of term.

My final week at the school was marked by an evening dinner party given by the headmaster and Mrs Rees where Judith and I were the guests of honour, and where Idwal Rees recorded my contribution to the school over the last four years and his personal sadness at my leaving. The second function was when the staff took me to the Bear Hotel for a farewell drink after school and presented me with an honorary old boys tie and blazer badge.

And so the four glorious years that I had spent at the school came to an end. Years that I will always recall with fondness, pride, and some degree of sadness, since looking back I often think of what might have been had the school been allowed to continue with its fine traditions in both the academic and sporting arenas, and not been subjected to the mediocrity of the comprehensive system.

Chapter Eighteen

When I took up my appointment in September 1960, courses available at the Llandaff Technical College were administered under six departments. These were the Departments of Building, Chemistry and Biology, Commerce, Electrical Engineering, Mechanical Engineering, and Science and Mathematics. The full-time staffing establishment of the college totalled eighty-six, of which nine were in the Chemistry and Biology Department. Student enrolments totalled 232 full-time students, 2,300 part-time day students, and 2,500 part-time evening students. Of the 232 full-time students, the majority were in the Departments of Science and Mathematics and Chemistry and Biology, with a significant number being from countries such as Egypt, Libya, Nigeria, Persia, and West Africa, pursuing the General Certificate of Education at Advanced Level in a combination of three subjects selected from Biology, Botany, Chemistry, Mathematics, Physics and Zoology. These subjects were offered as either one-year, or two-year courses of study, depending on the entry qualifications of the student, and used as a means of gaining university entrance in the UK.

It was into this very different environment that I stepped that September – an environment that was to change for ever both my professional career and my private life, although I did not know it at the time.

The nine members of staff of the Department of Chemistry and Biology were Dr Donald Lewis, who was the head of department and a chemist; Roy Vaughan-Williams, also a chemist, who was the lecturer responsible for the chemistry section; and myself as lecturer responsible for the biological sciences. The other biology staff consisted of assistant lecturers Heilig Jones, who taught Botany; my ex-university colleague Margaret Prethero, who taught Biology; and Heddwyn Richards, who taught Zoology. The chemistry staff consisted of three assistant lecturers, Dr Wyn Davies, who taught Physical Chemistry; Dr Brian Gibbon, who taught Organic Chemistry; and Mrs Mary Miles, who taught general and inorganic chemistry. In addition to the teaching staff there was technical support with each section having a technician.

Since the courses on offer were identical to those that I had taught for the last four years at Cowbridge Grammar School, I had no trouble in settling down and delivering the hour-long lectures and the two-hour practical sessions that the course timetables were based upon. As a lecturer I was required to teach eighteen hours per week, with the remaining twelve hours devoted to the administration of the section and preparatory work. Assistant lecturers were required to teach twenty-two hours per week with eight hours devoted to preparatory work. This workload linked to the almost doubling of my salary was a cause of much satisfaction, although the logic of the situation I considered to be questionable.

As I got to know colleagues in other departments and areas of work it became clear to me that the essentially school-type work of the two science-based departments was very different from that of the other sections of the college, where work was related to the post-war national trend of employers releasing their young employees to attend day-release courses at the colleges, and in so doing acquiring a better educated and trained workforce. Although there was one such day-release course in the chemistry section with young employees from the local chemical industry attending, no such provision occurred in the biological sciences.

My first task therefore was to identify and visit as many employers as possible whose work had a biological base. Such employers included departments at the University College and the Welsh School of Medicine, the Medical Research Council, forensic science laboratories, public health laboratories and the like. I soon discovered that there was a nucleus of around twelve employees whose employers would be prepared to release them for one day per week. My second task was to find a suitable course that would have national recognition and could be adapted to the needs of the employees involved. There appeared to be only one such biological course of two years' duration that was endorsed by the London-based Institute of Biology. This provision, which commenced in September 1961, was a completely new development for the Cardiff area, and its introduction coincided with the transfer of a two-year medical laboratory technician course from the Welsh College of Advanced Technology to the college. These two courses were the forerunners of follow-on provision that was to result in Llandaff Technical College becoming a centre of excellence in the United Kingdom for biological and paramedical sciences.

Alongside these course developments I had observed that the board of governors of the college consisted of representatives of Cardiff Education Committee and the chairmen of the various advisory committees established within the college to advise on the development of the various sectors of work. Since there was no such advisory committee for the biological and paramedical sciences, I contacted Professor Landgrebe to seek his advice and guidance. He was delighted with my suggestion and proceeded to recruit similarly minded colleagues from other university departments, medical research, forensic science and pathology laboratories as founder members of the committee. He also suggested that I extended the brief of the advisory committee, when established, to cover the areas of amenity horticulture and turf culture so that employees and employers at Cardiff parks and playing fields would be involved.

My next task was to prepare a submission to my head of department outlining a case for the establishment of the advisory committee, its terms of reference and initial membership. The following day I was called to the principal's office to be congratulated on my submission which he fully endorsed and which he would present to the board of governors at their next meeting. By September 1962 the Advisory Committee for Biological Sciences had been established with Professor Landgrebe as its first chairman.

Towards the end of the 1961/62 session the department was invited by the Department of Education and Science to submit an application to run a three-year full-time course leading to a Diploma in Dietetics. This was my second submission within a few months, and required an assessment of staffing, equipment and accommodation needs, detailed subject syllabuses, the recruitment of students, and how the timescale of the development would coincide with the building programme that the college was already engaged in. On its completion and submission, I was again called to the principal's office to be congratulated on a job well done.

The Diploma course commenced in September 1962 alongside first- and second-year intake of the Endorsed Certificate in Biology and the first-year intake onto Medical Laboratory Technology courses.

These course developments demanded additional staffing and accommodation and by September 1963 the number of departmental teaching staff had risen from nine to twenty-one, with appointments in dietetics, histology, haematology, microbiology and clinical biochemistry and horticulture. Additional accommodation had become available as a result of the third phase of the college building programme being completed, and the transfer out of the college of the Department of Commerce releasing much needed classroom space. September 1963 also saw the very first Higher National Certificate course at the college. This was in biology and was the follow-on provision of the two-year endorsed certificate in biology started in September 1961. The development of this advanced-level provision resulted in the college's staffing establishment qualifying for a senior lecturer appointment, and following an interview by a committee of the board of governors consisting of Councillor Iorworth Jones, who was now chairman of the governors; Professor Landgrebe; and Principal Cottrell, I was appointed as the first senior lecturer at the college taking up my appointment in September 1964. My promotion created a vacancy at lecturer level and despite the post being advertised in the national press and attracting considerable interest both inside and outside the college, Margaret Prethero, who had given me much assistance over the last four years, was appointed.

During the period 1960 to 1964, and in addition to my teaching and contribution to course development, I had become involved in assisting the assistant lecturer in sports with coaching the college rugby team and had officiated as referee at several college rugby matches normally held on Saturday afternoons. In

1963 I was elected as chairman of the College Staff Association. Principal Cottrell had always been keen on developing the social side of college life and with this in mind had established the Staff Association as a vehicle to encourage such activities. These social activities usually took the form of staff dances held on Saturday nights with canned music and refreshments where tea and sandwiches were the order of the day. These arrangements were not popular with many staff and excuses were made not to attend, so I attempted to persuade Principal Cottrell to allow Hancock's Brewery to run a bar at the next college staff dance. Although he was not in favour of alcoholic drinks on college premises, he relented, and when all members of staff attended the next dance, I believe he saw the wisdom of his decision.

During my quest for membership of the Advisory Committee, I met Dr Glyn Phillips, a chemist working in the Chemistry Department of the University College. Glyn, who originated from North Wales, was a fluent Welsh speaker and was involved with a science programme for children, broadcasted every Saturday between twelve and twelve thirty on BBC Wales Television. In my conversation with Glyn he suggested that since I was a Welsh speaker and a biologist I might be able to contribute to the programme through developing the biological aspects of science. This was a challenge, but after obtaining the principal's permission to take equipment from the college to the studio, I was able to perform various experiments suitable for primary school children, and those in the lower forms of secondary school. Since the programme went out live, there being no video recording available in the early 1960s, experiments involving live animals or live organs was very much a question of luck. A full rehearsal took place on the Friday evening with the programme televised live on the Saturday morning. At that time the BBC television studios occupied an old converted chapel located in the Broadway area of Cardiff, and facilities were fairly basic. The half-hour programme was usually divided between Glyn's chemistry experiments and my biological ones, and I shall always remember one Saturday in November when Glyn decided to demonstrate how to make some simple fireworks in preparation for Guy Fawkes' night. Although the rehearsal went fine the actual programme ended in clouds of black smoke that obliterated Glyn and filled the studio, bringing that Saturday's programme to an abrupt end.

Although I enjoyed my work on television, it was very time-consuming and eventually I decided to give it up, but not before I was able to persuade the producer to arrange an outside broadcast at Llandaff Technical College when all the different aspects of technical education would be on show. This programme was a great success, with the principal, staff and students enjoying the experience of appearing on television.

Towards the end of February 1962, almost a year after we had moved to Claude Road, Judith announced that she was pregnant, and our daughter Julia Ann was born at the Romilly Nursing Home on 24 November of that year. David Lawrence was now approaching three years of age and growing up fast to become a very likable little chap, and the apple of his grandfather's eye and spoilt by my aunt Catherine, who he referred to as Ano, for some reason I am not aware of.

This addition to the family necessitated a further change in the bedroom arrangements, with my father moving into the front top-floor bedroom and Julia Ann occupying his old bedroom, which being on the first floor was nearer for her mother and me to hear her should she cry in the night.

It was about this time that I fell in love again. Although the Citroen had given me excellent service and had become a well-known and recognised car throughout the college and neighbour-hood, I had always dreamed of owning a car that I had first seen back in 1953 when attending the University College in Newport Road. This car, which was always parked outside a doctor's surgery in Newport Road, was an Alvis TC 21 'Grey Lady' saloon in navy over pale blue, with blue leather upholstery and sun roof. It had a winged silver bird mascot on the radiator cap and twin air intakes on the bonnet. Rear-wheel spats completed, and set off, what I considered to be a really beautiful car. The car, which was now ten years old, had been traded into a garage in part-exchange, and although requiring some cosmetic work to the body and wings, still showed those features of class that I had noted some ten years earlier. Having obtained the name and address of the one previous owner, who was the doctor who had now retired from the practice in Newport Road, and having obtained from him a brief history of the car, I bought it subject to the garage giving it a full service and spraying the lower half, since the original pale blue was somewhat tatty. I then advertised and sold the Citroen to a local man who was a work colleague of Judith's aunt Dorothy. The family loved my new acquisition and it attracted considerable attention at the college where my addiction to unusual and future classic cars was beginning to be recognised.

A particular fan of such cars was Margaret, who at the time ran an early MG Midget two-seater sports with red coachwork and black hood and interior trim. Since our first meeting at university, where she had obtained a first-class honours degree, Margaret had lectured at the Welsh College of Advanced Technology, and had been transferred to Llandaff when the General Certificate of Education at advanced level studies were moved there in 1958. She was the only daughter of Dr John Prethero, who was the head of the Department of Chemistry at Ogmore Vale Grammar School and later became headmaster at the school. Like myself, her mother had died while still very young and her father, who by now had retired, had married again and was living in Bridgend.

During her stay at the Welsh College of Advanced Technology she met and married a fellow lecturer and widower, Hayden Jones. Hayden, a lecturer in economics, had lost his first wife in childbirth and having one daughter was at the time probably looking for a stepmother for his daughter Lena. Although Margaret was twenty years his junior she had taken on the responsibility of bringing up Lena, who was now approaching her teens and attending the private fee-paying Howells School for Girls at Llandaff.

It was during one sunny lunchtime shortly after I had acquired the Alvis that Margaret, in conversation, said that she would love to drive the car. I said she was most welcome and off we set through the leafy roads and lanes between Llandaff and Miskin. The steering on any 1953 car was never the most precise, and although I had become used to it, comparison with that of the relatively new Midget was something Margaret had not anticipated, and when power from the three-litre engine was turned on she viewed the car as having a mind of its own. Claiming that she was exhausted driving the Alvis she drew into a side lane and parked. Getting out we walked up the lane that in all probability lead to a farm, and on reaching a gate paused to look at the scenery that stretched for miles into the distance. It was quiet, the sun was warm and I felt very close to Margaret, and apparently she to me, for she suddenly turned and whispered, 'Kiss me, John.' We kissed, and I knew that things would never be the same again and that our working relationship would in all probability take on a new dimension. We walked back to the car hand in hand not saying a word, since words were not necessary. I drove back to college and we continued work as if nothing had happened, although we both knew it had.

One of the consequences of the college gaining approval for a Higher National Certificate in the Biological Sciences was that it could be recognised as a centre suitable for full-time or sandwich provision at Higher National Diploma level, and such a course, in Applied Biology, commenced in September 1966 alongside the part-time course leading to Graduate Membership of the Institute of Biology, the first degree-level course at the college.

Early in 1966 Donald Lewis, the head of department, announced his resignation to take up an appointment as principal at a north of England college. The resulting vacancy was advertised and following another interview at the City Hall, I was appointed from a shortlist of five applicants. Again the familiar faces of Councillor Iorworth Jones, Frank Landgrebe and Joe Cottrell were there to congratulate me and wish me well for the future. My appointment was a cause of much celebration among both the departmental and college staff, since it marked the first occasion in the history of the college that an internal applicant had been appointed as head of a department.

As head of department it was necessary to reduce my weekly teaching commitment, although I retained my teaching of physiology to the newly established Higher National Diploma and to certain aspects of the Graduate Membership course. My old post was advertised and despite some very strong competition involving both internal and external applicants, Margaret gave a brilliant interview and was justifiably appointed as the first woman senior lecturer at the college, and indeed in the whole of technical education in Wales.

By September 1966 David Lawrence was six years old and attending Marlborough Road Primary School, which was a two-minute walk from Claude Road, while Julia Anne, at four years of age, was attending the nursery provision at the same school. Both were happy children and gave their mother and me no trouble. 25 May 1966 also saw my aunt Catherine celebrate her ninetieth birthday when we all had tea, sandwiches and cake followed by a glass of port.

Another family problem arose a few months later when Judith's mother, who had been sharing a flat in Pearcefield Place with a life-long friend, announced that her friend was returning to her place of birth in the Rhondda Valley and to what was left of her family, and that since she would not be able to afford the flat on her own she would be homeless. Since Ann's house was a modern semi and she now also had two children, her mother living with her was not a possibility, so the only option was her moving into 107 Claude Road. Having considered all possibilities, it was decided that changing the middle downstairs bedroom, which had an adjoining conservatory and was currently occupied by David Lawrence, into a bedsitter with adjoining kitchen was the best alternative, with David moving to the top floor bedroom next to his grandfather. This we did, and by Christmas of 1966 Gwyneth had moved in and we all had Christmas lunch together with David and Julia enjoying the Christmas tree, presents and crackers.

Following Julia's birth, Judith had suffered a great deal with female problems that culminated in her requiring a hysterectomy, which she had performed in 1970 at the Lansdowne Hospital in Cardiff. In the interim period our sex life was minimal and in some ways we drifted along with the cement that was holding us together being the children and members of both our families. My work load increased significantly with my becoming head of a department that now had a full-time teaching staffing establishment of twenty-five members, in addition to numerous part-time specialist lecturers, and a technical staff of eight servicing eight laboratories.

The developing Higher National Diploma in Applied Biology contained two innovative features. One was the fact that it contained two six-month periods when the students were in work placements arranged through myself as course tutor; and secondly, all practical work at second-and third-year level was conducted through the medium of six practical projects covering the course syllabus and designed to test the student's ability to plan, investigate, record and evaluate a topic under the guidance of his or her project tutor. To ensure that appropriate tutors and laboratory space was available, all Advanced Diploma and Certificate courses were timetabled so that all students, all staff and all laboratories were available for a continuous period of four hours every week. This nightmare task I placed in the capable hands of Margaret and very soon news of this new approach to practical work spread throughout the biological centres of England and Wales.

A consequence of these two innovative developments was that work placements became more student-friendly, with students during their six-month placements being able to contribute meaningfully to the work of their placement, and in most instances obtaining the promise of a job on successful completion of their studies, while on a personal level, I was invited to address various biological conferences organised by the Department of Education and Science, on the topic of practical project work and its assessment.

Visiting students on placements was both a demanding and rewarding exercise, and involved visiting biological establishments as far north as Edinburgh, as far east as London and as far south as Porton Down and Plymouth. To lessen my personal load of checking student progress in their placements, there were occasions when Margaret accompanied me, and on one of these occasions involving visits to three different drug companies in the London area, an overnight stay was necessary, resulting in our sleeping together for the very first time. We had waited so long and even before we decided that this was what we both wanted, we agreed that in no way would we wish to hurt our partners and families, and to this end we would exercise complete discretion, ensuring that family commitments always came first.

Our love-making was wonderful and released the tensions which we had both experienced over the years. We talked and held back no secrets, with Margaret admitting that she had been attracted to me when we were both at university, and how she had been envious of Sylvia during her secret relationship with me. This closeness was new to me since I suppose I had always retained an element of independence in all my other relationships with many decisions taken without reference to anybody else.

So my career as head of a thriving and developing department progressed, punctuated by family commitments and secret meetings with Margaret. Although there were occasions when we longed to share what we had with the world, these thought were swiftly dispelled by us both. There was one occasion, however, when some indication of our special relationship was detected by an outsider. The incident, which I will always remember, was when Judith and I and Margaret and Hayden attended a college dinner dance at the Angel Hotel. Sharing our table was Professor Landgrebe and his wife Margo, who had not met Judith or Margaret before and unwittingly made the assumption that Judith was Hayden's wife with Margaret being mine.

The development of biological science courses, numerous links with employers throughout the UK and a reputation for innovative work resulted in the Institute of Biology suggesting that a branch of the institute should be established in South Wales. Following consultation with a number of employers and university departments at both Cardiff and Swansea, the first meeting of the branch was held in May 1968 when I was elected as founder chairman.

At about this time the car bug bit me again when I saw a for sale advert in the local press for a Lagonda three-litre drop-head coupé. Remembering Professor Landgrebe's addiction to the make and remembering its basic specification, I decided to view the vehicle. A phone call later and I was on my way to Druidstone Road – a very select area of Cardiff, with large houses and residents with even larger bank balances. The car was a beautiful powder blue, aluminium-bodied coupé by Tickford, with a light grey hood and leather trim, belonging to a Miss Watkins, a middle-aged spinster who lived in an apartment in one of the converted mansion houses of the area. She took me for a trial run and I fell in love once again. There were two problems, however: one was that on inspection I could see that oil was present in the cooling system; and second, I could not afford the car without disposing of the Alvis. I drew Miss Watkins' attention to the oil problem and it transpired that her garage had suggested a major overhaul of the engine, although a quick telephone call to Professor Landgrebe reassured me that all that was required was a new cylinder-head gasket, and that this was a common problem with the twin-cam Aston Martin Lagonda engine, which had wet cylinder liners that were prone to moving slightly resulting in engine oil entering the cooling system. In respect of disposing of the Alvis, I enquired if, mindful of the problem with the Lagonda, she would be interested in a part-exchange, and was most surprised when she said that she liked the look of the Alvis and would take it as part of the deal. The next day, armed with £50 and the Alvis, I had acquired the Lagonda. A week later after I had solved the engine problem, cleaned and polished the coachwork and conolised the leather trim. I had a beautiful car that the children loved and was much admired where ever it went.

Events in 1970 were to change my life once again. By this time David Lawrence was eleven years old and in September commenced his studies at the Howardian High School. Julia was attending Marlborough Road Primary School, while Judith was working part-time at one of the shops in Albany Road as well as looking after her mother, who having been a heavy smoker all her life was now suffering the side effects. Having been hospitalised on two occasions due to lung infections, Gwyneth passed away in late January at St David's Hospital aged seventy-six.

During the previous year my aunt Catherine, who was now approaching her ninety-fourth birthday, had become less mobile and no longer could go shopping in Albany Road and was having difficulty with stairs, and following Gwyneth's passing, a further reorganisation of accommodation was undertaken.

My father and Aunt Catherine moved to the ground floor with my father occupying the front room and my aunt occupying the room previously used by Gwyneth, thus avoiding all stairs, while Julia moved to the top floor, occupying the bedroom previously occupied by my father. Judith and I occupied the rear bedroom on the first floor, with the middle bedroom previously occupied by my aunt being converted into a new kitchen.

A few months later my Aunt Catherine took to her bed and responsibility for her nursing fell on me, since she would not let anybody else touch her. The doctor diagnosed a failing heart due to age and viewed her passing as just a matter of time. Every morning I would change the bed and her nightgown, give her breakfast and then set off for work. My father would make her lunch and then in the evening on my returning from work, the morning exercise had to be repeated. On 25 May Aunt Catherine celebrated her ninety-fourth birthday, but it was not the Aunt Catherine of old; she was weak and fragile and her memory kept wandering back into the past. The following morning I attended to my aunt as usual, gave her breakfast and set off to work. I was half an hour into a practical physiology class when Margaret came in to inform me that the college had received a phone call saying that my aunt had passed away. With Margaret taking over my class, I set off for Claude Road to kick-start all the arrangements connected with the funeral.

Aunt Catherine had always expressed the wish that she should be laid to rest at Nevern, close to her beloved sister, mother and father. That was a wish that I carried out, and a week later the funeral service was held at St Brynnach Church where my aunt had worshiped for over fifty years and she was buried in the family plot that she had attended and cared for over the years. The funeral, while not being as large as that of my mothers', was well attended with many families who had known my aunt for over fifty years coming to pay their last respects since my aunt had been well thought of in the local community. We were all very quiet as I drove back to Cardiff, since both my father and I knew that we would miss my aunt, who had been so much apart of our lives for so long, and for me had made possible things that otherwise would have been impossible. Judith, although knowing her for a relatively short time, had got on with her very well and knew that both David and Julia would miss Ano.

Soon life returned to normal, and in August 1970 my father celebrated his eightieth birthday. There was little doubt that he missed his sister and one of the consequences of his feeling lonely was that he frequented the local public houses more and more, using up the best part of his pension on drink.

As Christmas approached I was called to the principal's office to be told that the Director of Education for the City of Cardiff wished to see me. Since the only other occasion that I had had any meaningful discussion with Alex McKay was when he requested that I give his son some tuition in the art of dissection in preparation for his General Certificate of Education at Advanced Level in Biology, I assumed that once again he was seeking my assistance for his son, who was now at medical school. This, however, was not the case, and his proposition was to have a major effect on my professional and personal life.

It transpired that under a recently published circular by the Department of Education and Science entitled Circular 7/70, colleges of the size of Llandaff and its sister colleges of food technology and commerce were to be granted new Instruments and Articles of Government and required that their management structure be strengthened by the appointment of full-time deputy principals. Although the situation as far as Llandaff College was concerned was straight forward, the situation in relation to the College of Food Technology and College of Commerce presented problems in that although they occupied a common site, they were effectively run as two separate institutions with the head of the food technology college, a baker, having the title of principal, and the head of commerce an economics graduate, having the title of vice principal. Circular 7/70 made this arrangement non-viable, and consequently the City of Cardiff Education Authority was required to establish a common management structure and board of governors operating under a single Instrument and Articles of Government. To implement these changes the newly established post of deputy principal would play a vital roll, and in our discussions Alex McKay was of the opinion that my application would be most welcomed by the authority.

Although my interview with Alex McKay was strictly confidential I had requested that I be allowed to discuss the matter with Joe Cottrell, since I felt I owed him my loyalty, and I also wanted to find out as much as possible about the personalities involved in food technology and commerce. My attention had now also been focused on the deputy principal's appointment at Llandaff Technical College.

Principal Cottrell's advice was that whereas the post at the College of Food Technology and Commerce could well be a 'bed of nails', he was confident that I would make a success of it. He would, however, be very sad to see me leave and asked whether I had considered applying for the Llandaff appointment – an application that he would welcome. The fact that both posts were non-teaching and would result in my having little or no contact with students he also emphasised, since he knew my love of teaching. I next discussed the issues involved with Margaret, who expressed the opinion that the invitation was only a just reward for all the work that I done over the last ten years and that I should apply. We then discussed our relationship and how my leaving Llandaff would affect the situation. It was at this point that Margaret made a suggestion that blew my mind. She told me that although she had achieved much in her career, and had a family that she would never let down or leave, the one thing that she had always longed for was having a child of her own and being a mother in all senses of the word. This was a side of Margaret that I had never seen before, and her sincerity and show of emotion over the issue was such that it resulted in us both crying and holding each other as if there was no tomorrow.

Although the two appointments were published together in the press, the closing date for applications and proposed interview date for the College of Food Technology and Commerce was one week before that of the Llandaff Technical College, so although I applied for both posts I knew that the outcome of the first would be the determining factor.

The day of the interview arrived and following a tour of the college premises, all six shortlisted candidates were invited to lunch in the training restaurant of the college hosted by the chairman of governors, Alderman Mrs Winifred Mathias and the principal, Leslie Smith.

Following lunch we were driven to the City Hall and for the fourth time in ten years I climbed the marble stairs that I had climbed as a university student, to a committee room where my future would be decided.

It was a large interviewing panel with representatives of both college governors, Education Authority and the Director of Education, with the one familiar face being that of Councillor Iorworth Jones.

I was offered the post and since an immediate response was required I could but accept, although I had many reservations as to what the future held.

Chapter Nineteen

I returned to the college at Llandaff with mixed feelings, told Margaret that I had accepted the post, then reported to the principal's office where Joe Cottrell congratulated me and wished me every success, while at the same time recording his sadness at my leaving. Returning home I told Judith, David, Julia and my father that I had a new job that would start the following September. All were very happy for me and we celebrated with a glass of sherry for the adults and lemonade for the children. The following day I was back in my office drawing up a long schedule of things that needed doing before I left.

One aspect of departmental activity that had expanded dramatically over the last few years was that of administration. This was directly related to the new Advanced Courses, the interviewing of prospective students, the placement of students in work situations and the production of examination papers that were externally assessed. These commitments, in addition to routine office administration, had resulted in the department requiring additional part-time secretarial assistance working alongside Mrs Diane Lambert, the departmental secretary. The person appointed was a Mrs Jean Davies, a married woman who had given up work to bring up a family of three children and was now ready to return to the workplace in a part-time capacity. Jean was a petite, blonde-haired, blue-eyed lady in her late thirties with excellent office and personal skills, and although having been in the post only six months had proved an asset to the department.

A consequence of Jean's appointment and excellent performance was that when I was later required to appoint a secretary for my new post as deputy principal, Margaret suggested that I ascertain whether Jean would be interested in that full-time appointment. Much to my surprise she said that she was, and following a lunchtime visit to the College of Food Technology and Commerce, when I was able to show her the office and general facilities, the usual internal advertisement of the post and the shortlisting of applicants, Jean was interviewed and duly appointed to commence duties in September 1971. Little did I know at the time how that decision would affect my life over many years to come.

My next task, at the principal's request, was to assist him in the shortlisting of applicants for my old post of head of department. By this time new Instrument and Articles of Government were in place and the college had, due to the rapid development of Advanced Level courses, been renamed the Llandaff College of Technology, while due to the dominance of the biological sciences, the department had been renamed as the Department of Biological and Chemical Sciences. These changes had created much interest and resulted in around forty applications being received, with my task being to reduce this list to the best six, who would then be interviewed by a staffing committee of the board of governors.

The outcome was that Dr John Juniper, head of the Department of Biology at one of the London polytechnics, was appointed. Although he appeared to be the best candidate on the day, both Principal Cottrell and Professor Landgrebe had their reservations, while Margaret, having met him briefly, viewed his appointment as not what the department needed at that time.

My last few months at Llandaff were punctuated by several farewell parties, the most memorable being the one organised by the department and held on a Friday evening at a hotel in Ogmore-by-Sea, a venue that I believe was suggested by Margaret. All the teaching, technical and administrative staff attended, having hired a bus for the journey to and from Cardiff. Margaret drove me there in her recently acquired white Triumph Spitfire, since the farewell party had been kept secret and not known to me until I arrived at the hotel. It was a great evening with live music, dancing and a buffet supper. On our way back Margaret drove the car onto a deserted beach and we made love in the moonlight.

The other farewell function was organised by the Staff Association that I had chaired during my early years at the college. This was a lunchtime event held in the college refectory and attended by most of the college staff, including the principal and my colleague heads of departments. While I had been presented with a carriage clock by the department, the Staff Association, mindful of my love of cars, presented me with the book *Great Cars of the World* by Ralph Stein.

In his tribute to my work at Llandaff the principal submitted an article to the college magazine *Snippets*, and the following paragraphs I will always recall with pride.

These eleven years have seen what can only be described as a 'biology boom' shattering all the traditional greenhouses of biology teaching as it has moved with what appeared to be supersonic speed through the educational centres. James wasn't driving the thing but sitting on the nose-cap developing courses, lecturing, obtaining the cooperation of industrialists and universities and lately rearranging teaching methods and systems and organising short courses. If he was head of electrical engineering, I would say he was a veritable dynamo; as a biologist, I do not know of an equivalent and can only reiterate what certain members of Her Majesty's Inspectorate have called his type – the 'bloody biologists'.

Consider this adjective 'bloody' in relation to James' Welsh ancestry. Obviously from his bearing, his handsome profile, his wavy locks, that diabolical laugh, now imagine all that in a Druidical red robe, what would he be in any circle but the hatchet-man. 'Come you in peace, boyo?' – demoniacal laugh – and out with the chopper. A stretch of imagination, of fantasy you say, but wait! What psychological urge is behind a man who buys a blue car the size of a baby *Queen Mary*, but that way back in history his predecessors used a chariot painted in woad which I understand is blue in colour? I warn the College of Food Technology and Commerce not to upset James or down will come the hood of the Lagonda, and down the avenue will roar the woad-coloured chariot and standing on the seat hair streaming, diabolical laugh strident on the cake-scented air will come the avenging bloody biologist himself.

Back to reality, I must stop my poetic pen and say with all sincerity, all good wishes to you, James, in your new post, a very sincere thank you for the excellent work you have done at this college. Your 'team' will miss you, the heads of department will miss you, and I will miss you – but be assured we all know where to find you.

It was with these plaudits ringing in my ears that I left Llandaff College of Technology after eleven successful years, and which I will always recall with fondness. Little did I know at that time that my leaving was not for good and that one day I would return.

Chapter Twenty

The College of Food Technology and Commerce, as it was now called, occupied newly-built premises in Colchester Avenue, Cardiff. The college had an enrolment of approximately 4,000 students with a mixture of full-time, part-time and evening-only students.

These students attended courses organised by five departments, these being the departments of Bakery and Confectionery, Catering and Hotel Administration, Science, Commerce and Social Work.

The college had a staffing establishment of 111 teaching staff in addition to the principal and deputy principal.

The major course provision was of a non-advanced type with an emphasis on bakery, confectionery and catering on craft-type courses leading to City and Guilds of London Institute examinations. The science department ran one of the few Advanced Level courses at the college, together with craft provision in hairdressing and domestic arts, while the Social Work Department provided the other Advanced Course provision through the certificate in social work and the diploma for teachers of mentally handicapped adults.

Upon arrival in my office on 1 September I was confronted by a pile of mail addressed to the principal but marked for my attention. I had been warned that Leslie Smith did not like to commit himself in writing, and that dealing with issues that required a detailed written response was probably going to be part of my role as his deputy. My second discovery regarding Leslie was that he was a very kind, likable man and although prone to making some terrible gaffs, had an inbuilt sense for survival. There was little doubt that in his time he had been a skilled craftsman, had written a book on the art of cake decoration, and been a very effective head of the Bakery Department at the old Cardiff Technical College, but now at the age of sixty he was prone to practically one hundred per cent delegation.

Leslie held weekly heads of departments meetings at which any issues not already delegated were passed on for attention. The five heads of department were familiar with this procedure and tended to use the meetings as a forum for domestic complaints rather than debating executive college issues, which had been my experience at Llandaff. The heads of department consisted of Edith Barnet, head of social work; Bruce Bullock, head of bakery and confectionery; Geoffrey Gogar, head of commerce; Victor Humphries, head of catering and hotel administration; and Donald Tucker, head of science. Departmental heads were as diverse in personality as the subjects they were responsible for. Edith Barnet was a professional social worker with a degree in sociology. She was a somewhat dominant spinster in her early fifties with ambitions of a career enhancement position within a local authority. Bruce Bullock was a tall, lean, well-spoken man in his forties who retained a low profile at meetings although in all probability was the most perceptive of the issues involved. Bruce was highly respected by both staff and students and was to become one of my closest colleagues. Victor Humphries was a short, stocky man in his early fifties and prior to entering education had been a chef with wide experience of catering both in the UK and abroad. He had a pleasant personality although in keeping with many chefs, had a short fuse when things were not going well. Donald Tucker was a dark-haired, handsome man in his late thirties, and a graduate biologist. Finally, there was the head of the commerce department, Geoffrey Gogar, a fifty-eight-year-old ex-army officer, a graduate in economics and the most senior of all the heads, having been a head of department at both the Cardiff Technical College and the Llandaff College of Technology before becoming head of department and part-time vice principal at the college.

I soon discovered that while my appointment as deputy principal was fully understood, there were concerns among the heads of department as to how my work might affect their role and responsibilities. Consequently, my first task was to remove these fears and build a working relationship with each one as individuals, promoting the view that I was there to give advice and guidance upon request, and assist in the development of

Advanced Level courses to the benefit of both students and staff. To further this objective I arranged weekly meetings with individual heads of department when informal discussions could take place, and I could begin to understand the workings of each particular department and they in turn could get to know me. With the exception of Geoff Gogar, and to a limited extent Miss Barnet, these meetings proved successful, and the feedback that I received from Jean via the college grapevine was encouraging.

Under the new Instrument and Articles of Government of the college, resulting from the implementation of Department of Education and Science Circular 7/70, the college now had an academic board, with an elected member of the board being its representative on the board of governors. At the first meeting of the board I was elected as its representative on the governing body and for the first time in my career experienced its workings, while at the same time getting to know the political membership of the board.

These changes initiated by Circular 7/70 were of considerable interest to me, since I often wondered if the advent of an academic board, with a brief of overseeing and controlling the academic work of the college, would have a significant effect on departmental development and departmental academic staff, and whether the involvement of both academic and non-teaching staff on the board of governors would have any significant effect.

My first initiative in terms of developing Advanced Level courses at the college was in catering and hotel management, and working alongside Vic Humphries I was soon able to persuade him and the departmental staff that a Higher National Diploma run as a three-year sandwich course with two six-month periods in the work situation would be the way forward. Although the subject matter was alien to me, the basic structure and staffing of the course was an exact replica of the Applied Biology provision that I had initiated at Llandaff. Although a full-time Diploma submission had been rejected in the past, on this occasion the Department of Education and Science had no hesitation in approving the scheme, subject to the appointment of a senior lecturer who would be responsible for the course and the placement of students in the work situation. This early success did much to enhance my reputation in the field of academic developments and the other departments were soon knocking on my office door seeking advice, guidance and assistance. Piloting the schemes through the academic board and board of governors was, I found, relatively easy and again my reputation was enhanced.

My overall workload at the college was comparatively light as compared with my work as head of department, with the result that I was able to get away and see Margaret on at least two occasions during most weeks. Although she said little I guessed that her role within my old department had changed considerably, since it would appear that John Juniper undertook all timetabling himself, and did not seek a great deal of advice as to how things had been organised in the past. It was during one of these meetings just before Christmas of 1971 that Margaret announced that she was fairly certain that she was pregnant and was going to see her doctor the following week. A week later and her pregnancy was confirmed. Margaret was obviously delighted and when I asked her what Hayden thought of the news and what she intended doing, she surprised and hurt me by saying that everything was all right and there would be no problems, and nothing would change between us.

My first year at the college ended with an invitation to Leslie and Gladys Smith's only daughter Janet's wedding. This was a grand affair held at Llanishen parish church on a Saturday in July, with over a hundred guests and a reception as the Cedars Hotel. Judith and I were very well received and made most welcome by Gladys Smith, a short, auburn-haired lady with the most pleasant of smiles, and we were introduced to the other guests as Leslie's deputy and wife. That day I realised that Leslie Smith did appreciate the work that I was doing at the college and the loyalty to him that I had been required to exercise on numerous occasions during that first year.

On 28 August 1972 at Cardiff Royal Infirmary Margaret gave birth to a baby girl that she named Bethan. 28 August was also Judith's thirty-ninth birthday.

I started my second year at the college determined to undertake a project of my own as opposed to work aimed at meeting the needs and wishes of others. Having approached Professor Andrew Taylor, Professor of Education at Cardiff University College, and declaring my interest in evaluating the possible effect of Circular 7/70 on college management, it was decided that I would undertake a Master of Education degree by thesis with Andrew Taylor as my tutor. The principal was very enthusiastic at this development, and on enquiring I discovered that all the college staff would be happy to complete the questionnaires that I would be circulating seeking their views of the changes involved. At the principal's suggestion I also made an application to the Education Authority for a grant to cover the university's tuition fees and was pleasantly surprised when I was informed that my application had been approved. My only remaining problem was the typing involved in the production of questionnaires, the tables of results, the analysis of results and the final preparation of the thesis itself. During one of my many daily discussions with Jean, I told her of my problem and she immediately agreed to undertake the work during any spare time that she might have outside her normal secretarial duties.

During this time I noticed that Jean talked more and more about her family and how her husband, John, did not appreciate her domestic duties, her views and her involvement in looking after the three children, who although now at school still required a great deal of support. This topic of conversation soon became a daily occurrence and on reflection should have given me cause for concern. As it was, however, I made reassuring comments that usually resulted in Jean commenting as to how different my attitude was to that of her husband and how working with me had boosted her confidence.

In March 1973 my father died. He had returned home around ten o'clock following a few drinks with his friends at the Claude Hotel and had fallen in his bedroom, cracking his head against the chest of drawers. Although he appeared to be all right when I helped him to bed, the next day I called the doctor to give him an examination, and although the doctor could find nothing wrong, he suggested that due to the blow to the head, I take him for an X-ray. I was eventually able to persuade my father to come with me to the Cardiff Royal Infirmary, where following an X-ray he was admitted for further investigation. A day later on 10 March he died of a fractured skull and internal bleeding. So within two years I was again following a hearse to Nevern where my father was buried next to my dear mother and Aunt Catherine.

By the end of my second year at the college, David Lawrence was thirteen and attending the Howardian High School, whose playing fields adjoined the college premises, while Julia Ann was in her last year at Marlborough Road Primary School and would be joining her brother at Howardian in September.

Judith continued to work part-time at the store in Albany Road while I spent many hours collecting data from the questionnaires that had been completed and returned by staff and applying statistical significance to the figures so obtained.

During the summer of 1973 I completed my thesis entitled 'An assessment of some of the effects of Circular 7/70 on Technical College Administration' in readiness for its submission to the University of Wales for a Master of Education degree. Since the period normally attributed to completing a Masters degree was two years, I had to delay the actual submission for a further six months, then by special dispensation from the Education Department it was submitted in March 1974 and I was awarded the degree at a graduation ceremony in July of that year.

During this time Jean, as a consequence of our close working relationship on both college and personal projects, had become very possessive and saw her role as my secretary as also being that of an 'office wife', advising me of the college gossip and what in her opinion I should be doing in my capacity as deputy principal. Her vivid account of her domestic life and how her husband did not value her became a daily issue and eventually I felt almost sorry for her. Then one day when I was on the point of leaving my office she told be that she had fallen in love with me and wanted me as a lover. On reflection, and mindful of the fact that Judith and I had grown apart and that I had not seen or talked to Margaret since around the time of Bethan's first birthday, Jean's approach flattered me and although I knew at the time I should have walked away, I took Jean out for a drive in the Lagonda, stopping at a rural inn for a sandwich before returning to the office. So my relationship with Jean blossomed, and although at the time I had visions of it being similar to that which I had with Margaret, it turned out to be very different, with Jean having a very different agenda from that I had enjoyed with Margaret. I soon discovered as our relationship progressed that Jean was very temperamental, with a tendency to fly into a rage very quickly, and was a very different person from the highly professional secretary that I had appointed three years previously. Since the dye had been cast, and although there were many occasions when I wished the relationship had never started, I went along with the situation with Jean promising to tell Judith all about us should I ever decide to end our relationship. Our love-making was torrid and usually ended in an argument with my being accused of not really wanting her. Yet there were occasions where she could be tender, loving and everything most men would wish for.

In July of 1973 the Department of Education and Science issued another circular to Education Authorities and colleges. This was Circular 7/73 and it outlined plans aimed at amalgamating colleges of education with colleges of art and colleges of technology to form institutes of higher education. The objectives of this amalgamation were to reduce the teacher training component nationally, diversify course provision and thereby utilise staff previously engaged in teacher training in other fields of higher education, while at the same time creating institutions of optimum size with the resulting economies of scale.

As far as the College of Food Technology and Commerce was concerned my task was to guide this document and its recommendations through the academic board and board of governors, ensuring that in principle, the majority of academic staff and governors were in favour of the proposed amalgamation of the college with its sister colleges in Cardiff.

When this stage had been completed with varying degrees of success within the other five colleges involved, the new Education Authority, established as a consequence of the local government reorganisation of 1974, established a steering committee with three representatives from all the colleges involved to consider both the academic structure and administrative structure of the proposed institute. The chairman of governors, the principal and myself represented the College of Food Technology and Commerce. There then followed almost eighteen months of discussion, proposal and counter proposal with all the colleges fighting their own corner.

During my first three years at the college and in addition to the work connected with my research, I had successfully obtained approval for a Higher National Diploma in Hotel and Catering Administration, a Higher National Certificate in Public Administration, a Higher Diploma in Baking, a two-year course leading to the Certificate in Social Work, while the Diploma course in Dietetics was being reorganised into a degree course validated by the University of Wales.

To reduce the size of the Commerce Department and establish a service provision to other college courses in general studies, and develop further courses in journalism, a new department of Liberal and General Studies was established with its first head being a John Evans. John was a fair-haired, very pleasant man in his late forties, having graduated in English at the University College at Aberystwyth.

During this period I had not forgotten my ex-colleagues at Llandaff and occasionally invited one or two over for lunch in the training restaurant. This restaurant provided a full silver service in plush surroundings. Being open every lunchtime during term time it had a number of regulars, including the director of education – Alex McKay, and numerous councillors who were personal friends of Leslie Smith.

On several occasions I would collect Aunt Lois from Kenfig Hill and following her favourite sherry in my office, would take her to lunch, then take her to visit some of her friends in Cardiff, followed by a quick visit to Claude Road to see David and Julia, before returning home. These occasions my aunt Lois enjoyed very much, yet as always she was perceptive enough to question as to whether I was completely happy in my new job, and did I not miss my teaching and love of science.

In the autumn of 1974 the principal's secretary retired after many years of, as she used to say, 'looking after Leslie'. The post was advertised and Jean decided to apply since the salary was higher than what she currently earned as secretary to the deputy principal. I had no problem with supporting her application and in due course she was appointed. Although Leslie had expressed his concerns at my losing my secretary, I assured him that it was all right and that I could not stand in her way of improving her career prospects. The major problem arose when it came to her replacement working for me since Jean had a very jealous streak and having now been appointed to the top job did not relish the prospect of someone else working for me. Fortunately, the first advertisement did not attract any suitable candidates and so for the time being Jean undertook secretarial work for both the principal and deputy principal, a situation I allowed to drift for several months in the hope that Jean would eventually be more reasonable.

Following my being awarded my M.Ed. degree, Professor Andrew Taylor approached me with the suggestion that since the five colleges in Cardiff would soon merge into one, would it not be more appropriate if their origins and history could be evaluated as part of the overall development of further education provision within the City of Cardiff? This suggestion I took on board and eventually a thesis entitled 'An evaluation of the Development of Further Education provision within the City of Cardiff between 1916 and 1976' was agreed upon, leading to the award of Doctor of Philosophy.

Once again Leslie Smith was delighted with the prospect of my gaining another degree, since it would appear that other members of the academic staff were following my example and becoming interested in embarking on similar research projects. Since the advent of such research programmes was compatible with the college developing degree-level courses, this was seen as a trend to be encouraged. Jean for her part volunteered, without my asking, to undertake the typing connected with the research which, under the PhD regulations of the University of Wales, would take three years to complete.

Chapter Twenty-One

On a dark and dismal November morning in what was my fourth year at the college, Principal Smith, Jean and I were having morning coffee in Jean's office when I heard a noise that I had not heard since my childhood days on the farm when my father went out shooting – it was that of a twelve-bore shotgun. Although unsure as to the location of the shot, instinct took me running along the main corridor of the building and up the stairs to the first floor. In the centre of the first-floor stairwell stood a man holding a sawn-off shotgun. At his feet was a body in a pool of blood that was gradually spreading as I looked. Although on reflection my actions could have proved highly dangerous, I walked towards the man, took the gun from his hands and although he offered no resistance, I gripped his arm firmly and with my other hand broke open the shotgun, revealing one empty and one loaded barrel. I then asked the obvious question, 'Did you kill him?' since it was obvious to me from looking at the victim that a twelve-bore shotgun at short range in the chest would most certainly be fatal. His response was, 'I killed him.'

By this time several students were hovering around the stairs on their way to the college refectory for their morning coffee, so I shouted to one to go to my office and get a tablecloth to cover the body, and another to let the principal know that there had been a murder and to call the police.

Elvet Lewis, a member of the Commerce Department staff who arrived on the scene, was instructed to take the man, who I later discovered was a mature Social Work student, to an empty adjoining classroom and keep him there until the police arrived. The student with the baize tablecloth from my office arrived, and the body was covered, while fifteen minutes later the police arrived and the college was sealed for the next four hours with no one allowed to enter or exit. Having told the police inspector what I had witnessed and what I had done and been told, I returned to my office, shaken by the finality of death and wondering what had caused one human being to take the life of another.

It would appear on investigation that the murder was committed as a consequence of the murderer's friend's wife allegedly having an affair with the social work student while her husband was away. That, to his way of thinking, was an unacceptable situation and resulted in his murdering the student involved. In due course and before the case came to trial, he was deemed criminally insane and detained at Her Majesty's pleasure.

About six months later there was a knock on my office door. It was a police officer returning my baize tablecloth blood stains and all.

The early months of 1975 were particularly harrowing, in that Jean was constantly suggesting that I should move out of Claude Road and find a place of my own where she and I could meet. This I was not prepared to do at the time since David Lawrence was sixteen and studying for his General Certificate in Education at Ordinary level, while Julia was only thirteen going on fourteen and beginning the difficult teenage years. I loved them both dearly, and found even the suggestion of leaving them at that age completely at odds with my upbringing and teaching in family values. A few weeks later Jean was off work on sick leave for a week, and it was only then I realised the effect that the constant pressure that working close to her was having on my quality of life and how foolish I had been to enter into the relationship. One day, during her absence, I was looking for the official title and address of one of the employers in the Civil Service who was sending students to the college on a day-release basis, and was thumbing through the directory of senior civil servants when I came across the name Brian Grant, an engineer working for the Civil Service in one of the Home Counties. His work and home telephone numbers were listed, and on impulse I rang the home number. I recognised the voice immediately. It was Sylvia. She in turn paused for a moment then said, 'John, is that you?' We chatted for about twenty minutes, during which time Sylvia indicated that she would love to see me again, and suggested that since her sister now lived in Newport Monmouthshire, and she had arranged to come and stay with her over the next weekend, it would be a great opportunity for us to meet up again. Before I rang off we had arranged to meet the following Saturday morning in Churchill Way, Cardiff.

Saturday was a bright, sunny day and at 10.30 I was walking along the rows of parked cars in Churchill Way, having left my car in the Parade which adjoined the University College where Sylvia and I had studied. Right on time a blue Mini appeared, I got in, we kissed and the twenty years that had passed since our last meeting appeared as only yesterday. We drove round to the Parade where Sylvia parked her car and we got into the Lagonda, which was soon heading west out of Cardiff towards Cowbridge and the coast.

We talked and talked about the old days, the intervening years, and how life had treated us. Like myself, Sylvia had two children, a boy and a girl, and as a consequence of Brian having a well-paid position in the Civil Service she had not taken up full-time employment following the birth of the children. She viewed her life as reasonably happy and despite the ups and downs experienced by most married couples had resolved not to do anything that would jeopardise her husband's career.

On arriving at Ogmore-by-Sea we strolled hand in hand along the seashore recalling our days at university, the staff and our fellow students. Sylvia asked about Margaret, since she knew that she was teaching in Cardiff but did not know of her having a daughter and consequently giving up full-time work. I did not reveal our past relationship since I viewed the past as a closed book, despite my thinking of what might have been practically every day. Our day together slipped by with much laughter and the occasional embrace as we recalled past experiences and soon it was time to return to Cardiff with Sylvia driving off to Newport and her sister, and me back home. On the following Monday Jean returned to work and life slipped back to normal until shortly after lunch when I was visiting one of the departments and a telephone call came through for me which in my absence from the office, Jean took. It was Sylvia, who when told I was not available left a contact telephone number.

Upon my return to the office Jean wanted to know who this woman who had called me was and why she wanted me to call her back. I explained that she was at university with me and was probably seeking advice regarding a job. Jean was obviously not satisfied but let it rest. I returned Sylvia's call to find that she was staying in Newport for a further day and wanted me to join her that evening and, as she put it, 'make a night of it'. This development I considered to be fraught with danger and made an excuse that I would be away on college business for the rest of the day and evening. Although sounding bitterly disappointed Sylvia rang off and I was left with my own thoughts of what might have been, and the feeling that whatever relationship I had with Jean it was not based on love.

The early part of the 1975/76 academic year saw discussions involving the establishment of an institute by the amalgamation of colleges draw to a close, with the South Glamorgan Education Authority and Council finalising its proposals regarding future academic structure and management that bore little resemblance to the recommendations of the steering committee. The first post to be advertised was that of the principal, and although three of the principals in post applied together with two deputy principals, including myself, by November 1975 Dr Ernest Brent, principal at a London teacher training college, had been appointed. Ernest Brent was a slim, white-haired man of Austrian origin, having left Austria with his widowed mother following the death of his father and prior to the involvement of Austria in the Second World War. He had a most pleasant personality and he and I immediately established a good working and personal relationship, which was very much at odds with his relationship with other senior colleagues. Ernest had met a Welsh girl, Jean, while at university and had subsequently married her and now had a son, Richard, and a daughter, Caroline, both of school age. Jean, in the meantime, had returned to teaching. His first task was to finalise the management and administrative structure of the institute, which was to be called the South Glamorgan Institute of Higher Education, and to make the necessary appointments for the new session in September 1976. One such appointment was that of principal's secretary, and once again Jean sought my assistance in making an application for this post which she considered as the 'top job'. Her application proved successful with the appointment commencing in April 1976. Since the administrative centre for the institute was to be located at Llandaff, this meant that for the first time in five years Jean would be working at a different location to me and where, hopefully, I would not be involved, although she had insisted that she would still type the work for my doctorate degree in her spare time. Of the senior academic appointments, Joe Cottrell was appointed deputy principal with Leslie Smith and Derek Turner, principal of the College of Art, being made assistant principals, while the principal of the College of Education, left having been appointed as principal of Durham Institute of Higher Education. The four deputy principals were offered the posts of Deans of Faculty, with myself being appointed as Dean of the Faculty of Sciences, a position I was very happy with since it put me back into the environment that I had always loved, and involved my having responsibility for the sciences at three locations within the institute, including my old department at Llandaff.

In January 1976 David Lawrence celebrated his seventeenth birthday and announced that he had decided to join the Royal Air Force, since he did not wish to pursue further academic studies, and had no wish to end up in a desk job, and was anxious to pursue an active lifestyle while at the same time seeing a bit of the world. His General Certificate of Education examination results at Ordinary Level, his love of rugby and his athletic build were such that his acceptance into the Royal Air Force was a formality, and within a few months he left Claude Road for his initial training camp in Abingdon.

When David had turned sixteen, I had bought him a second-hand motorbike for his birthday, and following a very professional rebuild, which he undertook himself, he used it as transport between Abingdon and Cardiff on the occasional weekend at home.

We all missed David, myself most of all since the house appeared so empty. My mother-in-law had gone, my dear aunt Catherine had gone, my father had gone, and although David was not in that category his absence was nevertheless a factor that highlighted to me what the future held when Julia Ann would also no longer be there. I felt guilty regarding what I had in mind, which was completely at odds with everything that I had been taught when young, and despite everything I had no wish to hurt anybody. At this time my career prospects were uncertain and although I had never planned my future in terms of job opportunities and career progression, the reorganisation and amalgamation of the colleges over which nobody appeared to have any control was contributory to a general feeling of insecurity among all concerned. I was also aware that Judith would never leave her beloved Cardiff regardless of where my next appointment might be, while the constant reminders by Jean that I was worthy of something better were beginning to have the 'drip of water on a stone' effect, although I knew that a great deal of what she said had a self-interest component. Against this background of conflict and uncertainty I decided that my leaving Claude Road was the best option, although there was no way that I would abandon David and Julia, and would always ensure that Judith was secure financially and had a home for the children.

My first task was to locate a suitable property that I could purchase at a price commensurate with my limited finances and where mortgage repayments would be containable. Luck was on my side and I discovered a small block of six apartments that were in the final stages of construction, located within easy travelling distance of my work, Cardiff city centre and Claude Road. The development known as Cooper Court was situated at the end of a tree-lined avenue within a conservation area, and appeared to me as exactly what I was looking for. My next task was to contact once again Strad Jones to seek his advice and to instruct him to act on my behalf in the purchase of 3 Cooper Court. He was saddened when I told him of my decision to separate from Judith while at the same time recognising that it was my decision and my life.

By July 1976 the apartment was completed and shortly afterwards I moved in. My first house guest was Julia, who at the age of almost sixteen and still at Howardian High School, worked part-time on Saturdays at Littlewood Stores in Cardiff, and called in at Cooper Court on her way home. This link I treasured, since to some extent it lessened the feeling of sadness and guilt I had experienced throughout the whole process of separation.

Number 3 Cooper Court consisted of a good sized lounge/diner, a fitted kitchen, a modern bathroom with bath and shower and two double bedrooms, one of which had a balcony. During the following months I gradually bought some furniture including a lounge suite, a bed, dressing table and wardrobe, since the only items that I had taken from Claude Road was the grandfather clock that my grandfather had bought in 1875 at Llangennech together with some china that belonged to my grandmother and had been stored in the attic of Claude Road ever since we had moved there. Carpets and curtains were another essential and slowly the place began to look lived-in.

In 1975, and probably as a consequence of the unsettled atmosphere that prevailed at home and at work, coupled with the fact that the Lagonda, which I had now owned for over five years, was in need of considerable body work attention in order that it passed its MOT, I decided that following this remedial work being carried out professionally, I would sell the car.

Within a few days of the advertisement for the sale of the Lagonda appearing in the motoring press, I received a phone call from a gentleman from New Zealand who was currently in London and wanted, upon his return, to take back a Lagonda drop-head coupé to New Zealand. Having viewed the car, which was now in good order, and the large amount of spare parts that I had acquired over the years, a deal was struck and the Lagonda, with its roof down and the rear seats accommodating boxes of spares, was driven away for the then princely sum of £850. This money I banked, less £200 which was to buy my next car.

Prior to the sale of the Lagonda, I had noted a white Mark 2 Jaguar 3.4 saloon in a garage in City Road, and although not displayed for sale, I was given to understand, open to offers. The car, I discovered later, belonged to a lady who had been its only owner, with the car being serviced from new at the garage that now had the task of selling it on behalf of the owner. With cash in hand I was able to negotiate a price of £200 plus a free service. So my love affair with Jaguars came about, one that, with a few short breaks, persists to the present day.

Chapter Twenty-Two

September 1976 saw the first students entering the South
Glamorgan Institute of Higher Education. As Dean of the Faculty
of Sciences I was responsible for seven science-based departments, including Bakery and Confectionery, Catering and Hotel
Management, Food Science and Nutrition, Biological and
Chemical Sciences, Mathematics and Physical Sciences, Science
for Teachers, and Mathematics for Teachers, with a full-time
teaching staff complement of two hundred and five, and in excess
of three thousand students.

My heads of department were all known to me, with the exception of Dr John Juniper, my successor at the old Llandaff
College of Technology, who I had had little contact with since his
appointment, and the two heads from the Teacher Training
sector – Miss Nan Bowen a biologist, and Mr Dewi Thomas, a
mathematician. I immediately instituted weekly heads of department meetings and these gelled to become an effective forum for
developing faculty strategy and the parallel development of
degree-level courses from the existing Higher National Diploma
and Certificate provision. Since all such degree courses were to be
validated by the University of Wales, the format for presentation
was standard and reduced the room for error while at the same
time unified the various departments of the faculty.

During the first two years the faculty successfully submitted
proposals for sandwich degree courses in Applied Biological
Sciences, Medical Laboratory Sciences, Dietetics, Speech
Therapy, Hotel and Catering Management, and Food
Technology. The existing advisory committees of the individual
colleges were amalgamated to two, representing the work of the
faculty, and with the chair of each committee being a member of
the board of governors of the institute. Since all proposals
required both academic board and board of governors approval
before being submitted to the University of Wales for validation,

197

the process was long and tedious and as light relief, I pressed on with my PhD degree thesis, thus avoiding getting involved in the 'domestics' of the institute and its staff.

Although working for Dr Brent, Jean still met me most lunchtimes and continued to type the numerous chapters of my dissertation, which was rapidly nearing completion. Part of her duties as secretary to the principal was to prepare the monthly newsletter that Dr Brent had initiated. This involved collating a whole variety of newsworthy items submitted by the various departments of the institute and presenting them under specified headings. Jean found this task daunting and since Dr Brent assumed that she was up to the job with little or no input from him, Jean sought my assistance, and in exchange for the typing work she did for me, I became the 'secret editor' of the institute's newsletter.

Although my moving out of Claude Road had pacified Jean's constant nagging on that topic, she soon found a new one which related to my meeting David and Julia and having them round to the flat for the occasional bite to eat, a feature she was not in favour of. This upset me greatly and our future meetings at Cooper Court always ended in quarrels with bad words exchanged by us both. Eventually, I told Jean that my seeing or not seeing David and Julia was not up for debate, and as far as I was concerned if she insisted on my not seeing them, our relationship was over.

The Christmas of 1976/77 was a very lonely one. David had some leave and spent Christmas Day, Boxing Day and New Year's Day with his mother and sister Julia; Jean was at home with her family; while my other work colleagues had their own plans, and I was left with only memories of the past, and how exciting Christmas on the farm and when the children were young had been. I can safely say those days alone at Cooper Court with only my music centre and television for company were the longest and loneliest that I have ever experienced.

During 1977 Judith filed for divorce, giving unreasonable behaviour as the cause. This I did not challenge, and instructed my divorce solicitor to finalise the division of property and other financial considerations as soon as possible. The final agreement was that Judith had the family home at Claude Road; I kept Cooper Court, which in valuation terms was approximately equal, while I agreed maintenance for Judith and Julia at £200 a month, which at that time was a significant amount of money.

A consequence of this settlement was that the cost of running the Jaguar was putting a strain on my finances and it was necessary for me to consider a more economical vehicle. Parting with the Jaguar was a wrench since in terms of power and speed it was the best car I had experienced. ENY 75C with its 3.4-litre overhead cam engine with manual gearbox plus overdrive was a joy to drive, while the black leather interior and sunroof made motoring a pleasurable experience. If the car had one drawback it was its heating system, which in winter was very inefficient and resulted in driver and passengers having frozen feet on cold days.

Once again I advertised in the motoring press, and once again I had an immediate response, this time from a couple living in London. Having viewed the car and given a trial run a deal was agreed and ENY 75C was driven off for the sum of £450, which represented a £250 profit on the purchase price.

Not having to cater for a family, my quest for a new car centred on the two-seater, rag-top, small-engine sports car, a vehicle that I had never experienced. Within a few days I had located a suitable model in a small dealership in Cardiff, and after a trial run decided it was for me. My new acquisition, which cost £250, was a bright yellow 850cc Austin Healy Sprite with a black stripe down its bonnet and boot, black hood and interior and a great-sounding exhaust note.

My appearance in the open-top Healy caused much comment within the institute, many comments harking back to the open-top Lagonda, and suggesting that this was an offspring of that car. What the Healy did, however, was to cut down my fuel bill and made my commuting around the three sites of the institute to discuss issues with the various departments a financially viable proposition.

David and Julia loved the little car and there were occasions when all three of us crammed into the two seats on short journeys. Jean, on the other hand, was not really taken with the car but was fully supportive of my objective of saving money.

Now that I had a new address and had installed a telephone, it was necessary to let friends know of the changes. My aunt Lois was among the first to be told and true to form her comment was, 'Remember how I told you it was not too late to pull out, when we were on our way to your wedding?' I also called in on Professor Landgrebe, who had helped me so much over the years, and although he had only met Judith once, he thanked me for letting him and his family know.

By September 1977 my PhD thesis was completed, due mainly to the assistance and encouragement given by my tutor, Professor Andrew Taylor, and the typing undertaken by Jean. Copies were then submitted for binding according to University of Wales Regulations, with bound copies being available shortly after Christmas of 1977/78. A month later there was the meeting with the external examiner appointed by the university who, in the presence of my tutor, quizzed me as to my knowledge of the subject matter contained in the thesis. He was pleased with my answers and at the conclusion of the meeting I was advised that I had met all the requirements for the award of a Doctor of Philosophy degree.

Professor Taylor was warm in his congratulations and I returned to the institute in high spirits knowing that I now held four degrees of the University of Wales. My colleagues at the institute were equally congratulatory in their comments, with Dr Brent including his congratulations as an item in the institute's newsletter.

In March 1978 while looking through the various articles and advertisements in the *Times Educational Supplement*, I came across an advertisement for the appointment of principal at the Howel Harris College, Brecon. Not being particularly busy at the time since I was missing my research work, I sent away for an application form.

Details of the college, its location and spread of work, which was in the main at craft and technician level, with a minor input of farm management, appeared very attractive although very different from the work I was currently engaged in.

I applied using Dr Brent, Leslie Smith and Professor Landgrebe as my referees. Two weeks later I was called for an interview and was on my way to Brecon driving along the A470 through such valley villages as Quaker's Yard, Edwardsville, Aberfan, the site of the disaster of 1966 when 128 children attending primary school were buried by a coal tip collapse, and Merthyr Tydfil, which in the 1800s was the largest town in Wales, and became known as the steel capital of the world. The A470 then climbs onto the Brecon Beacons before dropping down into the market town of Brecon situated on the banks of the River Honddu which gives Brecon the Welsh name of Aberhonddu.

There were five shortlisted applicants, one being the current vice principal of the college, while another was principal at Brecon's smaller sister college at Llandrindod Wells – a well-known Victorian spa town. Following a introductory chat with the retiring principal Mr B H Roberts, who informed us that he had often been mistaken for a shorter version of the Duke of Edinburgh, and a short tour of the college, we were taken to a committee room at the Brecon Museum, where the preliminary interviews, conducted by the chairman and vice chairman of governors and the county's director of education, took place with the objective of reducing the number of applicants to three for the final interviews that would be held in the afternoon. I must have given a good interview since I was through to the final stage along with two other applicants from outside Wales, while the vice principal and principal from Llandrindod Wells had been eliminated.

The afternoon interviews were before the county's Further Education Committee of fifteen elected members, and although there were several difficult questions asked, my responses must have satisfied the committee since I was eventually called back and offered the appointment, which I had decided to accept. Following warm congratulations from various committee members and governors, I drove back to Cardiff in high spirits and in the knowledge that once again my life was about to change.

News of my leaving spread through the institute very rapidly, with the heads of department within the faculty bemoaning my imminent departure since over the two years we had formed a competent team that worked well together. Dr Brent, while being warm in his congratulations, expressed sadness at my leaving since he apparently valued my friendship and academic knowledge of the work the various colleges had been involved in prior to his appointment.

There then followed various dinners and presentations held to mark my leaving and the retirement of Leslie Smith, who on learning of my departure had decided to retire although he could have continued for a further year. One of the gifts presented and which gave me much satisfaction was that of a Grog cast in a self likeness complete with a Wales rugby shirt, mortar board and arm bands depicting Cardiff University colours and the South Glamorgan Crest, with my name engraved on the base. Grogs were made at a pottery near Pontypridd, and were very popular in the 1970s with a series depicting members of the Welsh rugby team of the 1970s much in evidence in most shops. To have a special Grog commissioned for me was a great thrill and much appreciated. Another gift very much treasured was a carriage clock presented by colleagues from the Llandaff campus of the institute.

Julia and David were very excited at the news that I was going to Brecon and to the top job of principal, and I had to promise that I would take them there as soon as I had settled in. At that time I had no plans to move to Brecon since a daily journey of just over an hour each way was not to my mind excessive travelling, especially when one considered the wonderful countryside I would be passing through. Jean also wanted to see my new college, but I kept making various excuses, and following one bitter argument I said she would never see the college. This proved to be a decisive step towards a split-up which I now saw as the only way forward.

By this time Julia had completed her General Certificate at Ordinary level and having gained the necessary number of subject passes, decided to apply to the institute to pursue a Business and Tourism course. Whether this choice was brought about by the news that I would no longer be a member of staff of the institute I never discovered, although like all young persons she and David had always been conscious of my involvement in education and the fact that their tutors were also aware of this fact.

My final task before leaving education in South Glamorgan was to present a copy of my PhD thesis to the chairman of the council at a council meeting, since it gave an historical account of the development of vocation, further and higher education within the City of Cardiff from 1916 to 1976.

Chapter Twenty-Three

During the July and August of 1978 I visited Brecon and the college on numerous occasions, since my work at the institute was finished and I was anxious to discover as much as possible about the town of Brecon and the Howell Harris College before the session commenced in September. There was also the need to upgrade my office since B H Roberts appeared to have done all his filing on large notice boards that dominated the walls of his office, and where I discovered letters covering most aspects of college work with scribbled notes on them indicating what action had or would be taken. This was not my scene, and I instructed my new secretary, Christine Forbes, who was a most pleasant young married woman in her late twenties, to acquire some new filing cabinets so that she could set up a filing system that both she and I could use. This she welcomed since as I discovered Christine was an extremely competent and efficient secretary. I then requested that she contact the County Architects Department and have all the notice boards removed and the room redecorated with carpeting, curtains and a new desk and chair. This she did with great enthusiasm, since in her view the college needed a shake-up and these changes would be a visual representation of change.

While these changes were being implemented I spent many a day strolling around the town, checking out the various points of interest and shops. Brecon proved to be a town where one could lose oneself, with its narrow streets and passageways lined with Georgian and Jacobean shop fronts which gave it a sense of timelessness. One such shop was a bookshop owned by Gwyn Evans and his wife Ann. Gwyn had been a local government officer who had taken early retirement following the local government reorganisation of 1974 and had set up the business that was also his hobby, since he was extremely knowledgeable of antique maps, books and the history of Brecon, and was known locally as 'Gwyn the books'.

Gwyn was a short, stocky man in his early fifties with a pleasant smile and a good sense of humour, and when he discovered who I was and that I would shortly be taking up an appointment in Brecon, he was most enthusiastic in giving me information as to what places to visit and what reading would best acquaint me with the history of the town.

It would appear that since the Iron Age the site of the present-day town had been prized in that it was situated at the confluence of the rivers Honddu and Usk and sheltered by the Beacons and the Black Mountains. Now Brecon was the commercial centre of the southern part of the county of Powys, which had been created under the 1974 Local Government Reorganisation Act, and was a traditional mid-Wales market town with a population of around 9,000.

There were several special features of Brecon that Gwyn drew my attention to, one being the cathedral, the origins of which dated back to 1093, when the half-brother of William the Conqueror captured the town and built a fortification on the present site. Three hundred years later the priory that he established within the fortification became known as the Priory Church of St John the Evangelist – being half church of God and half castle against the Welsh. The Priory Church later became Brecon Cathedral. I visited the cathedral and viewed the monastic buildings that lie within the embattled walls, and discovered in talking to the dean that the Bishop of Swansea and Brecon was none other than Benjamin Vaughan, previously Bishop of Belize, the second son of Mrs Ann Vaughan of Hendre Farm in Newport, Pembrokeshire, who was a cousin of my father and Aunt Catherine, and on whose farm I worked during my summer vacations. The second place I visited was the South Wales Borders Museum at Brecon Barracks, which traces the military links that Brecon had since the Napoleonic wars when French prisoners were incarcerated in the town, and where trophies and memorabilia of the heroic battle of Rourke's Drift of 1879 when 140 soldiers of the regiment faced more than 4,000 Zulu warriors were displayed. My final port of call was Christ College – a leading secondary school that like Cowbridge Grammar School was part boarding and part day boys, played rugby and whose team I had refereed on one occasion while at Cowbridge. Christ College dates back to 1541 when Henry VIII dissolved the existing monastery and founded the school.

The Howel Harris College was a much more recent development, although its name reflected the origins of agricultural training as far back as the 1700s when Howell Harris, one of the principal leaders of the Methodist Revival which began in 1735 and swept Wales from its allegiance to the Anglican Church, who was also involved in farming at a farm known as Trefecca on the outskirts of Brecon, became the first known person to issue certificates of competence to farm workers who had become skilled in such tasks as sheep-shearing, herding, droving and ploughing. The college, situated on a hill overlooking the town, shared a campus with Brecon High School, and was a low, sprawling, flat-roofed building, with a mixture of one-and two-storey accommodation, with separate workshop and lecture provision for Agriculture, Construction, Catering, Motor Vehicle Engineering and Horticulture. The administrative centre, adjoining the main entrance, consisted of a general office, a photocopying room, registrar's office and principal's office. Other communal accommodation consisted of an assembly/ function hall, a dining hall and adjoining kitchen. An out-centre for agriculture located at Llandrindod Wells, provided education and training for students from mid-Powys since the distances involved made it impossible for them to attend the Brecon site.

The college was built in the 1960s to meet the rapidly expanding demand of employers in terms of off-the-job training for their apprentices, and the needs of the various training boards that, at that time, were playing an important part in providing a growing economy with the necessary trained workforce. Initially the college had been classified as a Rural Technical Institute (RTI) in keeping with the rural needs of Agriculture, Horticulture, Building, Carpentry and Joinery, Farm Machinery and Motor Vehicle Engineering. It was only later that technician level provision was introduced in Business, Catering and Caring. It was into this environment and against this background that I made my entrance in September 1978.

In terms of its academic structure and management the college was a mixture of small sections with the lecturers in charge of sections being directly responsible to the principal, and one department of Business Studies with a head of department, Geraint Jones. The vice principal, a Walter Price, although a most pleasant man in his mid-fifties did not appear to have any specific duties other than assisting the principal as and when required. In addition to the teaching staff there was a registrar, Gwillym Griffiths, and two administrative assistants based in the general office, and various technicians based within the sections. A caretaker, kitchen supervisor and a variety of cleaners and kitchen attendants made up the rest of the staff.

My first task was to arrange personal interviews with all the lecturers in charge of sections, the head of department and Walter Price, the vice principal, to ascertain their views of the present position and the future of the college. I also contacted the HM Inspectors Department at the Welsh Office requesting that they conduct an inspection of the college with a view to ascertaining its strengths and weaknesses. Alongside this exercise of collecting information, I sought to find out as much as possible about the various employers who sent their trainees to the college, and how they viewed college provision and would they be interested in contributing by becoming members of the advisory committees I intended to establish.

Within the first six months of my being at the college I was able to present a detailed development plan to the board of governors. Based on my research, the views of HM Inspectors and employers, the new management structure of the college would consist of three departments, namely: Departments of Agriculture, Building and Engineering Studies; Business and Computing Studies; and Catering and Caring Studies. Each department would have a head of department with the existing head of Business Studies becoming head of the new Department of Business and Computer Studies; the agriculture advisor for South Powys becoming the head of the Department of Agriculture, Building and Engineering Studies; and the post of head of Catering and Caring Studies being advertised. The existing post of full-time vice principal would be phased out upon the retirement of the current holder with the limited duties being undertaken by one of the heads of department on a vice principal allowance. Each department would have an advisory committee with its chairman becoming a co-opted member of the board of governors.

The chairman of the board of governors was an ex-army lieutenant colonel, John Stevenson, who previous to his retirement had been Commander of the Sennybridge Training Camp in the Brecon Beacons. John Stevenson was a medium-built man with a receding hairline and searching eyes typical of a senior army officer used to giving orders and having them carried out. His vice chairman and close friend was Val Morris, a local farmer with a fresh complexion, ready smile and a most pleasant personality. Other members of the board of governors were in the main elected councillors representing South Powys. Both John and Val were complementary of my development plan and congratulated me on a job well done. This resulted in the plan being approved by the board with little or no debate with the result that a new college prospectus could be drafted incorporating all the changes approved with a foreword by myself and an introduction to the work of each department by its head. A glossy cover with photographs interspersed among the text completed the presentation and new image of the college. By May 1979 Dr John Fletcher had been appointed as head of the Department of Catering and Caring Studies, while I had negotiated with Walter Price a meaningful job description in line with his position as vice principal.

My next task was to assess the accommodation provision of the college and prepare a schedule of additional lecture and specialist accommodation that was urgently required, since the existing provision was poor and lacking in equipment. This aspect of the college had been commented on by the HM Inspectors during their visit and with this as a basis, a building programme was agreed upon with the County Architect, which received the governors' approval. The method of achieving the various workshops and specialist accommodation fell into three categories. Firstly, the new Agriculture Unit, consisting of lecture rooms and farm machinery workshops, was put out to tender.

Secondly, the new Brickwork Shop was to be built by the students with the blessing of the Construction Industry Training Board and to specifications agreed by the County Architect; while the third category involving restructuring of existing accommodation was to be carried out as minor works by the direct labour department of the county. With these changes in hand it was time to consider the provision for agriculture students in the Llandrindod Wells area, which was even worse than at Brecon.

While visiting Llandrindod on one occasion I met Martin Pugh. Martin was a large man in every since of the word and had been for many years regional officer for the Young Farmers Clubs of Wales. He was a very approachable person with a good sense of humour which he considered essential in dealing with young people. Martin's current problem related to very inadequate office space with no facility to hold committee meetings of representatives of the various clubs in Wales. I in turn recorded the lack of suitable accommodation that the college had at Llandrindod Wells, and it was from these initial exchange of views that a joint development plan incorporating workshop and lecture room accommodation for the college, and a suite of offices for the Young Farmers of Wales, was formulated. Following the board of governors' approval and approval by the Young Farmers Clubs of Wales, the development plan received County Council approval. Since the plans incorporated a community provision, it qualified, in part, for European Economic Community funding, which allowed certain refinements to be added to the initial proposals. The problem of where the new development would be built was resolved upon my visiting the chief executive of the Royal Welsh Agricultural Society at Builth Wells. Unknown to me, the society was anxious to develop a site which at that time was only used for the annual Royal Welsh Show, and the prospect of having a permanent building on the site housing both agriculture students and young farmers throughout the year was a most welcomed suggestion that was greeted with open arms.

With a major building programme underway, my final short-term project was in relation to the college acquiring a farm where the skills taught and illustrated in the college could be put into practice. Having been given to understand that current practice was for college staff to take students out on to commercial farms for such work, the advantages of a college farm situated between the college at Brecon and the out-centre at Builth Wells was an attractive proposition. I was advised that one of the high schools in South Powys and located at Three Cocks had inherited a farm that had originally been part of the estate of the manor house that now housed the school.

Upon visiting the school and meeting the headmaster, a Mr Huw Jones, I further discovered that the school had little use for the farm in terms of its teaching programmes, and since the farm bailiff, who lived in a cottage on the farm, and farm worker, who lived nearby, had protected contracts with the education authority, he would welcome the opportunity of getting rid of it. Huw Jones was a short, dark-haired man in his late forties; he was married to Marline, and together with their two school-aged sons they lived in the school house that had been built in the grounds of the school. Huw was a very pleasant person and we got on well together and soon became firm friends, so much so that following two further meetings we had prepared a detailed joint report for submission to both the board of governors of the high school and the board of governors of the college. A consequence of this joint report was that it was agreed by all concerned that the day-to-day management, financial management and the responsibility for future development of the farm became that of the college, and in so doing provided agriculture students at both Brecon and Builth Wells with an invaluable teaching resource, not only in the teaching of farm skills but as a case study in the teaching of farm management courses available to farmers' sons and daughters anxious to acquire management skills in running family farms.

With the raft of building programmes in the pipeline and the taking over and development of the farm an equally long-term project, I viewed the need to establish some form of shorter-term initiative as essential. Two such developments that I had experienced while at Llandaff Technical College came to mind. One was an Annual Carol Service of nine readings and carols for staff, students and invited guests, while the second was a Celebration of Achievement Evening, when students who had obtained some form of national qualification the previous session were presented with certificates or diplomas before an audience of fellow students, family and friends. Again the board of governors were most enthusiastic of these proposals and as my first year at the Howell Harris College drew to a close, I was well satisfied with the progress that I had achieved and was looking forward to their implementation in the years to come.

Chapter Twenty-Four

While I enjoyed travelling to and from Brecon on a daily basis, and enjoyed the journey through the Beacons in the Austin Healy Sprite – a journey that I timed to avoid much of the morning and evening traffic in Merthyr Tydfil – life continued in Cardiff and at Cooper Court. Most Saturdays Julia would visit me after she had finished her Saturday job at Littlewood Stores, or if David was home for the weekend, or was based at the RAF camp at St Athan in the Vale of Glamorgan, all three of us would meet in the Cardiff city centre visiting one of the many bars and restaurants for a lunchtime snack and chat. These meetings I valued more than words can tell, and were a source of much comfort to me. Jean, however, could not come to terms with my approach and what was left of our relationship soon turned sour, and although we saw less and less of each other, Jean soon became engaged in stalking me at every opportunity. This I found very unsettling and at times frightening – so much so that on one occasion when she entered the flat with no prior warning I demanded, and eventually was given, the set of keys for Cooper Court that I had foolishly given her when I bought the property.

One of the bars that we frequented on those Saturday mornings was the Savoy Restaurant and Bar situated at the Queen Street end of Churchill Way. The Savoy, as it was known, was a family-run business owned by John and Jane Williams and previously by John's mother, Anna. John's mother was Italian, and having met and married a Welshman, Jack Williams, while he was serving in Italy during the Second World War, had returned with her husband to make their home in Cardiff. John Williams was a tall, well-built, dark-haired man in his forties, having left university in 1952 with a degree in mining, a degree that he never used, choosing instead to enter the family business upon the death of his father. His wife Jane was an attractive blonde ex-model who had given him four children – three boys and a girl.

The Savoy Bar, situated on the ground floor of an impressive three-storey building, was run by John and a working partner, Dorothy Dawney, while the silver service restaurant and bar situated on the first floor was run as a separate enterprise by John and Jane Williams. Kitchens and staff rooms occupied the top floor of the building. Dorothy Dawney was a slim, middle-aged, married woman with a good business sense, a great personality and sense of humour, and with the ability of making all customers feel welcome and special. These qualities rubbed off on David, Julia and I, and as the weeks went by the Savoy Bar became our regular meeting place at lunchtime on Saturdays.

One Saturday in February 1979 while enjoying the usual drink and sandwich, we noticed that there was another girl working behind the bar. Julia commented on how pretty and attractive she looked, and I could but agree, while admiring her olive skin, dark-brown eyes that were constantly smiling, black shoulder-length hair and trim figure. Dorothy introduced us to Maria – an introduction that was to change my life once more.

Maria Leca was a Portuguese citizen who had left her home on the island of Madeira to take up employment with John Williams' mother, Anna, in October 1966. Maria was the eldest of eleven children and the early years of her life had been spent helping her mother, who worked full-time at the local health clinic, bring up her eight brothers and sisters, since two of her brothers had died within weeks of being born. At the age of twenty-one she had left home to take up employment as a cook in a doctor's house in Funchal, the capital city of Madeira. Following three and a half years in that position and a further eighteen months as cook/housekeeper with a wealthy family in Lisbon, she had decided to seek her fortune outside Portugal and arrived at Cardiff at the age of twenty-six. Although across a public bar is not the ideal venue to carry out any kind personal conversation, over the weeks and months that followed I was able to ascertain that February 1979 had seen her return from Argentina where she had been visiting her sister and family who lived in Buenos Aires, and that since her arrival in Cardiff in 1966 she had arranged for her three younger sisters to come and work in Cardiff, and although one had married a Spaniard and gone to live in Valencia in Spain, the other two lived with her in a house that she had bought through much hard work and careful financial management over the last thirteen years. During our brief snatches of conversations I was able to tell her that I was separated and awaiting my divorce to go through, that I lived on my own, and that Julia and David, who she thought were great, were my only close family. After several months I plucked up enough courage one Saturday to ask her would she consider going out with me. She said that she was too busy, did not go out with customers and was married. Although Dorothy had told me that she was not married and did not have a steady boyfriend, she confirmed that she did not go out with customers and that her social life was very family-orientated. I let the matter drop for a few weeks and it was not until the autumn of 1979, and my second year at Brecon, that I broached the subject with her again. Dorothy had suggested to me, after ascertaining that my intentions were honourable, as she put it, that an invitation to afternoon tea or coffee would be a better option than an evening date, since she informed me that in addition to working at the Savoy, Maria also worked some evenings as relief chief at the Angel Hotel, and consequently her evening time was limited. This suggestion I took on board and a few days after my birthday, I left Brecon early, picked up Maria in the Austin Healey and we drove to Penarth where we had afternoon tea at one of the sea-fronting restaurants.

Although Maria kept on insisting that her English was not very good, this was not the case, and I reassured her that as her second or third language it was excellent and how I wished that I could speak Portuguese, Italian and Spanish as she could. We were served tea and Maria instantly adopted the role of organiser and hostess by pouring the tea, adding the sugar and milk and even stirring my tea, something that I had never experienced before. As we talked Maria noted my ruby ring and recalled how her uncle in Madeira had a similar ring given to him by some lady friend who he had met in the Far East, before he returned to live in Madeira. I in turn recalled that my ring had been given to my grandfather by his seafaring brother and had been handed down to me at his death. The next few hours sped by and soon it was time for me to drive Maria back to the Savoy where in the evenings she was the assistant chief in the restaurant's kitchen. And so our very first date ended, but with a promise that we would go out again soon, although Maria drew my attention to the fact that Christmas was fast approaching and that she would be working every day and every evening during the weeks leading up to Christmas Day and would in all probability be back in work on Boxing Day or the following day.

As the end of term and Christmas approached, the tempo at work also increased with compiling the guest list for the first College Carol Service, to be held in Brecon Cathedral, being one of my many tasks. This list included members of the board of governors of the college, officers of the Education Department, the mayors of Brecon Town and Brecknockshire, the headmasters of the four feeder schools of the college and numerous other local dignitaries. I was given a great deal of support by both staff and students, the latter who volunteered as members of a college choir under the guidance of Brian Williams, a Business Studies lecturer, while two members of staff, David Handly and Tony Jenkins, who I was given to understand had great tenor voices, volunteered to undertake sole performances as part of the programme. I invited the dean of the cathedral, the Rev. Alwyn Jones, to lunch at the college and finalised the programme of nine readings and carols. Alwyn Jones was delighted with this new development and suggested that following the service readers and members of the choir be invited to the deanery for coffee and mince pies.

The service was a great success, with all students after registering for lectures walking to the cathedral, which was about half a mile from the college campus. The response to my invitations had been excellent and the cathedral was full. The choir, under the direction of Brian Williams, who also played the cathedral organ, were outstanding while the solo performances by David Handley and Tony Jenkins were of professional standard. The three female and three male students who read the first six lessons performed well with the last three readings being given by Colonel John Stevenson, chairman of governors, the dean and myself. Following the service the choir, readers and governors enjoyed mince pies and coffee at the deanery. So the tradition of an annual carol service at the cathedral was established, a tradition that provided many students with an experience that they might never again encounter in their adult lives, as well as bringing together the local community at a time of celebration. This tradition was to continue until my leaving the college ten years later.

After the pre-Christmas activities at the college, the days leading up to Christmas were very quiet and especially so at Cooper Court. I met David and Julia for a Christmas drink in the Savoy and had a brief chat with Maria. Both David and Julia were spending Christmas with their mother at Claude Road. I had not made any special plans and could only hope that the Christmas of 1979 would not be as lonely as that of 1978. On Christmas Eve I bought and gift-wrapped a small bottle of Tia Maria, which I delivered to Maria at the Savoy. I could see that she was delighted with a Christmas gift, and leaning over the bar gave me her first kiss, a kiss that I recalled over the following days as I listened to Christmas music and TV programmes.

The January and February of 1980 were cold months with occasional falls of snow that made some morning journeys to Brecon somewhat hazardous, especially after leaving Merthyr Tydfil and climbing up and over the Beacons. February also marked my first proper date with Maria, when after she had agreed to come out on one of her few free evenings I took her to Cowbridge for a meal at the Bear Hotel. The restaurant at the Bear was located in the original cellars of what was a famous coaching inn, and provided very different surroundings to those experienced by Maria while working at the Savoy and Angel Hotel. We had a lovely meal and after a bottle of wine the conversation flowed and soon it was time to go back to Cardiff. When we came out it was snowing and we hurried to the Healy, which was already smothered in a blanket of snow, hoping that we would not have problems driving back. Our concerns were ill founded, and although if we had left our journey any later it might have been different, I had no problems in driving Maria home to Keppoch Street where, after further conversation and a goodnight kiss, we parted, with the promise that we would do this again very soon.

My next task in relation to college development was to establish a Cerebration of Achievement Evening. Many students entering the college onto craft courses had left secondary school with little or no qualifications, yet by pursuing vocational studies which were of interest to them, the majority were highly successful in gaining craft qualifications. These successes I believed needed to be recognised. A date in March was arrived at, and with all certificates and diplomas now in the possession of the college, invitations to students who had been successful in their examinations of the previous year, and their families, were sent. A guest speaker had to be chosen, and since it would be the very first celebration of its kind I was determined that it should be someone known and respected in the community. Mindful of the developing links with the Royal Welsh Agricultural Society and the development of joint college – Young Farmers' facilities on the society's showground, Lord Gibson-Watt, chairman of the board of governors of the society, was invited and was delighted to accept. Lists of successful students were prepared under the headings of the three newly established departments, with the head of each department being responsible for calling out the names and inviting individual students to step up onto the stage in the main hall of the college to receive their certificate or diploma from the guest speaker. The evening arrived, and the guest speaker and other VIPs were directed to my office for a pre-event sherry. Once students, their families and friends were seated, the VIPs were escorted to the main hall followed by the platform party, consisting of the chairman of governors, guest speaker, college principal and the three heads of department. It was with much pride that I extended a warm welcome to all present and presented a report of college achievements over the last eighteen months. Following the presentations Lord Gibson-Watt gave his address in which he applauded the development of the college, the successes of the young men and women who had achieved nationally recognised qualifications, and the ever increasing role of the college in the community at large and its links with rural industries and organisations. There then followed a vote of thanks by the chairman of the college governors, with proceedings ending with the singing of the national anthems. All invited guests were then escorted to the newly refurbished and extended college training restaurant where catering students had prepared a finger buffet with coffee to round off the evening.

That evening was to me the highlight of my first eighteen months at the Howell Harris College.

In April 1980 the decree absolute of my divorce came through, and although I felt sad in many ways, I was now free to begin life again, although I knew I would never forget my yesterdays. To mark the occasion I took Maria to London the following Sunday, leaving Cardiff at the crack of dawn and driving along the M4 at a steady fifty miles an hour. Having parked the Austin Healey in Hyde Park we visited the various places of interest including the Houses of Parliament, Westminster Abbey and Buckingham Palace, and where I attempted to give Maria a potted account of the history of the various buildings and institutions that make London unique. We had an early evening meal in one of the few restaurants that in those days were open on Sunday evening, and set off on our return journey to Cardiff. It is a day that I shall always remember since I had not felt so relaxed for many a long year, and Maria's cheerful presence generated a feeling of closeness that I had not experienced for a very long time. We arrived back in Cardiff tired but happy and I felt that it was the first step on the road to tomorrow.

Following our visit to London we established an arrangement that allowed us to meet most days. This was achieved by my collecting Maria from work at around midnight, and returning to Cooper Court where I would have prepared a light meal. We would then make love for about an hour before I drove Maria home at around 2 a.m. Since I usually left for Brecon at around 7 a.m., this schedule necessitated my having a few hours' sleep between returning home at around 5 p.m. and collecting Maria at midnight. For her part, since her working day started at noon the extra hours of sleep were easily achievable. On Sundays when Maria and her two sisters, Rita and Sandra, were not working, I was usually invited over to Keppoch Street for Sunday lunch. The three sisters took it in turns to cook such lunches that were typical continental in style and duration, usually starting at 1 p.m. and ending at around 5 p.m. This was a completely new experience for me and an introduction to being part of a large and very happy family.

Chapter Twenty-Five

By early June of 1980 I had asked Maria to marry me and she had said yes. We chose an engagement ring together and following a visit to the register office in Park Place, Cardiff, decided on Saturday, 26 July for our wedding. There then followed weeks of unprecedented activity during which time Maria planned her wedding with her two sisters, arranged for her parents to fly over from Madeira, and organised the reception, while I decided upon the best man, the flowers for the bride and bridesmaids and the honeymoon.

Since all my university friends had long since moved to other parts of the UK and we had lost contact, I decided that the only man who I wished to stand with on 26 July had to be Frank Landgrebe, who had contributed so much to both my academic career and my professional career since leaving university. Professor Landgrebe was both shocked and delighted when I called in at his home in Miskin and told him of my impending marriage. He and his wife Margo wanted to meet Maria and so I arranged for them to visit Cooper Court during a weekend in early July. Maria took the Saturday afternoon off work and prepared a wonderful meal with French onion soup for starters, followed by fillet steak 'Rossini', cream caramel for sweet followed by cheese and biscuits and Gallic coffee and mints. It was a wonderful evening with Maria being complemented on a superb meal and myself on having found such a talented, attractive and sweet-natured girl.

The following week Maria's parents arrived. Maria and Manuel da Silva Leca had been born in Madeira, Maria das Neves from a moderately wealthy family from the Camara de Lobos area of the island, while Manuel da Silva Leca came from a poorer family background living in the Arco da Calheta region of the island. Upon their marriage they had moved to Arco da Calheta were they had brought up eight children, six daughters and two sons.

Maria's mother was a short, plump lady with short, greying hair, dark smiling eyes and a tanned complexion reflective of someone who had lived all her life in sunny climes. Her father was of medium build with deeply tanned skin and receding hairline and dark, friendly eyes. Neither spoke any English although they understood many words, but their welcoming smiles and hugs when Maria and I met them at Cardiff General Station needed no words, and I immediately felt that I had become a member of a very close-knit family. This was not their first visit to the UK, since when Maria's younger sister Regina had married in 1973, Maria had paid their fares to come to Cardiff, as a wedding surprise for her sister. This previous experience enabled them, having landed at London Heathrow, to get a train to Cardiff with little or no difficulty.

Although due to the late hour only Maria and I had met them at the station, upon our arrival at Keppoch Street, Rita and Sandra had prepared a three-course meal which in true Portuguese style was not over until the early hours of the morning. I took myself off at around 3 a.m. to return to Cooper Court and snatch a few hours sleep, before setting out for Brecon and work.

The reception was to be held at the Cardiff Post House Hotel situated on Eastern Avenue. Maria had selected this particular venue since there was a large patio outside the dining area that could be used for dancing or sitting out should the weather be suitable. Her choice of menu was a prawn cocktail starter, followed by grilled steak, a sweet trolley, cheese and biscuits, coffee and mints and was to prove very popular with guests, while red wine for the meal and Champagne for the toasts rounded off what she regarded to be a reasonable reception.

Having chosen the rings and flowers, all was ready for the big day. The wedding ceremony was for 11 a.m., Professor Landgrebe collected me from Cooper Court at 10.30 and we were at the register office in good time. Maria, in a cream ankle-length dress with a floral headband and cream carnation bouquet accompanied by her two bridesmaids in pale blue dresses, arrived exactly on the hour looking radiant, and within thirty minutes we were man and wife. Since the reception was not until 2 p.m., all the guests had been invited back to Cooper Court for pre-reception drinks and for various photo opportunities. We had hired the white Mercedes that had brought Maria and her father to the Register Office to take us on to Cooper Court so we were able to welcome all our guests as they entered our new home. At around 1.30 everybody set off for the Post House Hotel in party mood. The reception was a great success with the food, wine and speeches being of the highest order. Professor Landgrebe as best man sang my praises and toasted the bridesmaids, while John Williams spoke on behalf of Maria's dad by saying what a great girl Maria was and how he and all present knew that she would make me a wonderful wife. The sun had shone throughout the day and following the speeches and toasts we all moved onto the patio for drinks, music and dancing. I shall always recall Dorothy Dawney dancing with Maria's father, who after a few glasses of wine danced with the best, and recalling in Portuguese that the marriage of his eldest daughter was his happiest hour. As the sun dipped over the horizon and we bid our guests goodbye, we drove back to Cooper Court in the back of Frank and Margo Landgrebe's open-topped Triumph Vitesse, and with the warm July wind blowing in our hair it was the end to a perfect day.

We had decided that the following day, which was Sunday, would be a day of rest and of final preparations for our drive to Valencia, where we would spend our honeymoon with Maria's sister Regina. Due to her first pregnancy being in its eighth month, Regina and her husband Leon had decided not to visit Cardiff for our wedding, but alternatively had insisted that we visit them after the wedding and stay in their apartment in the City of Valencia. Since neither of us had been to Spain before it was an invitation that we could not refuse.

The next day we set off on the first stage of our journey to Valencia, arriving at Dover in time for the night ferry to Calais. We docked at Calais around midnight and decided to drive to the outskirts of town before having a sleep in the car. This was a mistake, since on leaving the centre of Calais we soon found ourselves on a country road that after passing through a few small villages petered out into a field. We then had to retrace our journey back to Calais where at one o'clock in the morning some difficulty was experienced in seeking guidance as to the best route to take for Normandy and the west coast of France. We saw what appeared to be a bar which was still open and I went in to see whether there was somebody there who could give us guidance. What I did not know at the time was that this bar was the base for a large number of ladies of the night, and in my limited French of asking 'the way', some confusion may have occurred resulting in my beating a hasty retreat back to the car being the best option. We then decided that heading for Paris was the only practical option, and after an hour's driving we pulled into a lay-by for a few hours' sleep. The following day we motored through north-west France keeping to the 'N' classified roads, passing through Bordeaux and eventually reaching Bayonne just north of the Spanish boarder, where we booked into a travel lodge for a much needed rest. The next morning we crossed into Spain at one of those 'one man and his dog' custom posts that existed in the 1970s. Having negotiated the mountain roads of northern Spain we then followed the N121 to Pamplona and then the N232 to Zaragoza. The N330 and then the N234 saw us arriving at the outskirts of Valencia at around 10.30 p.m., a total of eleven hours' driving. Although we had the address and telephone number, neither of us had any idea where her sister's apartment in Padre Vinãs was located. We decided to continue towards the city centre in the hope of finding some directions and a petrol station since the tank was now quite low. After a further twenty-minute drive we came across a petrol station which was open and at which point I told Maria that I had no intention of driving any further, since I was exhausted, hot, sweaty and in need of some sleep. Having filled up the car I showed the attendant the address that we were looking for and discovered that by sheer luck we were within fifty yards of Padre Vinãs. My delight at this news was obvious and to complete my relief the attendant took it upon himself to telephone my sister-in-law's number so that they could walk over and collect us. The next few hours were a blur what with enjoying a much needed shower and the wonderful meal that Regina and her husband Leon had prepared, and then sinking into a great big double bed, for one of the best sleeps I had experienced in days.

The City of Valencia, with a population at that time of around 600,000, had, I discovered, origins dating back to the Bronze Age, having been founded as a city by the Romans in 138 BC receiving the name of Valentia. Originally it was a walled city but expansion creating suburbs outside the original walls were soon established with the walls eventually demolished in 1865. One of the city's major problems was the series of devastating floods created by the River Turia that ran through the city. The last of these occurred in 1957 and caused so much damage that it was decided to divert the river bed and so avoid any further problems, while at the same time gaining about one million square metres of land, now used for recreational installations, and at a later date cultural facilities.

The first week of our honeymoon was spent visiting all the various tourist attractions of the city, including the cathedral located in the Plaza de la Reina and housing what is claimed to be the very same chalice used by Jesus Christ in the consecration of the Last Supper. Not far from the cathedral is the Palau de la Generalitat, the headquarters of the autonomous government of the Valencian community, while the bullring, the Valldigna Gate, which is the last remaining of the twelve gates that once gave access to the city, and the central market situated opposite the ancient Lonja Market or exchange deemed the best civil Gothic building in Europe, were other places that we visited.

The following week Leon and Regina took us by car to visit the surrounding areas of Valencia, with its orange groves, vineyards and olive groves. Then disaster struck.

One morning Maria complained of very strong period-type pains and soon it was evident that this was no ordinary period and when excessive bleeding accompanied the pains it was time to seek medical assistance. I only have a vague recollection of driving Maria to the hospital under the instructions of her sister, of parking the car at the door of the emergency and accident unit and helping her to be carried in. Maria was having a miscarriage and the doctors operated immediately to prevent further loss of blood, since in their view there was no chance of saving the twelve-week-old foetus. Although Maria had not been aware of her pregnancy, not having experienced any of the normal symptoms of early pregnancy, the next few days were very sad days for us both since we both felt that we had lost something that could not be replaced. Two days later Maria was out of

223

hospital, and showing remarkable powers of recovery, was soon her normal happy self again, although I knew that inwardly she was grieving over her lost baby.

The remaining week of our honeymoon was a low-key affair, since Leon had returned to work. I spent some time checking over the car in preparation for our return journey, while Maria spent hours talking to her sister about times gone by and the impending birth of her first child.

The day of our departure arrived, and with much hugging and kissing we set off for Cardiff. Not wishing to follow the same route home, we had decided to drive east along the southern coastline passing through Castellón, Tarragona and Barcelona, and crossing into France at Le Boulou, before heading north for Paris. Following a long day's driving we arrived on the outskirts of Paris as dusk was falling and most Parisians were heading for home, or so it seemed by the volume of traffic. Needless to say this was when we got lost and spent considerable time before we found the route out of the city leading to Calais and the ferry. By now it was dark and having followed a detour that had added many kilometres to our journey we stopped at a roadside hotel for the night. Following an early coffee and brandy we set off to catch the midday ferry, arriving just in time to avoid a seaman's strike that would have delayed us for many days on the wrong side of the Channel. Arriving back in Cardiff we were both exhausted and very tired, and although it had been a wonderful experience it was, and has remained, tarnished by a great sadness that we had left something most precious, and as it proved, irreplaceable, in Valencia.

Although nobody at the college were aware of my marriage, Christine Forbes immediately spotted my new shining wedding ring, and in her forthright and direct manner enquired if I had got married during the vacation. As expected, the news spread through the staff like wildfire and a few days later Walter Price, my vice principal, came along to enquire if I was amenable to the staff contributing to a belated wedding present. I was very touched by this gesture and by the concern he expressed that nobody wanted me to feel that such an initiative was an invasion of my privacy. For my part I was able to assure him that both myself and Maria would be delighted by the staff's kindness and that he was free to pass on the news of my getting wed to both governors and others with interest in the college.

And so the 1980–81 college year commenced with a shower of congratulations and good wishes for the future, with many invitations for Maria to visit Brecon, since I could sense that many were curious as to what the principal's new wife looked like and was like. Shortly after the commencement of term, which was now characterised by my meeting all the teaching staff on the Friday prior to the commencement of the session when any future college developments were outlined and announcements made, all full-time students on their first day at college and all part-time day students on their first morning at the college, when they were told what to expect in terms of tuition, guidance and the level of behaviour expected of them, Walter Price came to my office and presented me with the staff's wedding present, which turned out to be a framed early map of Brecknockshire by the famous map-maker John Speed. This gift apparently had been selected by the staff on the advice of Gwyn Evans, who had given me much assistance and help when I first visited Brecon following my appointment, and who had remembered that while browsing in his shop I had declared an interest in antique maps. I was very touched by their kindness and issued letters of thanks that were posted on the staff room noticeboard and the departmental noticeboards.

It was shortly after this event that Walter turned up at my office with some bad news. He had apparently been visiting the local medical practice for several months and following numerous tests he had now been diagnosed as having Multiple Sclerosis. Although over the last few months I had noticed that he was rather unsteady when walking, the progressive nature of MS gave me much cause for concern since it would in the longer term affect his work and duties as my deputy. After much thought I decided that to help him cope with the initial stages of the illness nobody else at the college should be told of his condition. I advised John Stevenson, the chairman of governors, of my decision, emphasising that I would ensure that all duties that Walter could no longer carry out would be covered by myself on the pretext that I wanted to familiarise myself with the adult education classes that were Walters main responsibility. Colonel Stephenson was most understanding and complemented me on my decision. And so my third year at the college commenced with Walter being driven to and from the college by his wife, Gladys, on the pretext that he had hurt his foot and was unable to drive, and myself, with a great deal of assistance from Christine Forbes, who I felt sure suspected an ulterior motive, organising the initial enrolment of adult education classes.

Chapter Twenty-Six

Ever since coming to work in Brecon, and especially since meeting Maria, I had been looking for a suitable property to purchase, since although I enjoyed my daily journeys in the Healey I was very aware that in terms of a social life and community activities I neither belonged to Cardiff nor Brecon. One morning as I was driving up the road towards the college I noticed that a gateway had been made in the tall stone wall that bordered the road and that behind this new entrance was a newly built bungalow with a for sale notice. Upon enquiring of Christine I was informed that it was a development in the garden of a large house that had been built by the company that her husband worked for and probably would not be on the market for long. I immediately contacted the estate agent involved, viewed the property that afternoon and agreed a price before returning to Cardiff, since I was sure that Maria would love the location, the new kitchen, bathrooms, lounge and three bedrooms.

That night after collecting Maria from work at around twelve thirty, I told her that we now had a brand new home in Brecon, that we would need to sell the apartment and that she would have to hand in her notice to John Williams at the Savoy. Once she realised that I was serious, I spent the next few hours describing in detail what the bungalow was like, where it was, and how soon she could see it.

The following Sunday having made arrangements with the estate agent to have the keys over the weekend, I drove Maria to Brecon to view our new home. She loved it and wanted to know how soon we could move in. We returned to Cooper Court in high spirits and in the knowledge that our lives would once again be changed.

Selling Cooper Court turned out to be problem-free with my using the same estate agent that I had purchased it from, while once again I consulted Strad Jones regarding the legal issues pertaining to the sale. To expedite matters at the Brecon end, I used a local solicitor who knew the estate agent and vendors and was able to obtain a completion date in early January. The estate agent was kind to me in that once a completion date was established I was given a key and could gain entry for carpets to be fitted, curtains to be hung, and some walls papered since every room had been decorated in magnolia and somewhat lacked personality. Much of this work I undertook after work and before returning to Cardiff so that by the actual day of moving all the rooms were ready to be furnished. On 26 January 1981, six months to the day after our wedding, we moved to Brecon and to the bungalow that we subsequently named 'Bemvinde', being the Portuguese word for welcome.

The 26th being a Saturday allowed us to get most things organised during the remainder of the weekend, and on the Monday morning I was able for the first time in over two years to walk to work. At work over the next few weeks I received many comments as to how pleasing it was that I had decided to come and live in Brecon, since it would appear that many viewed my appointment as principal at Brecon to be short-term, with every prospect that I would soon be moving on to a larger and more prestigious establishment. The fact that I had never planned or even thought of such a move appeared strange to many I talked to, but I could in all honesty say that during the whole of my professional career I had never planned ahead, always recalling a favourite saying of my grandfather that 'tomorrow belongs to no one'.

The early months of 1981 were cold and frosty and by late February the snow arrived with a vengeance. It started snowing at lunchtime on a Tuesday and by 2 p.m. the Education Authority had called in the transport to take pupils from the high school and students from the college home before the roads became impassable. I closed the college at 3 p.m. and walked home through the drifting snow to find Maria at the patio window gazing with wonder at the snow that was gradually building up against the window.

The winters in Cardiff that Maria had experienced since arriving there in 1966 had, with one or two exceptions, been relatively mild with snowfall restricted to a dusting that rapidly disappeared, so continuous snowfall for two days was a completely new experience for her, and for me brought back memories of the snowfalls in Pembrokeshire in the 1940s. By the second day the snow had almost reached the top of the patio doors and when it eventually stopped we spent many hours digging ourselves out of the front door and eventually through the gates to the road, which were just about passable thanks to the very efficient snow-plough teams that operated throughout the area.

The next few days were somewhat unreal in that although I struggled up the hill to the college campus I found everything was closed. The caretakers had not reported for duty and since the majority of staff lived outside the town they had little chance of being able to drive in to college. It was four days later that student transport was able to operate on the major roads and the college resumed its normal routine. So our first winter in our new home became something of a landmark and represented the first of many memorable experiences that Maria and I shared during our stay in Brecon.

The next memorable event as far as Maria was concerned was her attendance at the 1981 Celebration of Achievement Evening which was held in late March just before the Easter vacation. Fired by the success of the previous year's event I was determined to make this one even better. The examination results from the previous academic year had been good and the response to the invitations to attend from both past students, governors and representatives of both the town council and borough council was excellent. Adopting the theme that the guest speaker on these occasions should reflect the work of the college, I was able to persuade Lord Gordon Parry of Neyland, who at that time was chairman of the Wales Tourist Board, to be our speaker. This choice highlighted the role of the college in promoting tourism in the rural areas of South and Mid Powys and as a means of diversification within the agricultural community.

Lord Parry arrived at the college in his chauffer-driven car shortly after lunch accompanied by Lady Parry and a large collie dog which apparently travelled with them on most occasions.

Since the Celebration Ceremony was not scheduled to start until seven thirty I had no alternative but to give Maria a quick telephone call telling her to expect visitors within the next ten minutes, that it was a peer of the realm, his wife and dog, and could she entertain them for the next three to four hours. On returning home an hour later I discovered that she was doing a brilliant job, with the collie asleep on the kitchen floor having been fed and watered; the chauffeur having been given a cup of tea had gone off for a stroll around the town; while Lord and Lady Parry were exchanging views on Argentina with Maria – views based on their experiences during their recent visit to the Welsh community in Patagonia, and she on her visit to her sister in Buenos Aeries in 1978.

The evening proved a huge success with Lord Parry giving a most witty and informative speech addressed at both students and their families present, as well as indicating the importance of the roll of colleges in promoting rural tourism in Wales. The rapid development of the college, which I was able to summarise in my report, was endorsed by the chairman of governors in his vote of thanks that included all those involved. This being Maria's first public engagement since moving to Brecon found her being the object of much attention, with a large number of those present extending their personal welcome to Brecon and wishing her every happiness in her new home. Being a very social person Maria thrived on such attention and very soon I could see that she would be a hit with the people of Brecon. Having said our farewells to Lord and Lady Parry and having thanked all the staff and catering students who had provided a wonderful buffet, we drove home satisfied on a job well done.

By the end of the 1980–81 college year, the majority of the building programmes initiated in my first year were nearing completion. The new Agricultural Unit, with lecture rooms, laboratory and farm machinery workshop, was awaiting its furniture and fittings; the Motor Vehicle workshop had been transferred into the old farm machinery workshop; the training restaurant had been extended by utilising an adjoining classroom; an existing classroom had been converted into a computer suite, while the new brickwork shop being built by construction industry students was also nearing completion. On the Royal Welsh Showground the joint College – Young Farmers Clubs of Wales building was progressing apace, while a new cattle-rearing unit had been constructed on the college farm, were it had been decided to switch from milk production to store-cattle rearing, the latter being more in keeping with the farming practices of the area, and being less labour intensive than milk production.

While these developments were progressing Maria was busy putting her final touches to the bungalow, finding her way around Brecon, making numerous friends in the local community and scheduling visits by family and friends to see our new home. Among the first were Julia and David, Maria's two sisters, some cousins and friends, Margo and Frank Landgrebe, and Jean and Ernest Brent. They all loved Bemvinde and were all very pleased for us.

July and the college's summer vacation saw Maria and me fly to Madeira to visit her parents, since before they left for home after our wedding we had to promise that we would visit them the following July. Although now approaching forty-nine years of age I had never flown so the experience was completely new to me, and arriving at London Heathrow on a Sunday afternoon to catch an Air Portugal direct flight to Funchal, Madeira, was a tremendous buzz and a journey into the unknown.

Chapter Twenty-Seven

As the plane dipped out of the night sky and flew along side the rugged coastline of the island of Madeira I could see the lights from the various dwellings that dotted the hillside, and as the plane approached the runway I could see into the lighted living rooms of those houses perched on the hillside overlooking the airport. Then the plane touched down, the pilot applied maximum breaking and reverse thrust, passengers strained against their safety belts and the hand luggage moved in the overhead lockers. At that instant I thought that we were going to hit some obstacle on the runway or there was something wrong with the plane. What I did not know and Maria had not told me was that the runway at Santa Cruz Airport was, at that time, extremely short, beginning and ending in the sea, so that for the modern plane carrying over a hundred passengers a high level of skill was required when landing. On landing all passengers gave the crew a round of applause which I was told later was the custom at Santa Cruz airport.

After passing through passport control and claiming our luggage we made our way out of the airport and into the arms of Maria's mum and dad, who together with the local village taxi driver had come to meet us. We then started the longest taxi ride that I had ever experienced. From Santa Cruz the old Peugeot shooting break taxi wound its way along the twisting and turning road that hugged the steep hillside passing through the villages of Ponta do Garajau and Canico before winding down into the capital, Funchal. Having negotiated the cobbled streets of the city, passing its cathedral, the Savoy Hotel and Reid's Palace – one of the world's great hotels – the taxi headed north-west along the coast road, passing through the village of Camara de Lobos where Winston Churchill painted landscapes on his frequent visits to the island, then on to Ribeira Brava, Ponta do Sol until almost two hours later we arrived at Arco da Calheta where the family lived and where Maria had been brought up.

The house perched on the hillside above the road was accessed by means of a stony pathway that wound its way up between the vines which, it being late July, hosted bunches of black, succulent grapes. The house itself consisted of a kitchen-diner, a living room, bedroom and store on the ground floor with two bedrooms and a small sitting room on the first floor, the latter having been converted from a once open balcony. Our cases were taken upstairs to the bedroom and within a short time we were sitting down to a wonderful meal of green soup followed by fish, cheese and fruit. Despite the fact that it was now well past midnight the meal and conversation went on and on as the Madeira wine was drunk and the family celebrated the return home of their oldest daughter.

The following morning I awoke to the sound of a cock crowing, the sound of a church bell and sunlight pouring in through the shuttered window. Getting up and opening the shutters I was confronted with a panoramic view of the village of Arco da Calheta sweeping down to the brilliantly blue Atlantic Ocean beyond. Maria crept up behind me, put her arms around my waist and whispered, 'Do you like my home?' What could I say other than, 'Wonderful, how could you have left to come to Cardiff? But I'm glad you did.'

Breakfast was followed by a tour of the village during which Maria visited all her old friends and relatives and introduced me as her husband. Every such visit entailed our partaking of either a glass of home-made red wine, a large glass of Madeira or a very potent home-made liquor. Since Maria had warned me that to refuse such hospitality might offend, I ended the morning in a very happy frame of mind having formed the opinion that this was the place and way to live.

The days flew by with Maria helping her mother with the meals and her father and me spending a lot of time playing cards, once I had been instructed in the basics of a card game called 'Bisca'. Although Maria's dad spoke no English and me no Portuguese, we communicated very successfully through single words accompanied by signs and through this method we got to know each other fairly well. Outside eating, drinking and cards, the major part of my time was devoted to reading books that I had brought from home and reading about the history of Madeira and the Portuguese.

Portugal is one of the oldest nations in Europe, obtaining sovereignty in the eleventh century. The earliest settlers were believed to be the Celts around 700 BC, followed by the Phoenicians, Greeks and Romans. The Moors crossed from North Africa in the eighth century and ruled for around 400 years before being finally repelled during the thirteenth century. The first official alliance between Portugal and Great Britain was signed in 1386 and led many centuries later to Anglo – Portuguese forces fighting invasion from Napoleon in 1807. However, some of the most enduring of the nation's history is that of its seafaring tradition that once saw Portugal as the world's most powerful colonial empire.

One of the most renowned figures from this seafaring past was Prince Henry the Navigator. Born in Porto, of an English mother and Portuguese father King Joao I, Henry set up a school of navigation in the Sagres region of Portugal and trained and inspired some of history's best known explorers such as Vasco da Gama.

One of the great discovery stories that exist is the discovery of Madeira in 1419 by the Portuguese navigators João Gonçalves Zarco and Tristão Vaz Teixeira, a year after they had discovered the neighbouring island of Porto Santo, about fifty miles from Madeira. Historical records indicate that they landed at the part of the island where the village of Machico now stands and found deep forest. So the island was named 'Madeira' which in Portuguese means 'wood' – 'The Island of Wood'. Moving along the coast, they landed at another bay where they found large areas covered with fennel – *funcho* in Portuguese – thus giving a name to 'Funchal', now the capital of the island.

It was with background information together with what Maria had told me upon arrival that I viewed this most beautiful of islands and became determined to see and experience as much as possible of its scenery, culture and people.

One opportunity to do this occurred during the second weekend of our stay when we, together with Maria's mum and dad, joined a coach trip organised by the village to Madeira's

Agricultural Show held at Porto Moniz situated at the northern tip of the island. The coach was a pre-war Volvo bus with wooden drop-down windows that remained open all through the journey and served as an excellent substitute for air conditioning. The day being warm, several jars of wine were on board and these were passed round to anyone that wished to partake. To complete the scene three musicians, consisting of an accordionist, a fiddle player and a rather large lady on the tambourine played all the traditional Portuguese songs throughout the two-hour journey. The show itself was relatively small by UK standards but its location among the pine and laurel trees was beautiful. One of its many features was the stalls selling wine and meat, with a very large adjoining barbecue area where the meat on skewers cut from the bay leaf could be cooked. There was little doubt that this aspect of the show was much appreciated by those attending and contributed to a very party-like atmosphere. Following a barbecue lunch of beef washed down with a considerable amount of wine, we all got back on the bus, the music started and we were on our way out of Porto Moniz and along the cliff-hugging road on the eastern facing side of the island until we reached the village of Sao Vecente. Following a 'comfort stop' we turned inland with the road climbing to one of the highest points on the island before dropping down to the town of Ribeira Brava on the west facing coast, then north on another cliff-hugging road through the village of Ponta do Sol to Arco da Calheta and home. It was a great experience and one that I shall never forget.

A second opportunity to explore occurred when the family decided to visit the small adjoining island of Porto Santo. While Madeira has a population of around 300,000 inhabitants and an area which is 57 km long and 22 km wide, Port Santo has only 4,000 inhabitants and an area 12 km in length and 6 km in width. While Madeira is mountainous and of volcanic origin, Port Santo is flat with long, sandy beaches and regarded by the Portuguese as a holiday destination only. We left Arco early one morning, travelling by public transport to Funchal. Having had a traditional lunch of espada – a deep-sea fish only caught in the deep waters surrounding Madeira and Japan, followed by crème caramel and a small black coffee – we boarded the ferry to Porto Santo. The fifty-odd miles were covered in just over two hours and then we were walking along the jetty leading to the town of Porto Santo. The town situated on the sea overlooks the long beach and is shaded by palms and flowers that give it a tranquil if old-fashioned atmosphere. The beach, which extends some 9 km along the south coast of the island, is used extensively by locals and tourists alike, and the golden sand is reputed to have healing properties, as does the water, known as Agua do Porto Santa, and grapes grown in a soil with particular properties and in a very mild climate.

After checking-in to the accommodation that had been arranged for us we visited the local restaurant for a light evening meal and retired early. The following day we hired a taxi for a tour of the island, which for the most part appeared rather arid and very different from Madeira. The other difference was the airport, with its huge runway capable of handling jumbo jets and other large aircraft and very different from the short runway of Santa Cruz Airport. That afternoon we caught the return ferry arriving in Funchal at dusk, and Arco da Calheta at around eleven o'clock.

The final opportunity of experiencing life on Madeira came during our last weekend on the island when Maria and I decided to have a mini-break in a hotel in Funchal. Although very expensive, we decided that a two-day stay at Reid's Palace Hotel would be a fitting end to four wonderful weeks' holiday. We checked in on Saturday afternoon, had pre-dinner drinks on the balcony overlooking the sea and dinner in the fabulous dining room with its high pillars, crystal chandeliers and high French doors leading out to the balcony overlooking the sea and the lights of Funchal. The dinner consisted of the traditional Portuguese green soup, followed by a fish course, a main course of Beef Wellington carved at the table and washed down with some excellent Portuguese red wine, with crêpes and coffee to finish. As I sat in the elegant surroundings that had not changed since the time when Winston Churchill and other famous people graced the white, linen-covered tables, I had the impression that time had stood still at one of the world's great hotels. As we climbed the grand staircase to our first-floor bedroom, Maria considered the experience as one of the highlights of the holiday, and indeed her life, recalling how as a young girl she had passed Reid's Palace on hundreds of occasion but never imagined that one day she would be one of the guests wining and dining with wealthy tourists.

The following week we boarded the Air Portugal flight for Heathrow and returned to Brecon in readiness for the beginning of the 1981/82 college year.

Chapter Twenty-Eight

The 1981–82 college year proved to be very eventful. Early in September the new Agricultural Unit built across the road from the main college building was officially opened by the chairman of governors, Colonel John Stephenson, accompanied by the chairman of the Powys Education Authority, the director of education and a whole host of local dignitaries.

On 29 October 1981 the new £200,000 college Agricultural Unit and Young Farmers Clubs of Wales Centre was opened at the Royal Welsh Showground by the Prince and Princess of Wales during their three-day visit to Wales. The two-storey building with YFC (Wales) offices on the first floor with a balcony overlooking both show rings shared a main entrance lobby with the college leading to a student's coffee lounge, library and exhibition hall/ lecture area with an adjoining agricultural workshop with project bays used by college students during term-time and by the young farmers at show time.

Since the opening was scheduled for 9 a.m., Maria and I left Brecon at around 6.30 a.m. and after a rather lengthy wait standing in line were presented to Their Royal Highnesses as they entered the building to unveil the customary plaque.

Following a tour of the building the recently married couple were presented with a wedding present in the form of a black Welsh ewe that I had acquired from a local farmer, George Thomas of Trecastle. This gift proved very popular with the young couple and the college was complemented on its choice of gift and on the buffet that the catering students had prepared for the visit. Following the buffet the prince insisted on entering the preparation area and congratulating every student individually on their hard work and expertise.

As we drove home that afternoon Maria said, 'The princess is pregnant, you know.' Asking her how she knew, since there had been no press reports on any such event, she simply said, 'I know.' A week later there was an official announcement from the palace that Princess Diana was indeed pregnant.

The last week of the autumn term saw the College Carol Service taking place at Brecon Cathedral, with the attendance being such that extra chairs had to be brought in to accommodate all those who attended. A new initiative that I introduced on this, and subsequent occasions, was the Student's Christmas Party held between 2 p.m. and 4 p.m. on the afternoon following the carol service and open to all students and staff. Held in the main hall with suitable music and a DJ, this event proved very popular as well as being an additional source of revenue for the college refectory.

On 22 January 1982 the Parliamentary Undersecretary of State at the Welsh Office, Mr Michael Roberts, visited the college and toured the college departments, talking to staff and students and ending his visit with a lunch in the newly furbished training restaurant.

In April 1982 the college, in association with the Welsh Bee-keepers' Association, obtained financial aid from the European Community to establish a Welsh Beekeeping Advisory Centre at the college. Conversion of the old motor vehicle engineering workshop and adjoining staff room was approved, as was the appointment of a full-time advisory officer and tutor in beekeeping. Following an advertisement in the national press, one of my ex-students from Llandaff – Charles Dublon – was appointed to the post.

The annual Celebration of Achievement Evening, although held a little later than usual, proved highly successful with the guest speaker being Dr Tom Pritchard, director of the Nature Conservancy Council for Wales, who following his visit to Brecon insisted that I become a member of that organisation's steering committee whose patron was HRH the Prince of Wales. This involvement resulted in my meeting His Royal Highness on numerous occasions, both in Cardiff and on his farm in the Vale of Glamorgan.

In terms of student/course activities, I had actively promoted the work experience element in as many courses as possible, an aspect that had been well received by all staff members. The outcome of this initiative was that business studies students became involved in studying company operations and reporting back to the companies on shortcomings and possible changes; caring students ran day centres for the elderly at out-of-college venues in the town; while catering students and staff took over the running of various local hotels for weekends. One such exercise involved them taking over one of Wales's largest hotels, the Metropole Hotel at Llandrindod Wells, when the Secretary of State for Wales, Nicholas Edwards MP was guest of honour of the owner, David Baird Murray.

So my years at the Howell Harris College unfolded, season by season, term by term, with a kind of timeless rhythm which marked off in the college calendar the various established events which were now becoming part not only of the lives of college students and staff but of the Brecon community as a whole.

November 1982 saw the passing of dear Aunt Lois. Following her retirement and sale of the business, she had developed dementia and was living at a residential home in Kenfig Hill. Maria and I had visited her on a number of occasions and outwardly she was her normal, cheerful self, only giving herself away when making reference to visitors who we knew had long since died. The funeral saw our meeting with Aunt Lois's nephews Kelvin Marsden and Duncan Marsden, who I had not seen since their college days. I had always been very fond of Aunt Lois and all the help and advice that she had given me over the years was something that I would never forget. Her death also marked the last link with that generation of the Marsden Family.

1982 also saw the sudden and unexpected death of Margo Landgrebe. We had invited them up to Brecon to join us for a meal when Frank telephoned to tell us that Margo was had gone into hospital for a few days for some tests, and that their visit would be delayed by a few days. Three days later Margo was dead from a very aggressive form of leukaemia, the very same disease that had killed my mother.

In 1983 I was invited to join the Rotary International Club of Brecon, and although having no previous experience or knowledge of the movement I was persuaded by Howel Davies, who lived in the adjoining bungalow to us, that I would enjoy being a member and that Maria would enjoy membership of the Inner Wheel Club of Rotary Wives. Weekly meetings of the club were held at lunchtime on Mondays at the Castle of Brecon Hotel with the occasional social evening when wives were invited. Rotary is characterised by the fact that membership is restricted to chief officers or managers of the various local organisations, with only one representative from each profession or business. At the time of joining I was the only education representative, since the headmaster of the high school had in the past declined the invitation to join. The club of forty members represented all areas of community life in Brecon and soon I had got to know the majority of them, whose age ranged from forty to eighty years. The following year I was requested to chair the Community services committee of the club. This involved organising all those activities relating to the local community where Rotary International felt it could contribute and at the same time generate income for specific community projects. One such activity was the so-called Caledonian Market, which in effect was a gigantic jumble sale held in the Brecon market on a Saturday afternoon in the November of each year when hundreds of people from the local community came looking for a bargain or for some article that they required. Stalls selling second-hand clothes, electrical goods, furniture, bric-a-brac, books and endless items that could not be classified were set up on the Saturday morning to be manned by Rotarians, wives and partners when the doors opened at 2 p.m. and the queues that had formed outside rushed in searching for that elusive bargain. On the popular bric-a-brac stall Maria proved to be a born market trader and in around two hours had sold over £300 worth of articles, enjoying every minute of the experience.

In keeping with tradition, a Caledonian Evening was held the week following the market. This rotary function was aimed at thanking rotary wives for their assistance with the market and where the wives were the guests of the club. Although in the past this function had been held at a local hotel, I felt that the college training restaurant would be a suitable venue and that the function would provide catering students with practical experience of costing, planning, cooking and serving a meal for around eighty people. The dinner proved to be a huge success since in addition to the usual activities, I had arranged through the vice chairman of the board of governors for a male voice choir from Ystradgynlais in the Swansea valley to provide the after-meal entertainment. And so began a long association between the college and the Rotary Club. By belonging to the Inner Wheel Club, Maria got involved in their charitable work and very soon was delivering meals on wheels to those senior citizens who were in need of that service. Another activity involved supervising the hydrotherapy sessions of the physically handicapped children who attended the local special school. Maria loved this activity and loved the children, who she regarded as her second family.

At about this time the Jaguar bug struck again and I decided that it would be convenient if we had a second car, with Maria having use of our existing car and myself obtaining a Jaguar or Daimler – cars that I had always admired since the time I had the 1965 Jaguar Mark 2 with its 3.4 twin cam engine with manual gearbox with overdrive. After some considerable time and after viewing many so-called immaculate cars within my price range, I eventually spotted an advertisement in the local paper, the *Brecon and Radnor Express*, where a local small-time motor trader had a Daimler Sovereign 3.4 automatic for sale. Tom Cross was an elderly, white-haired man with twinkling eyes and a very cheerful disposition who, I was later told, was well known in Brecon for his charitable work, and who appeared to run his small yard full of second-hand cars more as a hobby than a business. The Daimler, it turned out, belonged to Tom's son who was an airline pilot and who only used it to commute occasionally between Heathrow and Brecon, while the first owner had been Christopher Chataway, the famous Olympic athlete of four-minute mile and 3,000 metres fame. After a test drive we decided that this 1977 Series 2 car in carriage brown with gold coach-lines and sage green leather interior was for us and the following day, which happened to be St David's Day, 1 March, I handed over the cheque for £2,300, this being the largest sum I had ever paid for a car.

1983 also saw my being elected as hon. secretary to the Wales and West of England branch of the Association of Principals of

242

Colleges. This association, which I had joined upon my appointment as principal at Brecon was, at the time, influential in presenting the collective views of all colleges in the UK on the various government white papers and similar issues of policy. The various branches were represented on the association's executive committee by the branch chairman and hon. secretary, and as such my duties involved regular attendance at the association's meetings in London. This work I enjoyed since it broadened my view of further and higher education and filled the gaps in my normal duties, which since the completion of the initial building programmes and the establishment of student work-based training were now much less demanding.

One major government initiative in 1983 was the introduction of the Youth Training Scheme, known as the YTS. This scheme in effect replaced the training responsibilities of the training boards that the government had to some extent disbanded, and was aimed at providing a standard pattern of on- and off-the-job training. To undertake such training, training agencies were established and the college was designated as one providing training in agriculture, horticulture, motor vehicle engineering and caring. Although in practical terms the off-the-job training programmes were not very different from those previously sponsored by the training boards, the involvement of college staff in monitoring off-the-job-training was a significant change reflected by the significant increase in funding that enabled the college to upgrade much of its facilities, especially in terms of farm equipment and information technology, which was an essential part of all the training programmes.

During the latter part of 1983 Walter Price's health deteriorated and he could no longer attend college or undertake any duties. I was greatly saddened by his departure since he had been a very loyal colleague from the first day I entered the Howel Harris College and although I had in effect carried him over the last two years, his leaving left a gap and a genuine sense of loss. Over the next year Maria and I visited him at his home but following a short time in the local hospital, Walter died, leaving a wife, Gladys, and two married daughters.

Although I had deliberately not sought an immediate replacement for Walter, his death prompted my requesting the governors to consider not filling the post, with vice principal appointment being given to one of the three heads of department as an additional responsibility. This was agreed, and at the next meeting my report recommended that the governors consider Dr John Fletcher, head of the department of catering and caring, for this appointment. This decision was probably my one and only error of judgement since arriving at the college, since it discriminated against the other two heads of department, and although Geraint Jones, the head of the business studies, had already declared no interest in the appointment, Iuan Evans, the head of the agriculture, building and engineering studies, viewed my recommendation as a vote of no confidence in him, despite my spending many hours explaining that whereas he was an excellent head of department and his work was greatly valued by me it did not mean that he would of necessity make a good vice principal deputising for the principal as and when required. The issue was, however, resolved by the board of governors who, while noting my recommendation, viewed it necessary to invite all three heads of department to apply for the position with the appointment subject to interview being made by a sub-committee of the board.

This approach was implemented and Dr John Fletcher was appointed as vice principal. But the damage had been done and my working relationship with Iuan never returned to what it had been.

The 1984–85 college year slipped by with the only memorable college event being when the training restaurant was invited to provide a luncheon for twenty American visitors to Brecon.

In 1965 the then mayor of Brecon had visited the city of Saline in the state of Michigan, and although the visit was initially to meet a relation working in the town it turned out to be the start of what was to become a twinning arrangement that in 1985 was celebrating twenty years of a sister city relationship. Following discussions with the town clerk – Don Stewart, a short, cheerful Scotsman who viewed the occasion as being one where there were no financial restrictions – the college put on a luncheon long remembered by those present. The mayor of Saline, Judge Donald Shelton, and his wife; the mayor of Brecon, Cllr. Arthur Bowley and his wife; together with the other visitors and their hosts in Brecon, sat down to a five-course lunch which was rated by the catering staff and students as the best they had ever produced and by the guests, which included myself and Maria, as one of the best anyone had experienced.

This event marked my introduction to Sister City Twinning, a close and long friendship with Arthur and Dilys Bowley and Don Stewart, and resulted in Maria and myself joining a party of Brecon citizens on a return visit to Saline the following year.

1984 was memorable on a personal level by my involvement in a new initiative aimed at establishing an annual jazz festival in the town.

Liz and Tony Elston were keen jazz fans – Tony was managing director of Elston Motors, the main Ford dealer in Brecon, and also a Rotarian, while Liz was very much involved in community work in the area. Together they had sought the assistance of George Melly, a jazz musician with an international reputation who had a country residence outside Brecon, and professional jazz festival organiser Jed Williams, who lived in Cardiff and who had numerous links with the music industry. They then decided that they required a publicity/promotion person with ideas on promoting the event. I was approached and after much thought decided that I would accept the invitation to become a founder director of Brecon Jazz, little knowing the impact the first festival, held on the first weekend in August 1984, would have on the town or that twenty-two years later the Brecon Jazz Festival would have an international reputation attracting musicians from all over the world.

Chapter Twenty-Nine

1986 was 'Industry Year', so designated by the government to highlight the achievements of the Youth Training Scheme in providing young trained personnel for business and industry. The director of Industry Year 1986 was Sir Geoffrey Chandler CBE, and with little hope of success I wrote to him inviting him to be the guest speaker at the 1986 Celebration of Achievement Evening where a significant number of Youth Training Scheme trainees would be present. Sir Geoffrey replied that he would be delighted to attend and another success was marked up for the Brecon College, since it turned out that it was the only college in Wales that Sir Geoffrey visited during his year of office.

1986 also saw my election as president of the Rotary Club of Brecon, this following three successful years as chairman of its Community Services Committee. This position resulted in Maria and I being invited to many social functions both Rotary and civic. One of the highlights of my year was attending the wreath-laying ceremony at the war memorial in Brecon town centre on Remembrance Day and laying a wreath on behalf of my colleagues in Rotary, then marching in procession behind a platoon of Gurkhas to Brecon Cathedral for the memorial service before finally returning to the Guildhall for refreshments courtesy of the mayor and town council.

During the six years since we had moved to Brecon, both David and Julia had been frequent visitors, as were Maria's sisters from Cardiff, her sister from Valencia and her father and mother from Madeira.

David, having decided to specialise in radar and electronics while in the Royal Air Force, found himself in 1984 on board a ship bound for the Falkland Islands and the war with Argentina. Based at a radar station at Goose Green he spent eighteen months monitoring Argentine aircraft and ships in the south Atlantic. On his return from what he described as a rather lonely phase in his life, he arrived at Brecon one weekend with a girlfriend in tow. Sandra was a Leicester girl of medium build with light brown hair, blue eyes and a pale complexion. She had trained as a carer and was at the time responsible for a day centre for adults with learning difficulties. She got on well with Maria and her first weekend visit to Brecon proved a success, with Maria promising that we would visit them in their flat in Leicester in the near future.

Julia in the meantime had decided that college study was not for her, and had left the institute to pursue a career in banking with Lloyds Bank – later to become Lloyds TSB. Still living with her mother who, following the sale of Claude Road had moved to a house in Inverness Place, Julia at the age of twenty-four had grown into a very pretty and attractive girl with numerous boyfriends and a large number of long-term girl friends. She visited Brecon on a regular basis, arriving at Saturday lunchtime and returning on the Sunday afternoon bus to Cardiff.

On one such visit she was accompanied by Steve, her first steady boyfriend. Steve was a very tall, dark-haired, handsome young man who had attended school with Julia and was now making a successful career for himself through buying, renovating and selling property. He immediately took to Maria, whose cooking he viewed as being the best he had ever experienced, while she in turn viewed him as eminently suitable as a boyfriend for Julia. One such visit involving Steve related to an invitation we had received to attend a Victorian Charity Evening at a local manor house, with all guests expected to be dressed in an appropriate fashion. While Maria and I dressed as a Victorian gentleman and his lady, Julia and Steve decided to attend as the Charles Dickens characters of Bill Sykes and Nancy. At six foot four with a very tall and battered top hat, Steve most certainly stood out in a crowd, with Julia as Nancy looking absolutely stunning. The evening was a great success, although getting Steve into the back of the car after a few glasses of wine proved to be quite a task, and the evening ended with Maria and Julia putting him to bed fully clothed and with his size twelve boots sticking out from the bottom of the bed.

When we visited David at Leicester, he and Sandra had decided to buy a house since paying for the small, rather cramped flat was not economically good practice. The house that they took us to see was in the village of Enderby a few miles outside Leicester and was one in a row of what had in the past been farm workers' cottages, and with an asking price just over their budget we thought it to be a reasonable buy. When we were told of the details Maria, in true businesswoman fashion, suggested that to fit their budget exactly they make a slightly lower offer. David, on returning to the property, made the offer, returning to the car with a great big smile on his face. Maria's suggestion had worked and the vendor had accepted the lower price. A month later they moved into their new home, and six months later we had the invitation to attend their wedding at the Leicester Registry Office.

The wedding was the first occasion that I had seen Judith since our divorce. She, together with her sister Ann and brother-in-law John, had, like us, travelled up to Leicester on the morning of the wedding, staying the night at a motel on the outskirts of the town before returning home on the following day. Julia had travelled up with Steve giving David's best man and old school friend Russell and his girlfriend a lift from Cardiff. Following the civil ceremony where David, in his Air Force uniform, accompanied by Russell, in Royal Navy uniform, made a striking pair, and Sandra looked every inch a radiant bride accompanied by her sister as bridesmaid, the wedding party gathered in a local hotel where a room and bar had been booked for the reception. This was a very jolly affair and with a free bar, conversation and laughter was the order of the day. Maria and I had a few brief words with Judith, Ann and John and for the rest of the time mingled meeting members of Sandra's family and friends. Following a buffet meal we checked in to the motel that David had arranged for us for a rest and a change of clothes before the evening disco. The disco, held in the same room as the reception, was a noisy affair and the night ended with Russell giving his impression of a male stripper, much to the amusement of all present.

The following morning Maria and I drove over to Enderby to say our farewells to the happy couple who had decided to postpone their honeymoon until a later date. Julia, Steve, Russell and his girlfriend Sharon had similar ideas, so that by lunchtime the house was full. Since Sandra was nursing a hangover and all present were hungry, Maria decide to raid the refrigerator to discover some steak, sausages and eggs, and within a very short time all present were sitting down to a wonderful mixed grill followed by cheese and biscuits and coffee. We took our leave in late afternoon, returning to Brecon happy in the knowledge that David appeared to have found himself a good partner.

The week following the end of the college session Maria and I, together with thirty other citizens of Brecon including the mayor, Councillor Arthur Bowley, his wife Dilys and the town clerk, Don Stewart, set off for America. Having obtained the necessary visas by visiting the American Embassy in London, we boarded the Trans World Airways (TWA) flight from Heathrow to New York. From JFK New York we took a connecting flight to Detroit where we were met by our hosts from Saline and driven to a meeting point in downtown Saline where we were introduced to our hosts who would be looking after us for the next ten days.

The Twinning Committee at Saline had done some research into the background of their guests, so that guests with a particular background and occupation were hosted by families with similar jobs and interests. Our hosts were Maurice and Carol Conn. Maurice was the superintendent of schools in Saline and was a graduate in the biological sciences like myself, while Carol was a graduate in physiology researching in exercise and the immune system at Michigan University.

We struck up a friendship immediately, a friendship that has lasted over the last twenty years. Maurice, like me, was the only son of a farmer who had emigrated from Germany in the 1930s to take up farming in the adjoining state of Ohio. He was a tall, well-built man in his early fifties with a great sense of humour. Carol was a short, attractive mother of four teenage children, three girls and one boy, who following bringing up the children had gone back to work at the university.

Their home in the Mill Pond Park region of the city was a typical American timber-framed bungalow with a huge basement overlooking the pond, and since they had only recently moved in and we were their first guests, it was decided that during our stay a house-warming party would be held so that we could meet all their new neighbours. Despite the fact that Maurice and Carol were out at work every day the party proved a great success thanks to the working partnership of Carol and Maria, with Maria making bread and a selection of cakes while I organised the drinks. On the night the highlight was Maria making and serving thirty or so glasses of Gallic Coffee. Irish whisky with hot strong black coffee topped with a thick layer of cream was a drink not familiar to those present, but greatly enjoyed by all, despite the fact that the July temperature was around 30 degrees.

Although this was a domestic function there were many others organised for all those who had travelled from Brecon. These included being the guests of honour at the fourth of July celebrations; attending a special meeting of the Saline City Council, where Maria presented a cloth she had embroidered in true Madeira fashion with the shields of the twin towns; visiting the state capital at Lansing as guests of the state governor; visiting Washtenaw Community College and Michigan University at Ann Arbour; visiting the headquarters of Domino's Pizza; the Michigan Space Center; the Ella Sharp Museum that depicted life in America in the late 1890s, and finally a sunset cruse down the Mawme River beginning and ending at Toledo.

So ten wonderful days slipped by and it was time to say farewell to our hosts and the many other friends that we had made during our visit. It was also farewell to the rest of our party, since while they returned to the UK, Arthur, Dilys, Don, Maria and I flew on to Long Beach, California, to spend a further ten days with two police friends of Arthur's who had visited Brecon in the past and who were anxious to return the hospitality. California was like another country with its exotic dwellings at Long Beach and the off-shore oil derricks masked as buildings, and of course Disneyland. One of the many highlights of our visit was the visit to Universal Studios; the *Queen Mary* docked at Long Beach and now used as a hotel and restaurant; the Crackers Night Club, Los Angles; and being guests of the El Bekal Temple Guard at their old fashioned steak fry. A personal highlight involved my being invited to address a group of students at a Los Angeles College on the UK system of education and where students could not believe that the average UK student did not pay any tuition fees, further and higher education being free at that time.

Our next port of call was Washington and we flew into Dulles Airport on 21 July. Our hosts there were Sonia and David Cowie, the daughter and son-in-law of Haydn and Audrey Sprague. Hayden had been a colleague of mine at the Llandaff College of Technology and more recently been involved with my establishing a series of short courses for teachers of agriculture, outlining the effect of the Common Agriculture Policy of the European Community on agriculture in the UK and Wales in particular. Sonia, a teacher, and David, a doctor, lived in Colombia, and their house was our base for the next ten days. During our stay we visited the National Aquarium at Baltimore, and as guests of Congressman Ford, who represented Michigan at Congress, we were able to visit the White House; the United States Senate Chamber; and the House of Representatives. Our final evening was spent at the famous Haussner's Restaurant with its array of original 'old masters' decorating the walls.

Saying our farewells to the Cowie family we boarded yet another TWA flight, this time to Boston and Maria's uncle and aunt – John and Connie Leca living in Rhode Island. We were met at Boston Airport by the whole family, consisting of the two daughters, Rosa and Fatima, and their husbands, and son Joseph and his wife. To accommodate us all the family had hired a large minibus which was used as transport during the visit. There then followed ten days of pure pleasure including visits to the famous Boston Harbour, scene of the Boston Tea Party; the Old State House, on the Freedom Trail; the replica of the *Mayflower* that brought the pilgrim fathers to Plymouth; the America's Museum of Pilgrim Possessions and replicas of original dwellings built by the Pilgrim Fathers.

In addition to sightseeing there were the family activities including barbecues, meals out and get-togethers that went on until the early hours and where considerable consumption of alcohol occurred.

All too soon it was time to say farewell not only to the Leca family but to America. We had experienced and enjoyed forty wonderful days in the company of wonderful and generous people, forty days that Maria and I would never forget.

On returning to Brecon it was the general opinion that the twinning visit had been a great success, and mindful of the hospitality extended by our American hosts, it was felt that an invitation should be sent to them inviting them back to Brecon for the 1987 Brecon Jazz Festival. To facilitate this project it was decided that rather than leave arrangements in the hands of the town council, a Twinning Association should be established with representatives from all the various fractions of Brecon society, and that this association would be responsible for all future visits between Brecon and Saline. At a public meeting held at the Guildhall Arthur Bowley was elected president and I was elected chairman of the association, a position I held until leaving Brecon, while my membership of the association continues to this day.

Our return from the States was tempered with sadness at the news that Frank Landgrebe had died. His funeral, which Maria and I attended, was marked by a very strange occurrence that I shall never forget. Following the service in the Chapel of Rest, those who had attended congregated outside while the coffin was loaded into the hearse. At this point one of the chapel ushers came out looking for a James Marsden, I indicated my presence to be handed a small leather-bound Bible that I had supposedly left behind following the service. I advised the usher that it was not mine, only to be shown the inscription inside the cover which read 'Presented to James Marsden with much love'.

At this point I accepted the Bible but immediately approached those present to ascertain whether they had inadvertently left a Bible in the Chapel of Rest, but to no avail, and I was left with a Bible bearing my name which I have kept to this day and which brings back memories of a rather special man who I was privileged to know.

Chapter Thirty

Early in the 1986/87 college session, Colonel Stephenson informed me that the wind of change was blowing in the political fields of the county and that he would not be re-elected as chairman of governors. I was very unhappy at this news since he and I had established a close working relationship over the past eight years and had achieved much in terms of the development of the college and its role in the community. True to his forecast he was not re-elected and Councillor John Williams became chairman. John was a Labour politician from Ystradgynlais in the Swansea valley and a gentle man, of slight build with greying hair and bright, twinkling eyes under black bushy eyebrows. I could not have asked for a better replacement, since we immediately established a good working relationship that soon extended to that of friendship. The down side, however, was that due to other commitments he was only prepared to hold the chairmanship for one year. John was married to the daughter of a very well-known and respected politician, John Hughes, who although long retired was a great character and had been the first chairman of the college as well as being chairman of the old Breconshire County Council before the local government reorganisation of 1974. He was therefore following the footsteps of his father-in-law. On one of my visits to Ystradgynlais to see John Williams, Maria and I were introduced to John Hughes who at eighty years of age lived on his own in a house opposite that of his daughter, and while I discussed college business with the chairman Maria was entertained by John Hughes with vivid stories of what life was like in the valleys of Wales at the turn of the century and of his long and sometimes turbulent political career.

During the following session several developments remain in my memory. One was the development of short courses for teachers of agriculture aimed at acquainting them of the effects of the Common Agriculture Policy of the European Community on agriculture in Wales. These short courses, although organised by the college in association with the Education Office of the EEC, were funded by the Commission from a generous budget that allowed me to select hotel venues and a reasonable level of hospitality that proved highly popular with no shortage of participants from colleges throughout Wales. Iuan Evans proved himself as an excellent tutor ably supported by Peter Guthrie, the senior lecturer in farm management.

Another development, again in terms of short courses, was in beekeeping, with weekend courses offered on a variety of topics by the now well established Welsh Beekeeping Centre, with Charles Dublon acting as course tutor assisted by specialist speakers brought in as and when required. These courses were designed to contain a high practical content and consequently were run at times of high hive activity and honey production. A popular aspect of the courses was that they all ended with a Beekeepers' Supper held on the Saturday evening in the training restaurant, and where mead produced by a local beekeeper was the house wine. Maria and I attended many of these suppers and greatly enjoyed the events.

A further development that, in a way, was a spin-off from the short courses on the effects of the Common Agriculture Policy was overseas visits by farm management students to other EEC countries to observe first hand their practices and problems. Two such visits where I accompanied the coach party were to Amsterdam in the Netherlands and Frechen in Germany. On these occasions the students involved were in the nineteen to twenty-five age group studying farm management and almost exclusively the sons and daughters of family-run farms, the vast majority of who had never been outside Wales and in some instances not beyond their local town. Needless to say their excitement was at fever pitch as they left Brecon on a Sunday afternoon to catch the midnight ferry from Dover to Ostend. On one occasion the coach stopped off in London, where the problem of getting everybody back on the coach in time for the crossing outweighed the advantages of any sightseeing in central London. These visits resulted in my making some long-term friendships with several Dutch and German colleagues who later visited Brecon. One such person was Marius Borma, the public relations officer to the Netherlands Atomic Research Institute who I met when he gave a talk to the students on the use of atomic energy in agriculture. The other was Peter Volter from the Frechen region of Germany who was head forester for the region. Both subsequently visited Brecon, Marius's visit coinciding with the Remembrance Sunday celebrations at the Cenotaph in London which he had attended every year since the end of the Second World War, and when he proudly wore his medals gained while serving in the Dutch resistance. Peter's visit coincided with the Brecon Jazz Festival when he and two colleagues were our houseguests.

A final development was the establishment of the University of the Third Age at the college. This, through a series of one-off lectures and visits, allowed professional retired men and women to gain information and become interested in a whole range of topics ranging from local history to archaeology, literature and many more. Shortly after David and Sandra's wedding Julia broke off her relationship with Steve and started going out with another young man who she had known from her schooldays. Peter Woolcock was a dark-haired, dark-skinned, handsome boy of medium build with a pleasing personality and a good sense of humour. His mother was Welsh and his father of Portuguese extraction – a feature that Maria, being Portuguese, felt was a big plus in his favour. After only a few months Julia and Peter became engaged and decided to buy a house and move in together. Since Peter had a good job in auditing while Julia's career progress at Lloyds Bank was financially rewarding, they were able to acquire and afford a modern terraced property in the Thornhill region of Cardiff.

On 21 May 1987, following a short engagement they got married at the Cardiff Registry Office. I collected Julia from Thornhill in the Daimler with Maria acting as chauffeur. The car, with its carriage brown body work with gold coach-line polished to perfection and decked with white ribbons, made a splendid carriage for a beautiful bride and we received many curious looks from passers-by as we drove from Thornhill to Park Place. Following the ceremony Maria continued with her chauffer role and drove us to the reception held at a hotel in the Roath Park area of Cardiff, with Julia and Peter enjoying the bottle of Champaign that we had provided in the back of the Daimler.

Following the end of the college session Maria and I set off for Madeira, since we had not seen her father and mother for two years. In keeping with my first visit this proved most enjoyable and gave me the opportunity to unwind from my commitments back home. Before leaving Madeira we arranged for Maria's mother and father to visit us over the Christmas period of 1987.

Returning to the college I was soon involved in the routine of yet another academic year, addressing the beginning of term staff meeting held during the week prior to enrolment, addressing all full-time students entering the college and day-release students on their first day of attendance, and visiting evening classes as and when the opportunity presented itself. Other tasks included establishing the calendar of meetings for the three advisory committees and board of governors; ensuring that preliminary arrangements for the carol service were in hand; and that a guest speaker had been obtained for the Celebration of Achievement Evening; and ensuring that my diary allowed my attendance at the meetings of the boards of governors of the four secondary schools of South Powys.

At the October meeting of the board of governors, John Williams stood down as chairman to be replaced by Councillor Marlene Roberts. She was a short, plump lady in her early fifties with brown hair and eyes and a pleasant smile but with limited knowledge of the workings of the college, so that for the following months I had to acquaint her with the overall situation and college needs for the future and their inclusion in the financial estimates for the following financial year. Marlene was an eager learner and we soon established a reasonable working relationship, although I often yearned for the return of Colonel Stephenson.

Mid-December saw the arrival of Maria's father and mother from Madeira and her brother from Venezuela. Frank had left Madeira at the age of eighteen to seek work in Venezuela and was now the part-owner of two successful restaurants – one in Macuto and the other in La Guaira. He had not see his parents since leaving home so there was a grand reunion upon his arrival in Brecon.

The Christmas season in Brecon was marked by several civic functions to which Maria and I were always invited. Two such events were the mayor of Brecon town's Christmas reception for community leaders and the Mayor of Brecknockshire's reception for those engaged in county activities. When Don Stewart, the town clerk, and Franklin Jones Chief, executive of the county, heard that Maria's family were staying with us the normal invitation was broadened to include our guests, who were given a warm welcome on arrival and provided with numerous drinks and 'bites' during the course of the evening. Safe to say that all enjoyed themselves although Maria's mum, who did not drink any form of alcohol, became concerned at the possibility that Manuel and Frank might overindulge the hospitality.

The other event that Maria's mother claimed she would never forget was her attendance at the College Carol Service at the cathedral. Being a Roman Catholic she was apprehensive at entering a church of another denomination, but with gentle persuasion by Maria she was happy and enjoyed the singing of the carols and the readings. On this particular occasion Bishop Vaughan of Swansea and Brecon was in attendance, reading the final lesson and giving the final blessing. Immediately following the blessing he came down from the altar on to the floor of the cathedral and proceeded to shake the hands of the dignitaries in the front row of the congregation. When he came to Maria and her mother he proceeded to kiss rather than shake their hands. Since Maria's mother had never experienced such an act by a priest, let alone by a bishop, she went home very happy, threatening never to wash her hand again.

Following their four weeks' stay at Brecon with numerous visits to Cardiff to see Rita, Susana and Sandra, who was now married to Pasquale and living in Richmond Road in Cardiff, I drove them to London Heathrow and saw them safely on to flights to Funchal and Caracas.

The 1988 Celebration of Achievement Evening saw Major General Morgan Llewellyn as the guest speaker. Based at the Brecon barracks he was GOC Wales and was in charge of all camps in Wales and as such was influential in the economy of many areas. Since his private residence adjoined the college playing fields, he and his wife were frequent visitors to the training restaurant, and his selection as a local guest speaker was very well received after the long list of imported ones.

In the months leading up to July '88 Maria was deeply involved in preparing for a surprise visit by all the family to Madeira to celebrate her mum and dad's golden wedding anniversary. This necessitated arranging and paying for a flight for her sister Julieta, who had not seen her family in thirty years, from Buenos Aires to London Heathrow and then arranging for her to fly to Madeira on the same flight as her sisters Rita and daughter Susana, Sandra and her husband Pasquale, Maria and me. On the same day she also arranged for her sister Regina, daughter and husband Leon to fly from Valencia to Madrid on to Lisbon and finally Funchal. These arrangements culminated in five of the six sisters and their families arriving at Arco da Calheta to the astonishment and delight of Maria and Manuel. Since the youngest sister Fernanda and oldest brother Jose both lived in Arco da Calheta and had been aware of the surprise visit, sleeping arrangements had been organised, and on the first evening the six daughters and one son and their families sat down to supper, giving a total with Mum and Dad of sixteen. The only son who was unable to be there was Frank since work commitments in Venezuela made it impossible, but since he had spent a month with his mum and dad at Brecon the previous Christmas, he was not too disappointed.

Organising sixteen people for a month is not an easy task, so various rotas were drawn up. There was a breakfast, lunch and dinner rota with two of the six sisters in the kitchen at any one time preparing the meals for all sixteen. Then there was the car rota where the 1960s Ford Cortina GT that I had hired from a local garage was allocated to different members of the family on different days. Although there were six drivers among us, a few, including Maria, were not very happy driving on the twisting roads of the island given the rather vague steering properties of the Cortina, and I can vividly recall one of my brothers-in-law returning from a day trip to Funchal promising that he would never drive that car again.

On the actual day of the anniversary, which was a Saturday, all the family and numerous friends walked to the church where a blessing ceremony was held. The little church was packed since Maria and Manuel were well-known and respected in Arco da Calheta and news of the special Mass had spread through the community with many anxious to wish the couple well. Following the service we all walked back to the family home for a celebration dinner, when fifty-two family members sat down for a meal consisting of freshly prepared chicken soup, courtesy of a few home-bred birds killed that morning, a beef barbecue involving half an oxen, and finishing with numerous sweets, cheese and grapes picked from the vines that surrounded the house. During the meal and in true Portuguese fashion vast quantities of red wine were consumed and the festivities, with music and dancing, continued far into the night. It was a wonderful occasion and brought home to me the fact that although members of the family were separated by distance they were an extremely close-knit unit that I was lucky and privileged to be a member of.

Soon it was time to leave, with Regina and family returning to Spain, while Julieta returned with us to the UK before eventually returning to Argentina. Little did we know at the time that we would be back in Madeira before Christmas.

Chapter Thirty-One

September 1988 saw the college electing it's forth chairman of governors in ten years. Councillor Dorothy James was a middle-aged, white-haired lady who, while being most charming on the surface, had the reputation of being rather devious in some of her dealings with fellow politicians. Her appointment coincided with the publication of the Department of Education and Science Circular 7/87 recommending the amalgamation of further education colleges to form larger and more cost-effective institutions. This circular, which had been long expected, was a follow-up to Circular 7/73 which had recommended the amalgamation of teacher training colleges with colleges of higher education and whose implementation had affected my career at Cardiff.

Although Circular 7/87 was received and noted by the board of governors, its adoption and implementation was a matter for the Powys Education Committee, and as such college input was limited, while the decision-making process of the authority would, in all probability, be a fairly drawn-out process with considerable political in-fighting between the old pre-1974 counties of Breconshire, Radnorshire and Montgomeryshire. Consequently I viewed this issue as one where one should keep one's head down, and not be drawn into political debate.

The autumn term slipped by culminating once again in the Annual Carol Service; the Students' Christmas Party; the exchange of Christmas cards; and the now established invitation to senior staff together with our friends from the Brecon community to join us for drinks on the Sunday morning before Christmas.

This took the form of mulled wine to Maria's recipe and home-made salt fish crockets, which were very popular with all our guests. The event usually started around midday and it had been known for the last guests to leave at dusk.

It was on the evening of 22 December that we received a telephone call from Madeira telling us that Maria's mother had died. Maria was devastated and just could not believe that the mother she had loved so dearly and who had celebrated her golden wedding anniversary a few months ago was no more. 'I am going to my mother's funeral,' she told me, and although the funeral was scheduled for Christmas Eve, and getting seats on any flights was very problematical, I set in motion the arrangements that saw Maria, her sister Rita and myself arrive at London Heathrow the following lunchtime. As anticipated there were no seats available on flights to Funchal direct or via Lisbon, despite Maria's pleadings the she had to get to Madeira on Christmas Eve. It was then suggested by a helpful airport information officer that we might try London Gatwick for possible flights. Following a telephone call when we were told that there were four seats available on an Air Gibraltar flight the following morning, we set out for Gatwick, securing three seats on the flight leaving at 9 a.m. for Funchal. Although exhausted, none of us felt like checking in to a hotel so we stretched out in the departure lounge in readiness for the next morning.

Our flight touched down at the Santa Cruz Airport at 12.45 p.m. local time. Since we had telephoned Maria's sister in Madeira from Gatwick Airport the previous evening, there was a taxi waiting at the airport to take us to Arco da Calheta. The funeral was scheduled for four o'clock – we arrived at the church at five minutes to the hour, walked in, and paid our personal respects to Maria's mother as she lay in the open coffin in front of the altar. In death as in life she looked calm and serene and the love and respect of the local community was reflected by the fact that the church was full with those paying their last respects. Maria's father had been devastated by his wife's passing and could not attend the funeral, wanting to see and remember her as she was and as she would always remain in his memory.

The funeral over the family returned home to comfort Manuel and share their sorrows and memories of a wonderful wife, mother and friend. This brought back for me memories of my mother's funeral twenty-two years earlier and the realisation of what both she and I had missed during those intervening years and how much I still missed her.

The next day, being Christmas, was a muted affair, with a mixture of happy thoughts and moments of sadness. The sun shone from a blue sky giving the day an unreal feeling of Christmas. Following lunch, which Maria and Rita prepared with their usual expertise, we all walked to the cemetery to visit the grave and say our silent farewells. A week later we were back home leaving Manuel in an empty house but secure in the knowledge that he would be well cared for by his daughter Fernanda, son Jose and their respective families.

News of Maria's loss had spread through the Brecon community and our return was greeted with numerous phone calls and letters of sympathy, since old and young alike had become very fond of Maria with her winning smile and happy disposition. The stress of travelling, the funeral and the initial worry about her father had taken it out of Maria, and a few weeks later she complained of not feeling very well. This feeling came to a head one Sunday afternoon when following lunch she felt really ill and asked me to call her doctor. Although he could not arrive at a specific diagnosis he noted that she had put on a considerable amount of weight and that her legs and ankles were swollen and referred her to a consultant at the Abergavenny General Hospital. Following a brief consultation the following week Maria was referred to the renal unit at the Cardiff Royal Infirmary.

The head of the renal unit and Director of the Institute of Nephrology at Cardiff was Professor John Williams, a tall, athletic man in his early fifties with a mop of long greying hair that made him look considerably older then he was, and blue twinkling eyes. Following an examination and a few routine tests Professor Williams suggested that Maria should be admitted, and when she asked when, the answer was, 'How about now?'

Within a few days Maria was diagnosed as having Nephrotic syndrome, a condition where kidney malfunction causes proteins to be excreted by the kidney, resulting in the protein level in the blood falling to such an extent that the body is unable to remove any excess water and becomes waterlogged. My qualifications in physiology together with some updating through a visit to the library gave me a fairly accurate picture of Maria's condition and its eventual outcome, which was total renal failure.

Following ten days as an in-patient Maria was allowed home on a course of steroid and diuretic therapy, with monthly visits to the day clinic. During her stay in hospital I had visited her every evening following work, slept on the settee at her sister Sandra's house, before returning to Brecon the following morning. Needless to say I had found that routine fairly demanding and highlighted probable problems that loomed in the future. On her return home Maria found that her levels of energy and feeling of well-being were not as they were, and more and more I was involved in tasks that she had in the past undertaken with no assistance.

As the college year ground to its conclusion, I was determined to give Maria a change of scenery, and in July 1989 I organised a visit to Madeira to see her dad. This visit made her forget her health problems, while seeing her dad, who appeared fit and well and coping with life after her mother, was a source of great comfort to her.

Returning home after four weeks in Madeira I was faced with the authority's policy that in compliance with the recommendations of DES Circular 7/87 the three colleges of the authority be amalgamated to form one institution. To facilitate this amalgamation it was recommended that a single board of governors be established and that a principal be appointed as a matter of urgency, with the current principals of the colleges at Brecon, Llandrindod Wells and Newtown invited to apply.

At about this time Maria had to return to hospital as an in-patient since one of the side-effects of the steroid therapy was type one diabetes, with consequential high blood glucose levels and sight problems.

It was decision time, and I had to consider whether to concentrate on being a full-time carer for Maria, or apply for the new post of principal with the associated problems of running three campuses sixty-three miles apart.

My first step was to consult Professor John Williams in relation to the longer-term prognosis of Maria's condition. This he confirmed to be end stage renal failure followed by dialysis which could be either Haemodialysis with three visits to the unit every week or Peritoneal-dialysis undertaken at home with bag changes at four-hour intervals.

My second step was to consult the Powys director of education, Robert Bevan, and his deputy, TAV Evans, regarding a possible alternative to my applying for the new appointment, in view of my personal situation and Maria's illness. Both were very sympathetic to the situation since both had met Maria on several occasions at the college and were very aware of the role she played in my life. Since I would be fifty-eight years of age the following year, it was suggested that should I wish to claim early retirement, this would be granted with the authority enhancing my contributory pension by seven years. This was in my opinion a most generous offer and I returned home in a much happier frame of mind to discuss the options with Maria.

Details of the post of new principal were soon available, and in keeping with my two colleagues I submitted a formal application since I wanted to appear before the selection committee and present them with the issues that I was faced with, concluding with my acceptance of the offer of early retirement that the authority had made.

Although not first alphabetically, Robert Bevan had arranged that I was the first to appear before the selection committee. Having thanked the committee for granting me the privilege of an interview and having explained that under normal circumstances I would be fully committed in seeking the appointment, since I felt that my previous experience of the amalgamation of colleges would be invaluable, I had come to the decision that my personal commitments were such that I would not be able to devote sufficient time to the post and consequently had decided to accept the early retirement package on offer. The committee chairman thanked me for my honesty and mindful of Maria's health congratulated me on my decision and wished us both well for the future. I returned to the college and let it be known that I would be leaving at the end of the college session in July 1990.

News of my immanent departure spread through both college and community with the normal workings of the college punctuated by the many expressions of sadness upon my leaving and good wishes for the future.

The authority had, upon the advice of the selection committee, appointed Bernard Wakley, principal of the Newtown

College, to be the first principal of the new college. This was a stopgap arrangement since at sixty-three years of age Bernard was only two years short of retirement. Donald Davies, principal of the college at Llandrindod Wells, had been offered the post of vice principal but had turned it down in favour of an early retirement package.

During the following months there was a climate of uncertainty among all the teaching staff, since they were all aware that changes were ahead, but unsure as to how these changes would affect them. Having experienced a similar situation at Cardiff in the months leading up to the formation of the institute, I was sympathetic to these concerns and implemented a staff development programme entitled 'The management of change' which was aimed at alleviating these concerns and worries as much as possible. My personal advice to those senior staff who approached me was to keep the head down and get on with the job in hand. News of this staff development initiative reached County Hall and together with my research experience on the effects of Circular 7/70 on college management, resulted in Robert Bevan requesting that I draw up the Instrument and Articles of Government for the new college and put forward a suggestion as to a suitable name. I was both flattered and pleased at this request and even happier that it was linked to a £2,000 honorarium payable upon completion.

In the eyes of many this involvement with the new college was an indication that had I not chosen early retirement, I would have been appointed as the first principal of Coleg Powys (Powys College) a Welsh title that I had suggested and that had been accepted by the authority.

As the session drew to a close I busied myself in ensuring that all administrative and management issues were up to date and that all college records were as I would have wished to find them. The board of governors organised a retirement buffet for me in the training restaurant, during which many kind words were said in relation to my twelve years at the college and I was presented with a Robert Vaughan map of the old Brecknockshire. The staff also organised a similar event when I was presented with a brass carriage clock. And so on the afternoon of the last day of the session I placed all my keys on my desk, said my goodbyes to my secretary, Christine, and the office staff and walked out of the Howell Harris College for the last time.

Another mile stone during 1990 was Maria's fiftieth birthday on 24 May. I had decided that following her recent health problems she should have a celebration that would be long remembered by those attending and one that she would never forget. It was scheduled as a garden party with drinks served in the garage, food collected from the kitchen and tables and chairs in the garden. I prayed for good weather and my wishes were granted with Sunday, 24 turning out to be a glorious warm day. Two of my ex-catering students ran the bar assisted by my brother-in-law. Maria's two sisters, Rita and Sandra, organised the fork buffet while music was provided by a local lady accordionist known locally as Big Brenda who played and drank white wine until dusk. Fifty guests attended including Arthur and Dilys Bowley; Harry Evans, mayor of Brecknockshire, and his wife Loma; Ernest and Jean Brent from Cardiff; and my St Teilo's Hall colleague David Pryce and his wife Pamela. Although I had lost touch with David for many years I discovered by accident that he was deputy director of education at Worcester and since then had visited him on several occasions, with Maria and Pamela becoming firm friends.

Everyone considered that it was a great occasion and the numerous birthday presents that Maria received were reflective of the way she had endeared herself to the people of Brecon.

Chapter Thirty-Two

As anticipated, Maria's health problems continued to give concern, and although on a high protein diet and steroid therapy, her kidney function continued to decline. Following several instances when I had to drive her over the Beacons at midnight for emergency treatment at the Royal Infirmary, I broached Maria with the suggestion that we would be better placed if we returned to live in Cardiff.

After much soul-searching we decided that while it would be more convenient to live in Cardiff, leaving Brecon and all the friends we had made during the last ten years could not be considered lightly, so the matter was placed on hold for the time being.

Christmas 1990 was spent in Madeira with Maria's father, while in the following May Maria's sister Julieta, having heard of Maria's health problems, decided to fly over from Argentina on a single ticket intending to spend a few months in the UK. August saw a return visit to Brecon Jazz of our friends from Saline, with Carol and Maurice being our house guests.

Towards the end of August Maria's sister Fernanda telephoned to report that Manuel was not very well and that he might have to go into hospital. Maria was immediately concerned and suggested a short visit to see him. On requesting clearance to travel from the renal unit she was, for the very first time, refused, with Dr John Williams forecasting that her kidney function was such that she would need to go on dialysis very shortly.

As forecasted, Maria entered hospital in early October to have the necessary tube inserted in her abdomen in readiness for the peritoneal dialysis which was the form of dialysis she had chosen. There then followed a series of minor disasters. The first tube had apparently been positioned in the wrong place and would not work. The second tube after insertion developed an infection and despite a course of antibiotics had to be removed and the infection treated. The third tube, although working appeared to have problems but at this stage and after three weeks' hospitalisation, Maria was sent home to recuperate.

During her stay at the Royal Infirmary, Maria was confronted with the tragic news that following his entering hospital in Funchal in early October and surviving an operation, her father had died suddenly. I shall never forget that morning in late October when accompanied by Julieta I had to visit the hospital and tell Maria that her dear father was dead. Her devastation was all the more in that she could not go to the funeral, but despite everything she insisted that her sister Rita go to Madeira to represent the family in Cardiff.

December saw David and Sandra celebrating their first child and my first grandchild – Carl Marsden. Carl weighed in at a hefty eight pounds, bearing many of the characteristics of his father, who by this time had left the Royal Air Force following his service in the Falklands and was now a fireman in the Leicester Fire Service.

Maria's period in hospital and the installation of the Tenkoff tube undoubtedly focused our thinking on whether we should move nearer Maria's treatment centre, and upon returning to Brecon we put Bemvinde up for sale. Within a week the bungalow was sold and Maria and I were on our way back to Cardiff to find somewhere to live.

After two days of viewing bungalows and apartments in the Penylan, Cyncoed and Rhiwbina areas of the city, Maria was exhausted and I was fed up with the whole experience until while at an estate agent's office in Rhiwbina I noticed a photograph of an apartment block very similar in appearance to our old home in Cooper Court. Upon enquiring we were told that it was in the village of Llandaff and was known as Cranmer Court. Since it was now late afternoon and getting dark we arranged for a viewing the following day.

3 Cranmer Court was a two bedroom, two bathroom first-floor apartment standing in its own grounds within a hundred yards of Llandaff high street and Llandaff Cathedral. The exterior resemblance to Cooper Court was, we discovered, due to its having been built by Rheidol Builders, the same builders who had

built Cooper Court. We were shown around the apartment by the owner, Peggy McGregor, who having recently been widowed had decided to move closer to her daughter who worked in the south of England. The large lounge with its windows overlooking Cardiff and Cardiff Bay housed a grand piano that the late Mr McGregor used to play, in addition to the other lounge furniture. The fitted kitchen/diner, bathroom with gold furnishings, two large double bedrooms with the master bedroom having en-suite facilities appeared to me to fit our needs perfectly. These feelings were confirmed when Maria turned to me and said, 'This is where I want to live.'

On 17 January 1992 we moved into Cranmer Court.

Once the news of our move became public knowledge, another round of farewells saw us being invited to numerous family functions. Our now traditional mulled wine and salt-fish croquettes party on the Sunday before Christmas had been a wonderful occasion, with more than fifty friends and colleagues calling by to wish us season's greetings and good luck for the future.

The Brecon – Saline Twinning Association organised a farewell party at one of the local hotels when the then mayor of Brecon presented Maria and I with a plaque depicting the coat of arms of the town and with an inscription that read – 'Presented to Dr John Marsden by the Mayor and members of Brecon Town Council, for services rendered to the Brecon – Saline Twinning Association – January 1992'. Another gift was a hand-coloured eighteenth century print of the bridge over the Usk, while the mayor and city council of Saline had sent a framed address signed by the mayor and various other dignitaries recording their appreciation of my contribution to the association. These kindnesses reminded me of the valedictory address presented to my grandfather by the people of Llangennech when he left to return to Pembrokeshire in 1891 and which still hangs in the lounge at Cranmer Court.

Within six weeks of arriving at Cranmer Court, Maria was on dialysis. Following three days' training at the renal unit and the delivery of thirty-five cardboard boxes each containing four two-litre bags of dialysing fluid, the routine of peritoneal dialysis commenced.

Bag changes were recommended every four hours with the evening change lasting until the following morning. Bags were warmed to body temperature on a special bag warmer, then connected to the Tenkoff tube immediately following the draining out of the previous bag into a measure that gave the volume of fluid removed from the body during the previous four-hour period, which in turn determined the amount of liquid that Maria could consume during the same period, and which amounted to around a pint per day. The disconnection of the old bag and the connecting of the new bag to the Tenkoff tube had to be undertaken under aseptic conditions by using sterile gloves and alcohol wipes. Failure to carry out this procedure correctly would inevitably give rise to peritonitis – an infection of the peritoneum and its loss of dialysing properties. Once the contents of the new bag had entered the peritoneal cavity by gravity – achieved by the bag being located in a position higher than the point of entry – the empty bag still connected to the Tenkoff tube was folded and stored in a cloth bag strapped around the waist until the next change was due.

Maria's bag changes usually took place at 9 a.m., 1 p.m., 5 p.m. and 10 p.m. Applying some flexibility to the timing we were able to fit in the changes without disrupting normal daily activities. The next stage in living with dialysis was to develop a safe system of bag changes away from home, since we were both determined that life should continue in as normal a way as possible. Soon we had put together a travelling pack consisting of a white plastic board, which could be wiped down with an alcohol wipe and that served as a table for the new bag during the change over; together with a pair of surgical gloves; a bottle of alcohol; a bottle of Hibisol – a surgical hand disinfection; some Betadine for cleaning the access site; and an insulated bag to keep the previously warmed dialysis fluid at the right temperature, which made bag changing possible at most locations and allowed us considerable freedom of travel.

Maria adapted rapidly to being on dialysis and with her improved health and my support she was soon venturing further and further away from home.

One such occasion was in July 1992 when we received an invitation to a Royal Garden Party at Buckingham Palace – an invitation that had apparently been initiated by the Lord Lieutenant of Powys following our departure from Brecon. We were both thrilled and honoured to have been invited and although we had met the Prince and Princess of Wales, Princess Anne, and Princess Margaret on numerous occasions, we had never met the Queen and the prospect of such a meeting was eagerly looked forward to.

Maria went out and bought a dress, matching jacket and hat, while I visited Moss Bros to be fitted for a morning suit with accessories. Having booked a room at the International Hotel in Cromwell Road, London, we drove up on the morning arriving at around midday. Having checked in, showered and changed, with Maria undertaking a bag change in readiness for the afternoon, we called a taxi to take us to Buckingham Palace.

It was a glorious afternoon. The sun shone; we drank iced tea, nibbled sandwiches and were privileged to meet the Queen, the Duke of Edinburgh and the Queen Mother as they strolled through the gardens. All too soon time was up and we had to return to our hotel for the next bag change, since we had decided that it would not be the done thing to request facilities for a bag change at Buckingham Palace.

The second and most ambitious journey took place the following December when Maria decided that she would like to spend the Christmas of 1993 in her beloved Madeira. We discussed the issues involved with Dr Gerry Coles, head of the peritoneal dialysis unit and he gave us the green light to go. The logistics of travelling abroad while on peritoneal dialysis are considerable and the holiday destination must be within three/four hours' flying time from the UK since bag changes during the flight would present problems. All the dialysing fluid had to be shipped out, received and confirmed by the holiday location before we could leave the UK. Additional antibiotics were provided to combat any peritoneal infections, while a supply of surgical gloves, alcohol, Hibisol and Betadine were an essential part of our hand luggage. Since we were staying initially at Maria's brother's house, the delivery of the thirty boxes of dialysis fluid was fairly straightforward, although the family were amazed at the shear amount of materials involved – Madeira not having any form of peritoneal dialysis at that time. While having spent

Christmas with the family, it was fairly easy to book into a hotel-apartment in Funchal for a week's stay with seven boxes stored in the boot of the car, with one collected daily. The families of Maria's brother and sister joined us in Funchal for the New Year celebrations and the midnight fireworks display that Madeira is famous for, and a great time was had by all, although Maria, on a restrictive fluid intake was on numerous occasions envious of those with no such restrictions.

Twenty-eight days passed quickly with Maria bag-changing in all kinds of locations, her favourite being the car with the draining out taking place while sitting in the passenger seat, the disconnection of the old bag and the connection of the new bag undertaken on the plastic board kept in the boot, while the draining in of new fluid was achieved by placing the bag on the roof of the car with the Tenkoff tube passing through the open window.

On our return I was asked to write an article on our holiday experiences for the newsletter of the Welsh Kidney Patients' Association, since the renal unit felt that an account of coping with peritoneal dialysis away from home might tempt other dialysis patients to venture beyond the shores of the UK, or at least take a holiday away from home. The publication of this article marked the beginning of my involvement with the Welsh Kidney Patients' Association that ended with my being its chairman.

The following year was fairly uneventful with the monthly routine of dialysis fluid delivery and visits to the dialysis clinic taking precedence. Following our move to Llandaff I had visited the lunchtime meetings of the Rotary Club of Llandaff on several occasions, since many members were ex-colleagues of mine from my days of working in the Cardiff colleges, and very soon I was invited to join, with Maria joining the Inner Wheel Club as she had done in Brecon. This involvement provided us with a social aspect to life in Llandaff, while the fellowship was something that we both appreciated.

As the winter months of 1993 dragged on and Christmas was approaching, Maria suggested that in February of the following year we might consider a further holiday in Madeira. Since these breaks were obviously improving her health I put the normal arrangements in place and we were scheduled to fly out on the second Sunday in February. Following the usual round of pre-Christmas parties and visits by David and Sandra, Julia and Peter and Maria's sisters, we spent Christmas Day with Sandra, Pasquale and their three children, Anthony, David and Michelle, while Boxing Day was spent with Rita and her husband Alfonso and her daughter Susana. A few days later Maria complained of pains around her waist and a rash and was diagnosed as having shingles. Normally this condition could be treated with a prescription drug, but due to her being on dialysis this was not possible since the dialysis would not remove the drug from her system. Consequently, the only treatment available was the painting of the infected areas with Herpid solution, a task that I performed with some relish since I claimed that I had never painted a woman before.

The onset of the attack of shingles put the planned visit to Madeira in doubt, and although by late January the worst of the attack was over, we decided to cancel. This cancellation, unbeknown to us at that time, was to change our lives for ever.

Chapter Thirty-Three

Sunday flights by Air Portugal from London Heathrow to Santa
Cruz, Madeira, take off at around 6.30 p.m. arriving in Madeira at
around 9 p.m. At 9 p.m. on the Sunday that, but for the shingles
attack, would have seen us landing at Santa Cruz, Maria had gone
to bed early while I was looking at a programme on the television
when the telephone rang. It was the transplant coordinator from
the transplant unit at the Royal Infirmary telling Maria that they
had a donor kidney for her. Had we gone on holiday we would
have missed this call and the following years could have been very
different.

Ever since Maria started dialysis and had her name on the
transplant list, we had a bag of basic items for a hospital stay ready
packed, and within twenty minutes we were at the transplant unit,
which occupied a top-floor ward with three single-bed side-wards
in the Royal Infirmary. The head of the unit, Professor John
Salaman, welcomed Maria and there then followed a whole series
of tests and report writing. Professor Salaman was a tall, lean,
grey-haired man in his mid-sixties who had pioneered kidney
transplantation in Cardiff since the mid-sixties and who was now
nearing retirement. The transplant team consisted of a further
two surgeons; Mr Griffin a short, balding middle-aged man; and
Miss Rosanne Lord, a newly-appointed surgeon from the London
Free Hospital. The support staff included a transplant coordinator, together with nursing and administrative staff.

Maria went down to theatre at 3 a.m. and seven hours later
returned to the ward. It had been a long operation, mainly due to
the donor kidney having poor blood supply connections, resulting
in the transplant surgeon having to graft on additional vessels to
ensure an adequate blood supply.

Kidney transplants vary in the time it takes for them to start
functioning, with some starting to produce urine immediately
while others take a few weeks. In Maria's case five weeks elapsed

before one night she woke up to find the bed soaked with urine. Although this marked a turning point in her condition, the previous weeks had been very traumatic in that Maria's Tenkoff tube became infected, due mainly to the anti-rejection medication that she was receiving to protect the donor kidney, and resulting in her having to go on to haemodialysis; she developed bed sores again as a result of her immune system being non-existent, while her general health deteriorated to a point that she was transferred to the intensive care unit and placed on continuous haemodialysis and antibiotic therapy.

This transfer I shall always remember because I had to remove all Maria's clothes and personal belongings from the ward and take them home, since nothing of that nature was allowed in the intensive care unit. Sitting in the car outside the hospital with her case and belonging by my side brought back vivid memories of similar incidents before my mother and father left me and at that moment I felt very alone and fearful of what the future might bring. Clasping the ruby ring on the small finger of my right hand I prayed long and hard for my Maria to be kept safe and to be back with me soon.

The head of the intensive care unit was a Dr David Wise who in addition to being a good physician was the kindest man I had ever met. Whenever I visited Maria, and that was morning and evening of every day, he would explain in detail her therapy and her progress and would allow me to be with her holding her hand for many hours, which was contrary to the normal rules of the unit. There were times when Maria was not aware of my presence as she drifted in and out of consciousness, but there was no way that I would leave her to fight alone, since I was now sure that we would see it through together.

After two long weeks Dr Wise was of the opinion that she could return to the transplant ward. Miss Rosanne Lord, who had made Maria her special patient, took personal responsibility for this transfer and to surgically remove the Tenkoff tube which was now non-functional, before she returned to the transplant ward.

Once the kidney started to function, Maria's condition improved dramatically, although having been bedridden for five weeks and fed by tube for several of those weeks, she had to learn to eat and walk again. Since Maria was having trouble with eating the standard hospital meals, my contribution at this time was to cook appetising but simple meals at Cranmer Court, drive across Cardiff to the hospital, run up the three flights of stairs to the transplant ward and help her feed herself. Walking was another major problem and I spent many hours supporting her as she attempted to walk around the small single-bedded side-ward that she had occupied since the transplant operation. To lift both our spirits I set a target date for when I predicted Maria would leave hospital. This was to be the Good Friday of Easter 1994, and although for several months she had to return to the unit at weekly intervals to have the wound left by the Tenkoff tube treated and dressed, Maria arrived home for Easter.

The following months were hard work and saw me doing the cooking, cleaning and caring as Maria slowly regained her strength. Walking proved the most difficult and when outside she had to use a wheelchair, which in addition to other aids such as shower grab-rails had been provided by Social Services. A suggestion put to us at one of the many day clinics was swimming as a means of improving walking and overall health. Since I considered the public baths as not very suitable we both joined a private leisure club run by one of the Cardiff hotels, and although initially Maria had considerable difficulty with swimming she persevered and was soon able to swim two and three lengths of the pool. Light exercise on the various exercise equipment available at the club completed the recovery and by Christmas 1994 Maria was back to full health, and as a consequence of my involvement in various exercises I was also considerably fitter.

Although during the difficult days when Maria was very ill no visitors were allowed, her coming out of hospital saw numerous visitors from Cardiff and Brecon calling in to wish her well. Her sisters Rita and Sandra, Julia and occasionally David when he could have time off from work all called to see her. Members of the Rotary and Inner Wheel Clubs of Llandaff also visited or telephoned to enquire as to Maria's progress, and this I found was a great comfort.

Living at Cranmer Court we discovered was living in a close community where help was always at hand although never obtrusive in any way. Our immediate neighbours were Eunice and Denis Collins. Denis was a retired army major who had served with the eighth army in the desert during the Second World War, and although now in his late eighties was very much an army man, being tall of stature with sleeked down white hair, small, clipped white moustache and bright blue eyes that missed nothing. Following the war he had gone into business in London where his father George Collins, later Sir George Collins, became Chief Commoner of the City of London and chairman of the Lands and Estates Committee. Denis later moved to Edinburgh where he established a clock and watches business, met and married Eunice and continued to live there until his retirement in 1974 when they came to Llandaff to be near Eunice's younger sister who had married a Welshman and lived in St Nicholas, a small village on the outskirts of Cardiff.

Eunice and her sister Dorothy came from a wealthy Scottish family and had been familiar with a high standard of living which they had brought with them to Wales, and the Collins's hospitality to Maria and me was always of the highest order and despite the age difference we, in addition to being good neighbours, became firm friends. In the 1970s Eunice, due to arthritis, had had her hips replaced and by the time of our arrival these were beginning to give problems, with the result that she was severely disabled mobility wise with Denis having to do much of the fetching and carrying.

Our other immediate neighbours were Don and Elsie Newns, Don being a retired tax inspector; Clifford and Susan Millensted, Clifford having worked in financial services in London before illness forced his early retirement; and Ramiz and Katherine Delpak, Ramiz being a reader in civil engineering at the Glamorgan University while Katherine was a practising physiotherapist. Other residents were a retired fruit merchant, John Hutton and his disabled wife May; a retired civil servant, Anne Dickson, who had lost her husband a few years earlier; a retired solicitor, Stewart Scobie, and his wife Vera; a young businessman, Paul Wilson, who spent most of his time running a business in South Africa in between crewing luxury yachts from the Cape to the West Indies; and David Tudor-Thomas, a solicitor who had been forced to retire following a nervous breakdown following the death of his father, Sir James Tudor-Thomas, who was knighted for services to medicine. It was into this small community that Maria and I settled and although different from the Brecon community we adapted and were soon accepted as members of the Cranmer Court family.

Early in 1995 Maria's sister Fernanda gave birth to her second daughter and fourth child, Anna. A few months later we received an invitation to be her godparents on the occasion of her christening at the church in Arco da Calheta, a church where we had experienced both happiness and sadness. This invitation we accepted and Maria and I once again set off for the Pearl of the Atlantic. With the exception of ensuring that we had sufficient immunosuppressant medication, this trip was considerable easier than the previous one when Maria was on dialysis. There was one thing missing, however, and that was Maria's parents and the family home that had now been sold with the proceeds divided between the eight children, and although Maria loved her sister and brother dearly, staying in working households was no substitute for the family home and her mum and dad.

Following my retirement I had invested a little money in buying one week's holiday every year in a time-share apartment in Tenerife, and through joining the time-share Residents Club International (RCI) I was able to 'bank' such weeks over several years and exchange them for holidays at any other time-share location registered under RCI anywhere else in the world. During Maria's illness and the associated problems of travel, especially to unknown destinations, we had banked four weeks' time-share and were now able to use these banked weeks as and when required. One such occasion was during this particular visit to Madeira when following the christening celebrations Maria and I left the village and had a week's holiday on our own at an exchange time-share apartment at the Alto Lido Hotel in Funchal. This marked the first of many such holidays, and although we did visit our apartment at Club Olympus in Tenerife on one occasion, all the other weeks were spent elsewhere.

On our return from Madeira Maria became ill with a severe attack of gall stones, which resulted in her requiring an operation to remove her gall bladder. The transplant team decided that the operation should be an in-house affair and one of the recently appointed transplant surgeons, an Adam Jurewicz, who had extensive experience of key-hole surgery, agreed to undertake the removal using this technique. Adam was Polish by birth but had spent much of his career in London hospitals before joining Roseanne Lord at Cardiff. The operation was a complete success and within three days Maria was up and around and within three weeks was declared fit to fly to Canada, to visit her uncle and his family in Cambridge, Ontario.

Chapter Thirty-Four

October 1995 saw us on a transatlantic flight from Cardiff International Airport to Toronto where we were met by Maria's uncle and his family. Uncle Luis Diniz and his wife Grace lived in Beverley Street, Cambridge, Ontario. Luis Diniz was Maria's mother's eldest brother and had immigrated to Canada in the 1940s. He was a stocky, white-haired man who following an industrial accident had been forced into early retirement. This injury had resulted in his losing one eye and his receiving a significant sum of money in compensation. His wife Grace, who was also Portuguese, had been born in the Azores and had given him four children – Maria, Judy, Manuel and Luis junior. With the exception of Luis all had married and were bringing up their families in Cambridge.

As was the case when we visited Maria's family in Rhode Island, all the family were at the airport to greet us since Luis had not seen Maria since he left Madeira and she was around eight years old, and had not met me at all. Cambridge is about twenty miles south of Toronto and the journey in the hired minibus was uneventful, with the family holding conversations in a mixture of Portuguese and English.

Cambridge, I was to learn later, has the largest and oldest Portuguese community in Canada and the city has numerous memorials to those who fought in the Canadian Forces during the Second World War.

Our stay of four weeks involved the third week spent with friends in Saline. This visit involved my hiring a Plymouth Sudan for the drive to Detroit and then on to Saline. Being autumn, the browns, yellows and reds of the trees were a sight to behold while the relatively empty motorway made driving a pleasure. Crossing into the States was a bit of a nightmare, with numerous toll and passport-control points. On entering Detroit we were advised by a kindly policeman to stick to the main routes out of the city and not to venture down side roads where car hijacking was not unknown. Taking this advice we arrived at Saline safe and sound where we were the guests of Paul and Jackie Tull who lived near where the Conns used to live, Carol and Maurice having left Saline to live in Albuquerque, New Mexico. Paul was a tall, lean, white-haired man who had been editor of the local newspaper, the *Saline Herald* for many years and was now nearing retirement. Jackie was a most pleasant lady who made us most welcome, giving us the run of their basement which consisted of a lounge with patio doors leading on to a terrace and swimming pool, a kitchen, bedroom and shower. Our stay was a mixture of parties involving many of those we had met while on our first visit to Saline and evenings at home with Jackie and Paul. Soon it was time to return to Cambridge, a journey we undertook on a Sunday morning when traffic was at its lightest and we arrived at Beverley Street by mid-afternoon. Since we had the car for a further week we took Luis and Grace to see Niagara Falls, while Maria and I visited Toronto to see the underground shopping malls and various other sites of interest.

Since Aunt Grace and I both had birthdays towards the end of October a joint birthday party was organised at a restaurant called the Red Lobster located a few miles outside Cambridge. The fish menu was excellent and we had a great time. On this occasion we travelled in Luis's car and although he was a very safe driver, only having one eye did affect his positioning of the car, resulting in his being pulled over by a traffic cop who suggested that not driving too near oncoming traffic would be advisable. We left Canada with many happy memories of yet another branch of Maria's family – a family that I was proud to be part of.

Christmas soon arrived and following a visit to celebrate Carl's birthday we divided our time over Christmas Eve, Christmas Day and Boxing Day between Julia and Peter, Sandra and Pasquale and their children, and Rita and her new boyfriend, Alfonso Pennasilico. Just prior to Carl's birth David and Sandra had sold their first home in Enderby and had bought a larger property in the adjoining village of Huncote, and it was in the new house that we celebrated Carl's birthday on 17 December 1995.

Although I had visited Madeira on numerous occasions I had never visited mainland Portugal, and since Maria had worked in

Cascais prior to coming to Cardiff, when I saw the opportunity to tour Portugal the temptation was too great to resist. An advertisement in the *Jaguar Enthusiast Journal* was the starting point. This was for a ten-day tour of Portugal organised by the Jaguar Club of Lisbon and billed as 'Jaguar Tour International, Portugal 1996'.

During 1995 I had taken the Daimler in for a major body overhaul by a Cardiff-based company that specialised in classic car restoration. This involved the replacement of numerous body panels, remedial rust prevention and a re-spray. For an eighteen-year-old car the overall condition was deemed as excellent so when the car emerged gleaming from the paint shop we were both delighted and viewed it as money well spent since Maria and I had decided that we would never part with UPA 860S. Although at the time I had no knowledge of the tour, the opportunity of using the restored car on such an occasion was an added incentive. At Maria's suggestion we contacted some friends in Brecon inviting them to join us as passengers since Maria was not keen on the prospect of being navigator for ten days. Clifford and Barbara Jones were keen motorists, with Cliff, who I had known since my school days in Cardigan, being an excellent navigator. They accepted our invitation on a shared expenses basis, and once the banker's draft was sent off to Lisbon there was no turning back.

I took the Daimler in to Paramount Cars of Cardiff for a full service, and to check that all potential problem areas were attended to; this included a new radiator to ensure adequate cooling, and new brake pads to ensure that we could stop. Having looked after the car for very many years, the technicians at Paramount were excited at the prospect of the car embarking on such a long tour and posed for photographs before the car left the premises.

Although the tour of ten days' duration was all-inclusive, with accommodation, meals and entertainments included, we decided that to extend our time on the continent would be a good idea. Consequently, although the tour was not scheduled to start until Monday, 20 May, we drove down to Plymouth and crossed by Brittany Ferries to Santander on Monday 13 May, spending the next six days touring the Costa Verdi of Northern Spain, visiting Gijón, Ferrol, Á Coruña la Coruña, and ending up in Santiago de Compostela, where on Sunday morning, 19 May we attended mass in the wonderful medieval cathedral.

On Monday morning we drove to the Spanish boarder which, due to EEC regulations, was non-existent, then on to Vila Nova de Cerveira and to Pousada D Dinis – the first of the many pousadas that we were scheduled to stay at during the next ten days.

The tour had attracted fifteen participants, including from Belgium Fernand and Micheline Derweduwe driving a modern XJ 300 Jaguar, and Rene Siomons and Marianne Forier driving an XJS Coupé. Germany was represented by Heinz Hoitz in an XJ 40, Kiaus and Ulla Stange in an E Type, and Peter Stange and Gabriele Allnoch in another E Type. The Netherlands were represented by Steven and Leonie Haverlach driving an E Type, while Michel and Catherine Roquet in a beautiful 1938 Jaguar SS100 flew the flag for Monaco. Denmark was represented by Christian Friborg and Christina Heinertz in a XJS V12 drop-head coupé complete with Christian's family coat of arms on the doors, while the host nation had five representatives in the tour organis- ers Joaquim Diniz and Isabel Tinoco in an XJ 6 Series 3, Manuel and Teresa Verissimo driving a XJ 6 Series 2, Jacquim and Joeo Olivera in an XJ 6 Series 2 Coupe, Raol Caralho and Alice Santos in a Daimler Series 2, and Francisco Nogueria driving a 1965 Jaguar Mark 2. Ours was the only Daimler Sovereign on the tour and the only car with four passengers.

When we arrived several participants were outside the Pousada Diniz giving their cars a final polish and fixing the tour number plates to their cars. We were crew number 3, and in addition to fixing the Jaguar tour of Portugal commemorative plate, I installed a small Welsh Flag on the nearside bumper. That evening, following a reception courtesy of Messias Wines, we all sat down to a welcome dinner of green cabbage soup (caldo verdi) followed by codfish (bacalhau) cooked in white wine, cheese and grapes and finally coffee.

The following morning after a buffet breakfast the tour got underway with the mayor of Vila Nova de Cerveira waving us off accompanied by the local band and a large number of villagers who had gathered to look at the cars. Our first destination was the fortress town of Valença, then on to the Brejoeira Palace followed by lunch at the Elevador Hotel in Bom Jesus de Braga. After lunch we drove to Abadia and then on to the castle at Póvoa de Lanhoso before ending the day at Guimaraes and the Pousada Sta Marinha da Costa where dinner was awaiting us. Our total distance travelled on the first day amounted to 233 km and I was happy to retire early for a well-earned rest.

Day three saw us leaving Guimaraes and after a short journey arriving at the Ducal Palace for coffee. We then drove 90 km to Porto where we were the lunchtime guests of Taylor's Wine Cellars, famous for their port. The winding street leading to Taylor's culminated in large wrought-iron gates with a speed hump that wreaked havoc on the exhaust systems of two E Types as they attempted to enter the courtyard beyond. Following a wonderful lunch and a tour of the wine cellars, I and my fellow drivers were faced with a journey of 165 km, with one break, believe it or not, for cocktails at the Messias's wine cellars. We arrived at the Palace Hotel do Bus Saco at seven thirty to be greeted at the entrance by a black-coated waiter holding a tray of sparkling Portuguese wine. That evening a black tie gala dinner was held in our honour followed by a group that entertained us with the traditional Portuguese fado singing. Needless to say after driving 259 km with coffee, lunch and mid-afternoon drinks plus the gala dinner and listening to fado singing until the early hours there were many exhausted drivers, myself included.

Day four took us on to Coimbra and its university, the monasteries at Batalha and Alcobaça and the sanctuary at Fatima where in May 1917 three children saw the apparition of 'a Lady more brilliant than the sun'. After lunch at the Arte Xavega restaurant in Nazaré and having strolled along the beach of the town, we motored on to view the castle at Óbidos and the monastery at Mafra before arriving at our next location, which was the Palace Hotel dos Seteais in Sintra. That day we had covered 306 km and were looking forward to the following day when there would be no driving.

The following day the cars were not used and we were taken by coach on a sightseeing tour of Sintra, Cascais and Lisbon.

Lunch was taken at the Cozinha Velha restaurant at Queluz, and following a lengthy and interesting tour of Lisbon we all sat down to dinner at the Sr Vinho restaurant in Lisbon. This being 24 May, which was Maria's birthday, the opportunity to enjoy a few extra celebratory drinks without the worry of driving was to me most welcomed and all the tour members joined in, drinking to Maria's continued health and happiness.

Lisbon proved a fascinating city that dates back to prehistoric times when man was attracted and captivated by the Tagus estuary and the hills sloping gently down towards it. According to legend, the Phoenicians were the first to establish a trading post in what they called Alis-Ubbo (Pleasant Haven). After the Phoenicians came the Greeks and as the city grew it changed its name to Olisipo. Then came the Romans, who made the city grander and more beautiful and called it Felicitas Julia. After the Romans came the Barbarian peoples of the North, followed by the Arabs who made their Aschbouna a truly opulent city. In 1147 a young lord of a county he had transformed into a kingdom obtained the help of the Crusaders passing through on their way to the Holy Land, and conquered Lisbon. The young lord's name was Alfonso Henriques and his recently formed kingdom was Portugal. Very soon Lisbon became the political decision-making centre and King Alfonso III made it capital of the kingdom. Later in 1383–85 the Aviz Dynasty came to the throne, and was instrumental in encouraging the Portuguese discoveries of the fifteenth and sixteenth centuries where voyagers left Lisbon to discover the New World and returned with wealth and spices. The Portuguese capital soon became a great metropolis with people of all nations in a cultural melting pot. The resulting economic boom of the time led to the construction of various palaces, monuments, convents and monasteries, many of which survived the earthquake of 1755 that destroyed almost two-thirds of the city. Some of these we viewed as we toured what is now the modern city of Lisbon which, following the 1755 earthquake, was reconstructed with an emphasis on wide streets, built according to a geometric grid plan consequently making finding one's way around relatively easy.

The sixth day of the tour saw us visiting the monastery at Arrábida before lunching at the Golf Trqia restaurant in Troia.

Following lunch and 153 km later saw us arrive at our next port of call, the Pousada Rainha Santa Isabel. Following breakfast the following day, which was a Sunday, we all walked to the Santa Maria Church and Santa Isabel Chapel which were next to the Pousada. The story goes that in the Santa Isabel Chapel you can still smell the scent of roses which were a gift by a lover to Isabel, with the perfume being a remainder of their undying love. Following a drive to the Vila Vicosa Palace we lunched at Saint Paulo's Monastery restaurant, before proceeding on to Monsaraz, Xarez and Évora, arriving at the Pousada Castelo in Alvito for dinner and a well-earned rest, or so we thought, since after dinner we were escorted by the locals to the village church to listen to regional songs performed by the village choir. Just after midnight we made our excuses of being very tired and retired to bed.

Day eight saw us leaving Alvito and driving the 126 km to Vila Nova de Milfontes where we lunched at the O Pescador restaurant before journeying a further 158 km to Vila Moura and the Vila Moura Marinotel – a modern hotel in one of the Algarve's popular holiday resorts. The penultimate day of the tour involved a drive to the western most point on the Algarve – the Praia de Rocha, which is also the most western point of the Continent. A visit to the castle and museum at Silves followed, before we lunched at the Vila Sodre Country House restaurant in Enxerim. Following a drive through the pine, eucalyptus and cork-oak-covered hills of Silves we returned to Vila Moura. That evening a black tie gala dinner had been organised to mark the end of the tour and when the results of the various competitions that had been held during the tour were announced. In addition to the traditional Concourse d'Elegance for the best car on the tour, won by Michel and Catherine Roquet with their SS100, there was the 'Passing of the Stone' tradition. This involved the team that had incurred the most navigational errors on any particular day being passed the Stone, which they were forced to accommodate in the navigator's footwell during the following day. This stone was in fact a large piece of rock weighing about five kilos. We had been passed the Stone on one occasion, as a result of Cliff deciding that we could take a short-cut to the next Pousada and could have a sleep before being first down for dinner, and this was regarded as a navigational error much to his disgust. The team with the most navigational errors during the tour was Klaus and Ulla Stange from Germany who had suffered the Stone under Ulla's feet for a total of three days, and which Klaus claimed would require a new floor-pan for the E Type. But it was all in good fun and the evening ended with all the participants recording their appreciation of the organisers' hard work and the excellent accommodation, food and drink provided during the tour and promising a return visit at the earliest opportunity.

During the tour we had made many friends, including Christian Friborg and Christina Heinertz from Denmark. Chris, as he became known to us, was the only son of a wealthy aristocratic family whose coat of arms he proudly displayed on the doors of his XJS. His occupation and hobby was the restoration of vintage and classic cars and his personal collection totalled around twenty cars, and in conversation I was amazed to discover that the engine restoration of the majority of these cars was carried out by a small company at Llanbister, a small village north of Llandrindod Wells in Powys, and that he frequently travelled to Wales to monitor the progress of the various restorations. Although he introduced Christina as his daughter who was convalescing from an illness, we all had our doubts as to the relationship and decided that she might be his young mistress taking a holiday with a rich man. They were, however, great company and we all agreed that our meeting would be long remembered, although Chris never took up the invitation to visit us in Wales.

The following morning, Wednesday, 29 May, saw our departure from Vila Moura heading for the Spanish boarder and on to Valencia and Maria's sister Regina and brother-in-law Leon.

Chapter Thirty-Five

Our journey from Vila Moura to Valencia was relatively un-eventful. After crossing the boarder into Spain we followed the motorway to Seville, crawling through that city at around 2 p.m. on what was probably the hottest day we had encountered. From Seville we followed the excellent Spanish motorway system to Granada, then Murcia, Alicante and finally the coastal motorway which brought us to Valencia, and following some excellent navigation by Cliff, to 98 Padre Vinãs.

Padre Vinãs always held bitter-sweet memories for me with the recollection of Maria and me on our honeymoon, her entering hospital and suffering a miscarriage and our leaving what might have been a son or daughter in Valencia. But as always our reception at 98 was warm and welcoming, with Regina having engineered a street parking place for the Daimler which, with its tour number plate and Welsh flag still in place, attracted much attention among the locals, with one gentleman volunteering to keep watch over it during our stay. Following our last visit to Spain, Regina's daughter, also named Regina, had been born and was now a very attractive and highly intelligent girl of sixteen. Her brother Manuel born three months after Carl and now aged six completed the family. Since we were four adults there was insufficient bedroom accommodation at Regina's apartment, and it was only through her negotiation with the owner of the adjoining apartment, which was empty at that time, that it was it possible for us to stay at Padre Vinãs over the next ten days. This arrangement resulted in our having our meals with Regina and sleeping in the adjoining apartment.

Once we had caught up on the sleep that we had missed while on the tour, we spent the major part of the time showing Cliff and Barbara around Valencia, while the one remaining weekend was spent at the bungalow that Leon had built in the village where his mother and father had been born. The village of Paraquallos, with a population of 200 residents was situated approximately midway between Valencia and Madrid and 15 km from the ancient city of Cuenca.

With Leon and Regina and family in their car and us following in the Daimler, we arrived at Paraquallos as dusk was falling, to be greeted by a scene reminiscent of one of those Mexican villages seen in Western films with empty streets, bordered by white-washed cottages, no cars and the only missing feature being the tumbleweed blowing into doorways.

Leon and Regina's bungalow was situated on the edge of the village and consisted of a large kitchen, living room, four bed-rooms and a family bathroom. At the front was an enclosed courtyard with wrought-iron gates and railings. Two vines occupied pride of place and supported by a metal framework provided a shaded area outside the entrance, as well as providing both white and red grapes.

At the back of the bungalow was a garage for two cars and a kitchen garden with the obligatory fig tree. It was obvious from the care and attention to detail that Leon and his father, who had been a master builder prior to retirement, had spent a great deal of time and hard work in constructing the property, which appeared to be the only new building in the village.

Once we had unpacked and settled in we were taken on a conducted moonlit tour of the village.

Paraquallos boasted one small general store, one bar that also served tapas, and one church, and we discovered during our tour that the villagers at that time in the evening were either in the store, bar or church. Needless to say we decided to spend the evening in the bar, ordering some of the local red wine and some plates of freshly cooked prawns. By this time Maria was feeling very tired so we decided to have a relatively early night, leaving Cliff, Barbara and Leon in the bar.

The following morning we set off for Cuenca, and although there were a few headaches recorded following the previous night's drinking, a pleasant day was spent viewing the ancient cathedral and the numerous antique shops of this once capital city. The following day we returned to Valencia and set about making plans for our return to the UK.

We left Valencia on 6 June, heading for Santander and the ferry on the following Saturday, 10 June. Heading north we passed through Teruel and then on to Zaragoza. Since we had two days to complete the journey we stayed the first night at a motorway hotel on the outskirts of Tudela before proceeding the following day to a little village called Abadiño on the outskirts of Bilbao where we stayed the night. The next day, following an hour's drive on the motorway, saw us arrive at Santander in time for the noon crossing of the ferry to Plymouth.

On arriving back in Cardiff and checking the mileage on the Daimler we found that we had covered 2,798 miles on what we all regarded as an unforgettable holiday. As promised, to the tour organisers in Portugal, I then proceeded to write an article for the monthly magazine of the *Jaguar Enthusiasts' Club* recording the events of the tour, which was published in the October '96 issue.

1997 proved to be a busy year in that I was invited to become president of the Rotary Club of Llandaff exactly ten years after serving in the same capacity at the Rotary Club of Brecon. At my installation, Lord Parry of Neyland was guest speaker and numerous Rotary friends from Brecon joined Maria and me at the Copthorn Hotel where the installation dinner with ninety guests was held.

The next eighteen months were punctuated by four deaths recorded in the *Western Mail* – a daily newspaper that my family had subscribed to over very many years. The first was that of Margaret's husband Hayden, who following a short illness had passed away at the University Hospital of Wales, Cardiff. Although I would have liked to attend the funeral just to see Margaret again, I felt that this would be inappropriate and contented myself with a simple sympathy card. A few weeks later, however, I had cause to pass the house in Wenallt Road and noted that it appeared empty with the curtains drawn and the garden in a neglected state. Stopping the car, I enquired of a neighbour as to the whereabouts of the family, to be told that daughter Bethan had married a few months before Hayden's death and had gone to live in the Shrewsbury area and that Margaret was in a nursing home somewhere in the Cardiff/Penarth area suffering from Multiple Sclerosis – a condition that apparently she had suffered from for many years.

I was shattered by this news since my memory of Margaret was of twenty-five years previous, and of a woman full of life and vitality who had recently given birth to a baby girl called Bethan – an achievement that had made her life complete. During the following months I telephoned the various residential and nursing homes in the Cardiff area enquiring if they had Margaret Jones as a patient. After numerous calls I struck lucky and discovered that she was a patient at a nursing home in Penarth. After much deliberation I decided to visit her, and one afternoon after a Rotary Club lunch I motored over to Penarth, to be confronted by someone who I hardly recognised. White-haired and withered, with a vacant look in the eyes, the person who I once knew sat in a chair in a single-bedded room overlooking the sea although I doubt whether she ever saw it. I discovered that the disease had affected her throat muscles and she could no longer eat or drink normally, being fed by a tube inserted directly into the stomach. After a little while she appeared to recall the past and who I was and started talking about Bethan, who was now twenty-four years old and had brought forward her marriage date once it was known that her father had only a short time to live. She also told me that Bethan, like her half-sister Lena before her, had attended Howells School in Llandaff, but unlike Lena, had then gone on to the Welsh College of Music and Drama where she graduated with a first class honours degree in music, follow-ing her mother's love of music and involvement in the National Youth Orchestra of Wales. Following her marriage she had undertaken further studies towards a law degree. As I left I gave Margaret one of my cards should she need anything and wished her well. Her response was, 'We left it all too late.'

Five months later, Margaret's death was recorded in the *Western Mail* with the funeral service being at Thornhill Crematorium in Cardiff. I was the only mourner outside the family at the funeral but felt that one last goodbye was appropri-ate. Lena, who I had met when she was a schoolgirl attending Howell's School, remembered me as a colleague of her step-mother and as the owner of a large blue Lagonda car, and introduced me to Bethan and her husband. Bethan, who I had not seen since she was a few months old, had grown up to be very like her mother with long auburn hair, hazel eyes and a tanned complexion and very unlike her half-sister.

The third death that severed another link with the past was that of Mona's sister Loma, who had been very kind to me when I was seeing Mona and she was staying with her in Newport. Loma and her husband, Jack Francis, had one daughter, who had qualified as a nurse and was working abroad in the Arab Emirates and the sudden death of a relatively young and fit woman was a great shock to the family. The obituary gave details of the funeral director involved and I penned a letter of sympathy to Mona and Jack care of the funeral director. A few weeks later I received a lengthy letter from Mona thanking me for my letter of sympathy and bringing me up to date on the forty or so years that had passed since we had last been in contact.

Apparently, after teaching for a few years at the school in Harrow on the Hill, Mona had returned to Pembrokeshire to teach at her old primary school at Glanrhyd. She had later married a Winford Phillips who was known to me as a contemporary at the Cardigan County School. They had one daughter, Susie, who was now working as a television presenter at the BBC Wales television centre at Llandaff. Following a long and painful illness Winford had died two years previously and Mona now lived on her own in Cardigan. Jack being unable to live on his own now, having lost his wife, was scheduled to go into a residential home, with his daughter returning to her post in the Arab Emirates. I felt the letter to be such that it deserved a reply in which I summarised my life to date and the fact that I and my dear wife Maria were now living in Llandaff and had seen Susie Phillips present many health programmes but until now never knew of the connection.

The fourth death was that of Sandra's mother, and although Maria and I hardly knew her having only met her twice before David and Sandra's wedding, there was little doubt that mother and daughter had a very close relationship and that her death after a long illness had a profound effect on Sandra. Although nothing was said she apparently started to take comfort in the drink, not made any better by the fact that David being in the Fire Service worked a shift pattern that often entailed his working nights and during public holidays. There is little doubt that depression and a certain reliance on drink was contributory to the eventual break-up of the marriage a few years later.

Now that Maria's health was greatly improved and she was able to undertake most aspects of housework I discovered that I had additional time on my hands, and when I read that the Welsh Kidney Patients' Association was requiring a secretary I decided to apply and in so doing contribute in some way to that sector of the Health Service that had given, through transplantation, Maria a new life.

Following a very informal meeting with Wayne Williams the then chairman of the association, I was appointed and welcomed as the new honorary secretary.

The Welsh Kidney Patients' Association had been founded in 1984 by a group of like-minded kidney patients and carers with the objective of enhancing the care of all kidney patients both young and old and, in particular, to promote the development of kidney transplantation within Wales. The association, with a membership that was free to around 1,200 patients and carers throughout South, West and Mid-Wales, was registered as a charity in 1992 and was governed by a management committee of fifteen under a written constitution. Its honorary president was Professor John Salaman, the recently retired director of the renal transplant unit at the Cardiff Royal Infirmary, with the vice president being Dr Andrew Williams, director of the renal unit at Morriston Hospital, Swansea.

I found the work of the association both stimulating and re-warding and although much of the work was routine, with membership issues and the publication of a quarterly newsletter, my previous experience of research involving questionnaires enabled me to influence the association in becoming involved in promoting patient surveys that would scientifically analyse the views of kidney patients and carers with regard to their treatment and factors associated with such treatment, resulting in the association becoming a valuable source of patient-based informa-tion.

Between 1999 and 2002 I was commissioned to undertake nine such surveys involving a total of around 700 kidney patients and covering the conditions of pre-dialysis, peritoneal dialysis, hospital- and home-based haemodialysis, transplant and including the views of parents of children with kidney problems. The findings of these surveys proved invaluable in the association, presenting patient views at the board set up by the devolved National Assembly Government in Wales to look at the renal services in Wales and establish a National Service Framework or NSF in renal care.

After three years as honorary secretary I was persuaded by the outgoing chairman, Neil Harvey, to stand as chairman, and in October 2001 I was elected to that position at the annual general meeting. This position I held for three years, resigning after that period in accordance with the association's constitution. During these three years I was privileged to represent the association on the NSF Board for renal care, Health Commission Wales, and at various meetings of the National Institute for Clinical Excellence (NICE). In addition, I was instrumental in establishing the Cross-Party Kidney Group of the National Assembly Government for Wales that provided the association with a vital political link in its quest for better patient services.

Chapter Thirty-Six

The summer of 1998 saw Maria's lust for travelling return, and since her last visit to Argentina to see her sister and her family had been in 1978, just prior to our meeting, she viewed that a return visit twenty years later would be most appropriate. Although she had seen her sister Julieta twice since that time, she had not seen Julieta's three daughters who were now grown up, married and had families of their own. Maria was also aware that her sister had not seen her brother Frank since he was a baby, and decided that it would be a good idea if Frank and his wife joined us in Argentina by flying direct from Venezuela.

Following much research on my part into the best way of getting to Buenos Aires, we eventually decided on KLM as the carrier and on 9 October we caught the flight from Cardiff to Amsterdam and, following a two-hour wait, the direct flight to Buenos Aires, arriving there at ten o'clock the following morning, where we were met by Julieta and her three daughters, Alcira, Edwarda and Margarita, together with Frank and his wife Fernanda who had arrived the day previous.

During my four-week stay in Monte Grande, which lies half an hour's drive from Buenos Aires, I learnt a great deal about the country and its people. Argentina is a vast country with the population concentrated in and around its major cities, with travel between cities normally being by air. The total population is of the order of 32.5 million made up of several distinct ethnic groups – the major ones being Spanish, Italian, Portuguese, French, German, British and South American Indian. The official language is Spanish although others are practised within the various groups including Welsh, which is still spoken in the Patagonian region. Buenos Aires is situated on that part of the South Atlantic known as the River Plate. The provincial capital and seat of the National Government is, however, in the adjoining city of La Plata, as are the official offices of the republic's elected president.

During our stay we experienced the transport system first hand, the alternatives being electric rail, bus, taxi or private car. The rail cars are very similar to the London Tube trains but above ground, with vast numbers of people getting on and off at all the stops. They are also used extensively by street traders to sell their wares. Buenos Aires has a huge number of registered taxis, 3,000 being registered in that city alone. Modern German, French and Japanese cars are plentiful in the city centres, while out in the suburbs and in the poorer areas the cars are '60s and '70s American gas guzzlers, most being held together with bits of string and all with some external damage. Petrol is by European standards very cheap and although during the military rule the then currency, the astralis, was constantly being devalued, the new currency of the paso, which at the time was linked to the US dollar on a one-to-one basis, has provided the country with much more financial stability.

Buenos Aires is a handsome city and in the springtime, October/November, is a blaze of purple thanks to the blossom of the numerous jacaranda trees. It is also a city of monuments, such as the 210 foot obelisk in the main thoroughfare which was built in 1936 to celebrate the 400th anniversary of the founding of the city. The statues of Manuel Belgrano, the revered military hero and designer of the blue and white national flag, are also in evidence, together with that of General Pablo Richieri, who was responsible for introducing conscription to Argentina. This wasn't abolished until the rule of President Carlos Menem who was in charge during our visit. Taking a tour of Buenos Aires reveals a city with three distinct and very European regions, such divisions being according to the original residents and their ethnic origins. There is the French area with expensive shops and apartments and the Café Tortoni reminiscent of Paris. Then there is the Italian quarter, with its corrugated iron houses painted in a range of bright blues, yellows, reds and green. This was the quarter where the Tango was born and where the streets are full of artists and craftsmen exhibiting and selling their wares, and although initially Italian, this area now houses much of the poorer South American citizens – the Italians having moved on to more up-market accommodation. The British quarter was identified until 1997 by a replica of Harrods store, complete with green awnings and expensive clothes and jewellery. Now the British community is recognised by its love of polo, classic car clubs and golf.

During the tour the other features worthy of note were the building and its first-floor balcony in the Plaza Mayor where Eva Peron gave her now famous speech; the Recoleta cemetery where its famous citizens are buried and remembered by huge statues of angels and crosses, and where President Peron and Eva are buried in a vault reputed to be twenty-six feet underground.

Another interesting feature of Buenos Aires at that time was the regeneration of its docklands reminiscent of the developments at London and Cardiff and where the old warehouse accommodation has been transformed into luxury apartments and up-market town houses.

During the second week of our visit I was privileged to accompany Edwarda, who was a primary school teacher, to her place of work and to gain an insight into the workings of the education system in Argentina. Both primary and secondary schools are run on a two-shift system. Half the pupils attend school daily between 8 a.m. and 12.30 p.m., while the other half attend between 12.30 p.m. and 5 p.m. The relatively short day of four and a half hours is made up by much shorter holiday periods of two weeks' duration. This system allows maximum usage of school buildings, which are occupied for nine hours daily, while teaching staff are allocated shifts that suit their particular circumstances and the needs of the school.

I was advised that universities do not adopt this system but due to there being no State grants the numbers going on to higher education is very much lower than in the UK.

The following day we took the hour's train ride to the old port of Tegra which backs on to a large expanse of levies and small islands on which have been built some very expensive properties with the area known as the Venice of the South. River taxis were in plentiful supply and a tour of this development where most properties have a jetty and its own boat or cruiser is to be recommended.

Adjoining Buenos Aires and Tegra is the River Plate that essentially separates Argentina from Uruguay, and by taking the ferry we were able to visit that country and its capital Montevideo.

Uruguay is a country with a population of almost 4 million made up of around 2.4 million females and 1.5 million males. It is a poor country with its cities giving a strong reminder of its colonial and Portuguese past. Indeed, Maria was able to recall a distant relative who lived in Uruguay for most of his life. Following my visit, two features of the country will always remain in my memory: the high number of 1920s and '30s cars still running and for sale in car lots; and the old style, ranch-type properties which have been developed as tourist attractions, and where you can go for a trip in a genuine covered wagon drawn by a team of four horses across the most uneven terrain imaginable. Following a typical ranch-style meal of barbecued beef and beer, this experience left me unable to sit comfortably for quite a few days.

The fact that a Rotarian from the UK was visiting a family in Monte Grande had been drawn to the attention of the Rotary Club of Monte Grande and within a few days Maria and I were invited to visit the club for one of their evening meetings. The hospitality that was extended to us was tremendous and involved our being collected by car, wined and dined in a warm and friendly atmosphere and then returned home at around midnight. Maria and I struck up a friendship with an Italian and a Scottish member of the club and between her Italian and my English we ended up receiving a return invitation to dinner and when it was time for us to catch our flight back to the UK both these gentlemen saw us off at the airport.

A feature of home life in Argentina is the drinking of vast amounts of 'mate'. Boiling water is added to the dried, chopped leaves of a relative of the holly. It is served in a hollowed-out gourd often decorated with intricate silverwork and sucked through a silver straw. During our stay the main family event was a dinner to celebrate my birthday on 30 October and when we invited all fifteen family members to be our guests at a local restaurant. Table flowers were provided by Alcira and her husband, who ran their own garden centre called Las Camellias, while the birthday cake was provided by Maria's sister Julieta. It proved to be a wonderful occasion that I shall always remember.

Although we had initially planned to visit Patagonia to visit some Welsh families, the addresses of which had been given us by Lord Parry during his attendance at my installation dinner, flying there was a daunting prospect so it was left for another time, as would be the visit to the Devil's Throat Falls, which we were led to believe are truly gasp-worthy.

Soon it was time to leave and on 7 November we boarded KLM Flight 792 for Amsterdam, eventually arriving at Cardiff airport at five o'clock the following day.

The year ended with the usual family gatherings: Julia and Peter for a pre-Christmas dinner; our visit to Huncote to see David, Sandra and Carl; Boxing Day at Maria's sister Sandra; and New Year's Day with her sister Rita and husband Alfonso, while all the family gathered at Cranmer Court on the Sunday following Christmas.

Chapter Thirty-Seven

On the morning of New Year's Day I received a telephone call from a distraught Julia who told me that her mother had just died in her arms. Apparently Judith had been unwell for a few days following Christmas and had been visited by her doctor and by a locum who both diagnosed a viral infection and prescribed aspirin. Julia had gone around to see her that morning and soon after her arrival Judith collapsed and died. My first task was to telephone David and then reschedule the remainder of the day. David was equally devastated by the news and to my mind his mother's death precipitated the series of events that ended in the break-up of his family.

A week later, following a funeral service at Summers Funeral Home, a place where she had worked for several years, Judith was cremated at Thornhill Crematorium. I accompanied Julia and Peter and David and Sandra to the funeral while Maria, with her innate sense of what was right, looked after Carl.

On 24 May, which was Maria's birthday, my family suffered the second death of 1999. Rita's daughter Susana had met, fallen in love with and gone to live with Carlos, a dark-haired, stocky Portuguese man who was her second cousin. Carlos, like so many young men, had left Madeira when a teenager to live and work in Venezuela. He and his brother had later come to live with his sister in Cardiff and there he met Susana. Initially they lived in a rented bedsit but later Maria, who felt that her niece deserved better, went and bought a one-bedroom flat which she rented to them at the same rent as the bedsit. After two years in the flat they decided to start a family and proceeded to buy a small house in the Splott area of Cardiff. It was there that their son Daniel was born on 26 May 1997. A year later Carlos started to complain of pains in the lower abdomen and on visiting his doctor and being referred to hospital underwent an investigatory operation a week later. Inoperable cancer was discovered, and after several months of chemotherapy and radiotherapy treatment he died at the age of thirty-three, two days before his son's second birthday.

One of the outcomes of our visit to Argentina was that Frank and Fernanda invited Julieta, Maria and me to visit them in Macuto, on the occasion of their daughter's wedding, and soon after our return home I was again involved in researching flights, costs and medical clearance for Maria to travel. When her sister Rita heard of our intentions and of the imminent wedding she and her husband Alfonso decided to join us and arrangements for four travellers were put in place. On researching the way of life in Venezuela I discovered that one of the favourite holiday locations of the locals was the island of Margarita, which is around forty minutes' flying time from Caracas Airport. On contacting the time-share organisation RCI, I discovered that I could exchange the week of our time-share at Tenerife, and which I had banked the previous year, with a week at a highly recommended resort on Margarita. So a holiday schedule involving three weeks' stay with Frank and his family and a further week in Margarita was finalised and on 17 October 1999 we boarded the ten-hour KLM flight, firstly to Amsterdam, and then on to Caracas.

On arrival at Caracas Airport we discovered that without the barcode on our luggage matching the barcode on our tickets there was no way we could have left the airport. This system had been introduced to combat bogus travellers claiming and stealing luggage. We were welcomed by Frank, Fernanda and his cousin Alfredo and soon the two cars were heading for the coast and the township of Macuto.

The first thing that struck me on leaving the airport was the wild and chaotic traffic situation, with much use of the horn and a great deal of pollution. Most cars I discovered were Fords, Chryslers, Mitsubishis, Renaults and Toyotas, all of which are imported as parts and assembled in Venezuela. Imported cars include Hondas, BMWs, Hyundai's, Peugeots and Volkswagens. There was little doubt that the car and motorcycle were the most popular mode of transport, with petrol costing 0.15$ to 0.2$ per litre, (8p to 12p in pounds sterling). This is the cheapest petrol in the world, despite a price hike of around 500% in 1997.

As I was to discover later, there are no passenger trains in Venezuela. The country did have a railway network but when oil was discovered and the oil boom came, it was largely discarded in favour of road transport. There were very many buses on the road and these apparently ran day and night between the major population centres and were very cheap, costing around 505 bolivars for one hour's travel (at the time the exchange rate was 815 bolivars to the pound sterling). It would appear that there were many bus companies with vehicles ranging from the very old to the very modern air-conditioned coaches. There was, I noted, lots of music on all bus rides, the volume and type of this music being at the discretion of the driver.

Arriving at Macuto, where we were introduced to Frank's three daughters – Sandra, Erica and Andrina – we sat down to a traditional Portuguese meal washed down with red wine followed by coffee and a great deal of family talk.

The federal republic of Venezuela is South America's sixth largest country with an area of 916,445 square km and a population estimated at 22 million, of which a fifth live in the capital, Caracas. It apparently has the highest population growth rate in South America at around 2.1%, with half being under the age of eighteen years. It is a country of mixed races with 70% being a blend of European, Indian and African ancestry. The remainder are whites (21%) blacks (8%) and ethnic Indian (1%). This population is scattered in and around the cities of Caracas, Valencia and Maracay.

During the first few days of our stay we enjoyed sightseeing in and around Macuto, visiting Maria's cousin Cecilia and her family who lived in the adjoining township of La Guaira, and visiting the two restaurants owned and run jointly by Frank and his cousin Alberto. One was a typical restaurant and bar in the business part of town, while the other was on the seashore catering for the more wealthy clients and the tourist trade. Both businesses were apparently doing good trade and we enjoyed the hospitality that the partners extended to us. No visit to Venezuela would be complete without one to the capital, Caracas, established over 430 years ago around the 1540s. Caracas is a huge city with every modern convenience and every third world problem. It is located in a long, narrow valley separated from the sea by a strip of wooded high ground, and covers over 20 km east to west, the area being linked by a metro. A curiosity of Caracas I discovered was the street address system, where it is not the streets but the street corners that bear the names – a feature that takes some time to get used to. Located in the centre of the city is the Plaza Bolivar with a statue of Bolivar on horseback being the dominant feature. I discovered later that this equestrian statue had been cast in the iron works of Ebbw Vale in Wales, shipped over in sections and assembled in Caracas ready for its unveiling in 1974.

Also in the Plaza is Caracas Cathedral, built between 1665 and 1713 to replace the original building destroyed by an earthquake in 1641. Next to the cathedral is found a beautiful restored colonial house which is open to the public as a reminder of the country's colonial past.

Caracas also houses the Presidential Palace, the home of the president who is elected by direct vote for a five-year term but cannot be re-elected for consecutive terms. The president has extensive powers, in that he appoints the Cabinet, the Commander-in-Chief of the armed forces and members of the Supreme Court. Based on the American model of government, Venezuela is governed by Congress made up of two houses – the 50-seat Senate and the 204-seat Chamber of Deputies. Elections to Congress are held at the same time as those for the president and members are elected for five years. Voting is compulsory for all persons over the age of eighteen years. Administratively, the country is divided into twenty-two states and the federal district of Caracas.

There was little doubt that Caracas was a dangerous city with a high incidence of muggings and theft. Gangs work the central districts during daylight hours, the usual weapon being a knife or gun. The method used is that you are stopped on the street by a man or a group of men, a knife or gun is shown to be better understood and either money and/or valuables are asked for or taken. This practice we experienced first hand, although it happened so quickly that hardly any of us knew that Alfredo, who was leading our party, had been robbed of his gold necklace and medallion. His account of the incident was that two men approached him; one dug a gun into his ribs while the other snatched the gold chain – the whole incident being over in seconds. He had not tried to stop them, escape or struggle since a passive approach is recognised as the best, since there is never any help from passers-by, while the police are known for their abuse of power, use of undue authority and corruption and should be avoided when possible.

We were all shocked by this incident and I quickly removed my grandfather's ruby ring from my finger and secreted it in my handkerchief for safe keeping. That night on retiring I slipped the ring back on my finger and had a most horrific dream of death and destruction.

Frank's house in Macuto was on a steep hillside with the road winding upwards towards the tree-covered mountainside that towered over the township. During one of my walks up the hill I came across the closed but still guarded terminal of the teleferico – a cable car system built in 1956 by a German company during the dictatorship of President Marcos Perez. This system, which was closed in 1988, consisted of two lines starting in Caracas then climbing 4 km and 2150 metres above sea level to El Avila and the 14-storey Hotel Humboldt before dropping down a further 7.5 km to Macuto. The hotel, which closed soon after the cable car stopped running, is now a striking landmark overlooking Caracas.

In talking to an English-speaking teacher, I was able to ascertain that the education system in Venezuela is based on six years' compulsory primary education for children aged seven to thirteen years. This is followed by a State-run, free but optional four-year secondary programme for thirteen- to seventeen-year-old children. For those wishing to enter university there follows a compulsory one-year university preparatory course. There are thirty-one universities in Venezuela. Some are State-run while others are sponsored or privately run. All universities involve students paying for their tuition.

The highlight of our visit was undoubtedly the wedding of Frank's oldest daughter Sandra, and after a whole morning and the best part of the afternoon spent in preparation, we gathered at the local Roman Catholic Church for the ceremony. There then followed an extensive photographic session and it was early evening before we were herded onto minibuses to be taken to the reception at a hotel on the outskirts of Macuto. With tables arranged around a large, open-air swimming pool it was the ideal setting on a warm evening and with live music, a hot buffet and a plentiful supply of Champagne we, and sixty other guests, partied until the early hours.

Soon our three-week stay was over and we returned to Caracas Airport for our 40-minute flight to Margarita. The island of Margarita is Venezuela's largest island with an area of around 950 square km. It is shaped like an hourglass with an eastern part which is the most populated; containing 95% of the island's total of 330,000, while the western part, which is very arid, is sparsely populated.

The island's capital is Porlamar, which also gives its name to the one airport. Porlamar has a population of 200,000, has a wide range of facilities and a good supply of comfortable hotels including a Hilton. Most of the hotels and holiday resorts are on the outskirts of the capital where there are plenty of sandy beaches and a warm sea.

The airport taxi took Rita, Alfonso, Maria and me on the half-hour journey to the Playa El Agua Resort. This resort, composed of a mix of apartments and small villas, with a restaurant, three outdoor swimming pools and a private beach about a mile long, was, like the majority of other resorts on the island, surrounded by 8-foot-high wire fencing with security guards at all the entrances. On arrival we were tagged with a plastic wristband without which re-entry to the resort would not be possible. Upon checking in we discovered that the RCI exchange had provided us with an air-conditioned penthouse suite with lounge, dining area, kitchen, four bedrooms with en-suite bathrooms, and a private roof garden complete with jacuzzi. This was way above my expectations but contributed greatly to the enjoyment of our stay.

During the following days we breakfasted and enjoyed the evening meal in the resort restaurant, having midday snacks in the apartment or on the beach. We hired a taxi to visit Porlamar while on another occasion we hired a taxi for a tour of the island. Margarita is a duty-free island with wine, spirits and gold being considerably cheaper than on the mainland.

We were scheduled to leave Margarita at 2 p.m. to connect with a 5 p.m. flight from Caracas to Amsterdam. As we were about to discover, the local airline operated a system whereby if there were only a few passengers booked on a particular flight that flight was cancelled with passengers placed on the next available flight. Consequently we left Margarita at 4 p.m. and only a call from the flight's captain to the KLM desk at Caracas requesting that our flight be delayed prevented us from losing the flight home.

We arrived in Cardiff on 4 December. Exactly one week later we received the news of the third family tragedy of 1999. Following three days of heavy rain and as a consequence of deforestation, a massive mud slide had occurred in the area of La Guaira with thousands of people dead or missing. The army had been brought in; Caracas Airport had been closed dealing with emergency flights only, while the whole area of La Guaira and Macuto were under 24-hour curfew. Among the families reported missing, believed dead, was Maria's cousin Cecilia, her husband, daughter and granddaughter – a family that we had visited and enjoyed the company of only a few weeks previously.

Chapter Thirty-Eight

As the new century dawned and we were involved in several celebrations connected with Rotary International and the Rotary Club of Llandaff, Maria's health took a turn for the worse and she began to complain of chest pains and a shortness of breath. On 7 January these pains got worse and on her doctor's advice she was admitted to hospital with a suspected heart attack. This proved to be a false alarm and she was discharged on 13 January with a referral to a consultant cardiologist. The transplant clinic that she visited on a regular basis immediately fast tracked this referral and within weeks she saw a cardiologist, who after clinical tests involving an echogram and an angiogram, diagnosed poor circulation in the cardiac arteries and a faulty aortic valve. This condition was, in the short-term, treated with a beta blocker and a Nitrolingual Pump Spray to ease any angina attacks. This condition, as Maria's consultant Dr Robert Penny explained, was progressive and would at some stage require surgery. So once again our lifestyle had to change, with Maria glad that she had travelled so much and seen so many members of her family since her kidney transplant, and looking forward to life beyond heart surgery.

In keeping with many other Rotary Clubs, the Llandaff Club decided to commemorate the new millennium and the writing of the club's history was prompted by a letter from a founder member, Tony Creighton Griffiths, to past president John Lewis, relating to the suggestion made by the ad hoc millennium sub-committee in June of 1998. This letter proposed that a commemorative booklet outlining the history of the club be produced and published. I was invited to undertake this work, an invitation that I readily accepted, little realising the amount of work and research involved.

As with any historical account, the introduction must include the origins of the organisation involved and its objectives and

Rotary International is no exception. Conceived and founded in Chicago in 1905 by a lawyer of that town named Paul Percival Harris, he, together with three friends – Silvester Schiele, Hiram Shorey and Gus Loehor – founded Rotary International and the very first rotary club. Initially the club was known as the Booster Club, but since the meetings were arranged in rotation at each other's offices or places of business, Paul Harris's suggestion of 'Rotary' was found to be a more suitable and acceptable title. Defined as a world fellowship of business and professional men and women united in the ideal of service, Rotary was a means by which such men and women could meet together on a weekly basis for the purpose of fellowship and service to others in a non-political and non-sectarian way.

The Chicago Club decided on an emblem, and one of the members, an engraver with the word 'Rotary' in mind, drew a simple wagon wheel with thirteen spokes. His fellow club members liked it and this emblem was adopted and appeared on the club's stationery until it was modified to a gear wheel in 1912 and in 1919 as a 6-spoke cogged wheel with twenty-four cogs and a keyway – a design which has remained unchanged to this day.

From these modest beginnings Rotary has expanded and at the time of my writing the history had 29,268 clubs in 162 countries and a total membership of around 1.2 million.

Upon researching the Llandaff Club I discovered that its inaugural meeting was held on 24 March 1964 at the Park Hotel in Cardiff, with an initial membership of twenty-six. At that meeting a president and other officers were elected and the club became a reality. Although a detailed account of my findings over the next thirty-six years of the club's existence would not be appropriate at this time, sufficient to say that recalling the club's growth, successes and failures in serving others gave me a great deal of pleasure, and probably gave me the inspiration to tackle a much larger but similar project a few years later. The monograph was published in September 2000 with copies distributed to all club members, past and present, and with sufficient copies remaining for all new members of the club to be presented with a copy at their induction.

In May of 2000 we were invited to Valencia again, this time to celebrate the first communion of Manuel. As always, we enjoyed the 21-day visit, meeting friends of Maria's sister, visiting now familiar places and of course the celebrations that went with the first communion. Maria's birthday on 24th also marked her sixty years of age and a party organised by her sister Regina at a nearby restaurant. Upon our return we discovered that our neighbour and now dear friend Denis Collins, who was now in his ninety-third year, had slipped and fallen while getting out of the bath and was at the University of Wales Hospital with a compressed fracture of the lower spine. Our other neighbour, Don News, was also unwell and following a brief illness died of pancreatic cancer, leaving his wife Elsie, who was in the early stages of dementia to enter a care home.

Following six weeks in hospital it was necessary for Denis to be found a suitable residential rare home since his wife Eunice, who was herself severely disabled, could not look after him. Eunice, Maria and I then spent several weeks touring the care homes of Cardiff until eventually finding a suitable place at St Winifred's Nursing Home in Romley Road. With his own room and some of his own items of furniture, Denis soon adapted to residential home life, much to the relief of Eunice and his widowed sister-in-law Dorothy. From there on my weekly routine included driving Eunice to St Winifred's to visit Denis.

During August David rang to let me know that he had split up with Sandra and was living with his new girlfriend, Melissa, in Markfield – a small town north of Leicester. Maria and I decided that a visit was in order. Melissa turned out to be a pleasant girl eight years younger than David with auburn hair and blue eyes. She had recently divorced her husband and was working as a unit receptionist at the cardiology unit at the Leicester General Hospital. She had met David when he was attending the hospital following an arm injury while on duty in the fire service and they had apparently been seeing each other for quite some time. In discussing the situation with David, I discovered that ever since Sandra's mother had died, she had become depressed and had taken to excessive drinking, especially when at home alone in the evenings. For the sake of Carl, who he loved dearly, he had left the house at Huncote for them to live in and in order that Carl could continue his attendance at the same school, while a monthly contribution for his upkeep eased his conscientious approach to life. I did, however, sense that not seeing Carl was not contributing to his new-found happiness.

Ever since she left Madeira in 1966 Maria had always kept in touch with the friends that she had grown up with or worked with and one such long-term friend was Gertrude Laricchiuta. When Maria came to Cardiff, Gertrude left Madeira for Brazil where she met and married an Italian, Manuel Laricchiuta. They had one son, Pasquale, and eventually the family returned to Italy to live on the Castellaneta Marina near Taranto. Having kept in touch since 1966 it was inevitable that they wanted to meet again and an invitation from Gertrude for us to visit Taranto was an opportunity that could not be missed.

On 16 September we boarded the Heathrow to Rome flight and then the Rome to Bari connection. Bari is a city on the eastern seaboard of the heel of Italy, and was a famous naval base during the Second World War. We were met at the airport by Gertrude and her son Pasquale and soon we were heading west across the heel to Taranto, Puglia and the Castellaneta Marina with its many beaches and holiday homes of wealthy Italians.

Gertrude, Manuel and Pasquale farmed two large vineyards covering many hectares which grew the largest black grapes that I had ever seen. Although the major part of the crop was sold on the vine as eating grapes, with the buyer responsible for the picking and crating, a small part of the vineyard was used to grow wine-making grapes with an annual output of around 2,000 litres. It being September, the grapes were rapidly ripening under the warm Italian sun and no meal was complete without a platter of grapes and cheese. Although most of the holidaymakers had returned home leaving their holiday homes shuttered for the winter, the weather and sea were warm and with the kilometre-long sandy beach that stretched from Taranto to Metaponto almost empty, all the ingredients for a relaxing holiday were in place.

We were taken on various visits by Pasquale since he was determined that his mother's best friend should see as much of his homeland as was possible. A visit to the ancient town of Matera, now being renovated with EEC monies, was one such visit, while ancient monasteries and convents gave another glimpse into the past. Castellaneta is itself a small town famous as the birthplace of Rudolph Valentino, the Italian immigrant who became a world-known actor, and to celebrate the myth of its famous citizen Castellaneta houses a museum in his honour. Soon it was time to return to the UK and on 27 September we boarded the return flight to London Heathrow.

October 2000 was a sad month for me. One evening, shortly after our return home, we received a telephone call from Eunice saying that she felt unwell and would we come and see her. Although she was in her favourite chair having had her usual gin and water, she looked unwell and I decided that a 999 call for an ambulance was the most appropriate course of action. I accompanied her to the A&E unit at the University Hospital, and after a rapid and thorough examination she was diagnosed as having a severe chest infection, which at the age of eighty-nine required immediate treatment and admittance to hospital. The following day when I and her sister Dorothy visited her she was feeling much better and was looking forward to getting home. At around midnight I had a call from the hospital informing me that Eunice had taken a turn for the worse and that either her sister or me should come to see her. I telephoned Dorothy but before we could decide a plan of action, a further call from the hospital confirmed my worse fears – Eunice had died, and Maria and I had lost a very dear friend. I was asked if I would go and tell Denis the sad news and although this was a task that I did not relish, it had to be done. In typical army fashion Denis received the news and although deeply saddened, recorded how glad he was that he and Eunice had spent over sixty years together. Their daughter Gaydon requested that I give the eulogy at the funeral, an invitation I was proud to accept, and in concluding felt that the poem 'Togetherness' by an anonymous poet would be appropriate.

> You can shed tears that she is gone
> or you can smile because she has lived.

You can close your eyes and pray that she'll come back
or you can open your eyes and see all she's left.

Your heart can be empty because you can't see her
or you can be full of the love you shared.

You can turn your back on tomorrow and live yesterday
or you can be happy for tomorrow because of yesterday.

You can remember her and only that she's gone
or you can cherish her memory and let it live on.

You can cry and close your mind, be empty and turn
your back
or you can do what she'd want: smile, open your eyes
love and go on.

When I had finished I noted that Denis, who had attended the
funeral in a wheelchair, had tears in his eyes. Eunice's death and
her daughter's return to work in Dorset resulted in my visiting
Denis twice weekly and dealing with matters previously undertaken by Eunice. These visits were much appreciated by both
Denis and his sister-in-law and I believe went a long way towards
his getting over his loss.

The other consequence of Eunice's death took everybody by
surprise, least of all Denis and Gaydon. It would appear that
Eunice had many years previously invested money in stocks and
shares in a range of companies and then forgotten about them,
and it was only following her death and a detailed investigation by
her solicitor, June Williams of Edwards Geldard, that it became
clear that she was a very wealthy woman, leaving a will amounting
to over £1,000,000. This money, together with the apartment at
Cranmer Court, which was in her name and was to be available to
Denis as long as he required it, was to be divided equally between
Denis and Gaydon and overnight Denis became a rich man. It
was at this point that Denis sought my advice on how he should
invest the half million he had inherited, and although June
Williams had suggested a colleague who was experienced in

money management he rejected this proposal in favour of my suggestion that he sought guidance from Lloyds TSB – a bank that he had used all his life. Since Julia had been working at Lloyds TSB ever since she left college, I sought her advice and soon the private banking service of Lloyds TSB in the form of its area manager visited Denis at St Winifred's, accompanied by Julia and myself. I shall always remember that occasion since Denis had insisted that he wore his best suit that had to be brought from Cranmer Court and that the meeting should take place in the matron's office at St Winifred's, since he considered his bedroom as inappropriate. He turned up in his wheelchair looking every inch an ex-army gentleman, and conducted his business in a way that surprised us all.

Three weeks later Maria and I boarded a morning flight from London Gatwick to Funchal having stayed the previous night at the Gatwick Meriden hotel. This visit coincided with our friends David and Pamela from Malvern being in Madeira, and while we were at a time-share apartment at the Alto Lido, they were staying at a hotel in the centre of Funchal. My hiring a car for the duration of our stay meant that we toured the island once again and visited Maria's family in Arco da Calheta. Pamela and David left Madeira on 20 November and although we were scheduled to leave on 29, bad weather and strong winds at Santa Cruz Airport resulted in our not leaving until 2 December. Although our extended stay was made very comfortable by British Airways with overnight stays at two of Funchal's five-star hotels – the Crown Plaza and the Madeira Palacio – Maria's supply of anti-rejection medication ran out and it was necessary to obtain a further supply from the local pharmacy. This proved relatively easy but very expensive and brought home to us how crucial these drugs are to any person who has received a transplant.

Just before Christmas Maria's heart problem resurfaced and she was again forced to enter hospital for two days in order to stabilise the situation. Leaving hospital two days before Christmas was a bonus and she and all the family enjoyed the first Christmas of the new millennium.

Chapter Thirty-Nine

Towards the end of January 2001 we visited David and Melissa in Markfield. Having chosen not to have an operation on his injured arm David had accepted early retirement from the Fire Service and was now undertaking casual work. Being versatile and using the expertise gained during his nine years in the Royal Air Force, he found this approach to working both interesting and rewarding. This kind of work also gave him the opportunity of perusing his favourite hobby of freshwater fishing, which he practised to competition standard, and reminded me of my grandfather and Uncle Robert, who were both keen fishermen.

In April of that year we spent the first of two short holidays in Torquay, staying at the Corbin Head Hotel overlooking the bay. The logic behind this new venture on our part was to have a change from home in a setting that did not involve excessive travel, since Maria was getting more dependent on her Nitrolingual Pump Spray in relieving her chest pains and we wanted to be within easy reach of medical attention should this prove necessary.

May saw my annual visit to Nevern to tend and place flowers on the family graves. These visits I had made ever since the family left Nevern in 1956, and stepping out of the car and walking through the church gates, past the famous bleeding yew and into the Norman-built St Brynnach Church, was a walk into the past. The font where I was baptised; the family pew where my mother, father and aunt sat almost every Sunday; the front pew where I was confirmed by the Archbishop of Wales; the gold lectern where the Reverend J D Roberts read the lessons; and the Celtic writing scratched on the stone sills below the arched windows of the side chapel all brought back memories of past yesterdays. Walking through the churchyard to the family graves I always sensed that one could feel the silence, broken only by the occasional cawing of rooks high in the trees above the church.

Our second visit to Torquay over the August Bank Holiday weekend was again enjoyable and we visited some old friends who lived down the coast at Paignton and who were friends of Ernest and Jean Brent. On our return to Cardiff, visiting Denis and my ongoing work for the Welsh Kidney Patients' Association kept me fully occupied until 25 October when once again we were found boarding an Air Portugal flight from London Heathrow to Madeira. On this occasion we were accompanied by Julia and Peter, since we had told them so much about Madeira that they felt they must see it for themselves. Staying in a two-bedroom apartment at the Alto Lido Hotel and with an Avis hired car, we were able during the two weeks we were there, to give them a fairly comprehensive tour of the island and take them to visit members of Maria's family and friends.

On our return, I visited Denis to find him in good spirits, although he had missed my visits and in my absence had run low on his supply of whisky, which I normally bought for him and which he kept in his wardrobe. His back continued to give him the occasional twinge when he moved around but it did not appear to give him undue problems. Early in December, Gaydon visited her father and called in at 3 Cranmer Court to see me with a very unusual request, namely, would I identify her father should anything happen to him? I assured her that this was unlikely in the short-term but agreed to her request, although finding it rather strange. At my next visit to see Denis, he was not his usual self and appeared agitated and his eyes had a glazed look about them. This prompted a further visit on the following morning, 17 December, when I found him confined to bed and when he hardly recognised me. As I was leaving I noted a hypodermic needle on his bedside table and requested a chat with Mrs Evans, the matron at St Winifred's. I discussed the obvious change in Denis and asked what the hypodermic was for. Mrs Evans, who appeared somewhat ill at ease, told me that following a visit by Gaydon and Dr Glasgow, a local GP, Denis had been prescribed morphine to ease the back pain that he complained of, and which up until that time had been treated with paracetamol. Mindful of the possible side-effects of morphine on kidney and liver function, especially on a ninety-four-year-old, I was horrified at this news. On returning to Denis's bedroom I enquired of the duty nursing sister what were her views of this treatment and like me she expressed some concerns at the use of morphine for what until now had been a long-term condition.

Within an hour of my returning home and recording my concerns to Maria, I had a telephone call from St Winifred's telling me that Denis had died. Although I was not approached in terms of identifying the body, the request that Gaydon had made earlier kept going around and around in my head, and I could but wonder if she had known that the treatment prescribed would kill her father. With an approaching Christmas there was a long delay before the cremation could take place, and it was not until 9 January that we could say our farewells to a dear man and good friend.

Once again I was requested to give the eulogy, which I felt privileged to do as the last task for a dear friend. On this occasion I chose Henry Scott Holland's poem which reads:

> Death is nothing at all;
> I have only slipped away into the next room.
> I am I and you are you.
> Whatever we were to each other that we are still.

> Call me by my old familiar name,
> Speak to me in the easy way you always used.
> Put no difference in your tone;
> Wear no forced solemnity or sorrow.

> Laugh as we always laughed at the little jokes we enjoyed together.
> Pray, smile, think of me, pray for me.
> Let my name be ever the household word it always was.
> Let it be spoken without effort,
> Without the ghost of a shadow on it.

> Life means all that it ever meant;
> It is the same as it ever was.
> Let it be so.

There is absolute unbroken continuity.
Why should I be out of mind because I am out of sight?
I am waiting for you for an interval,
Somewhere very near, just around the corner...

All is well, nothing is past, and nothing is lost.
One brief moment and all will be as before,
Only better, infinitely happier and for ever.
We will all be one together.

A few weeks later I received a telephone call from June Williams, the Collins's solicitor, to tell me that following Eunice's death Denis had made a new will in which he had left me £1,000 and the solid gold Half-Hunter dress watch that had been presented to his father, Sir George Collins, upon his retirement in 1929 as chairman and chief commoner of the City Lands Committee of the City of London. Knowing how much Denis valued links with the past and the position and status of his father in the City of London, the fact that he had given me this treasured possession touched me greatly, and although I rarely use the watch it is now one of my most treasured possessions.

The gold chain that came with the watch I gave to Maria, together with a matching hand-made Celtic cross of Welsh gold from the Clogae Mine in north Wales that I bought with part of the money left me, and in that way we both had something to remember our dear friends – Eunice and Denis Collins.

April saw Maria have her first consultation with her consultant cardiac surgeon Mr Peter O'Keefe. Mr O'Keefe was a tall, well-built man in his early forties with a smiling face and twinkling blue eyes, features that Maria instantly took to, and which appeared to generate an inner confidence in her, facing what was to be a major and potentially dangerous operation.

The pre-operation investigations resulted in further echo-grams and an angiogram being taken, with the latter causing considerable bruising at the point of entry of the catheter. Eventually it was decided that Maria required a triple bypass and the replacement of the Aortic valve, which had probably been faulty ever since Maria had rheumatic fever when she was nine years of age. The next decision to be taken was as to the type of valve best suited for Maria, with her being a kidney transplant patient. Two types of Aortic valves are available; the biological type that comes from specially bred pigs and the man-made mechanical valve. There are advantages and disadvantages with both types. In the case of the mechanical valve this has the advantage of never requiring replacement but the recipient must be on a controlled dosage of Warfarin for life. The biological valve, however, does not require the Warfarin treatment after an initial post-operative period of three months, but has a lifespan of around twelve to fourteen years and then requires replacement.

After consulting her transplant consultant and talking to some friends who had experience of the mechanical valve, we decided that the biological type was the most suitable in her case, since it avoided the strict regime of Warfarin therapy, and the possible noise factor that accompanies the mechanical valve. And so the scene was set for another operation that hopefully would see Maria restored to her old active self.

On the first Saturday in October at the annual general meeting of the Welsh Kidney Patients' Association held at the Seabank Hotel, Porthcawl, I was elected chairman of the association after completing three years as hon. secretary. This I considered an honour and a means of giving back to the service something in return for Maria's kidney transplant and resulting new life. Being chairman representing around 1,200 kidney patients in South and Mid-Wales involved being their representative on many other organisations involved with renal care. These included the recently established the National Assembly for Wales All Party Kidney Group involving politicians from all four parties of the Assembly; the National Institute for Clinical Excellence when it was conducting appraisals of home versus hospital haemodialysis and immunosuppressive therapy for renal transplantation; Specialised Health Commission for Wales; the Board of the National Service Framework for tackling kidney disease in the people of Wales; the National Kidney Federation Conference, and the Cardiff and Vale NHS Trust in its preparation of a business case for a new transplant unit at the University Hospital.

Other activities included establishing a parent group willing and able to help with the monitoring of paediatric nephrology at the University Hospital, and establishing a befriending service available to people with kidney disease, their families and carers living in South and Mid-Wales. This service, established in association with the renal unit at the University Hospital and later at Morriston Hospital in Swansea, proved to be very popular and although I am no longer on the executive of the association I have continued as a member of the befriending service, visiting pre-dialysis clinics at regular intervals to explain to those patients on the point of going on to some form of dialysis, what my experiences as a carer were, and that going on to dialysis is only the beginning, leading on, as in Maria's case, to a transplant and a new life.

During my three years as chairman, which I found most enjoyable and rewarding, the most difficult aspect of the work was chairing management committee meetings, and although I had chaired numerous other committees during my professional life all their membership had been of persons well versed in committee procedures and responsibilities. Not so the association's management committee, which consisted of kidney patients and carers all with very, limited knowledge of how a professional organisation should run. In some ways this was understandable since the association had started life as a group of patients and carers meeting to discuss personal issues, and it was not until it became a registered charity with a written constitution and with honorary officers and members of the management committee being elected annually as trustees of the charity directly responsible to the Charity Commission for its annual accounts, did the need for a professional approach become essential.

I was extremely fortunate in that a few months before taking over the chair a transplant patient who had, prior to taking early retirement, been the chief accountant for British Steel, volunteered to become the association's hon. treasurer following the death of the previous holder of the post. Tony Ford was an excellent treasurer and he and I soon established a good working relationship. We were both professional in our outlook and in order to ensure that the association's accounts could be audited professionally, submitted to the annual general meeting and published in the quarterly newsletter, several past practices and some sacred cows had to be sacrificed. Some members of the management committee found difficultly in understanding and accepting this need for change, and although well meaning, this lack of understanding of what were after all only the adoption of professional standards, frequently caused friction at meetings.

Another source of friction was in relation to the format and content of the association's newsletter – *Kidney News*. Having appointed a young transplant recipient, Rachel Jones, to act as editor shortly after becoming chairman, I was forced, following the publication of the second issue, which was subjected to massive criticism at a management committee meeting, to suggest to Rachel that she should modify her content and presentation. As luck would have it a few days before I was able to acquaint her with the views of some committee members, Rachel announced that she had accepted a more demanding full-time job and did not have the time to continue as editor. Following a nil response to an advertisement for a new editor, I was forced to take over editorial responsibility myself, and since I now had a fair knowledge of the ongoing work of the association while the other source of information was from the patients themselves through letters to the editor, there was no lack of material for publication. This task I greatly enjoyed, and I was able, as the months went by, to bring *Kidney News* up to professional standards in both content and presentation. The ultimate accolade came when it was decided that the findings of the board established by the National Assembly Government in Wales to look at the renal services in Wales and establish a National Service Framework would be published in the November 2003 edition accompanied by a request for the views of patients, carers and relatives.

On 11 October 2002 Maria entered University Hospital for her heart operation, performed by Peter O'Keefe and his team. It was the longest day of my life, a day that I spent working in the Welsh Kidney Patients Office at the University Hospital, and where Peter O'Keefe would contact me as soon as the operation was over. At around 4.30 p.m. the call came through. The operation had been completely successful and Maria was in the recovery room before being transferred to intensive care.

An additional dimension to Maria's operation and post-operative stage was the care of her donor kidney, and here the medical staff of the renal unit worked in close lesion with the cardiology team in ensuring that kidney function remained stable. Maria came out of intensive care five days later and was discharged from hospital on 22 October in time for my seventieth birthday. As predicted by Peter O'Keefe the operation was 100% successful and Maria could look forward to another life, free of cardiac problems.

Chapter Forty

Although the first half of 2003 was relatively quiet with Maria slowly regaining her strength and vitality following what had been major open-heart surgery, the second half was the exact opposite, with several memorable events.

The first of these was the celebration of the National Kidney Federation's twenty-fifth anniversary held on the terrace of the House of Commons on the evening of 2 July. Like the Welsh Kidney Patients' Association, the federation is a patient-run registered charity dedicated to promoting the care of kidney patients both young and old throughout England and Scotland. Having travelled in the Daimler from Cardiff that morning and booked into a hotel, we hired a taxi to take us to the House of Commons. This trip reminded us both of our previous visits to London – firstly to the House of Commons as guests of the then member of Parliament for Brecon and Radnor, Richard Livsey; and later to the garden party at Buckingham Palace, when Maria was still on dialysis. As we made our way through the seventy or so guests gathered on the terrace overlooking the Thames, Maria and I were warmly welcomed by Gordon Nichols, chairman of the National Kidney Federation and introduced to many of the dignitaries present, including the Health Minister, who later in a brief statement of welcome pledged her support for the work of the federation and all those patient-led organisations involved in the care of patients with kidney disease. After several glasses of wine and an excellent cold buffet we returned to our hotel happy in the knowledge that the Welsh Kidney Patients' Association was a recognised force in promoting the welfare of patients.

A few weeks later saw us attending the wedding of Sian Jones, daughter of our dear friends Barbara and Cliff Jones, at Brecon Cathedral, with the reception held in a marquee on the lawns of their home at Battle – a small hamlet outside Brecon. One of the highlights of the occasion for me, as an avid classic car enthusiast, was that the bride was driven by her father to the cathedral in the groom's beautiful 1976 red E Type Jaguar, while she was driven back to the reception by her new husband in the same car. The fact that the Daimler was parked next to two new Ferraris – one belonging to the groom and one to the best man – was an added bonus to a most enjoyable occasion.

A week later, accompanied by our friends David and Pamela, we set out in the Daimler for a short tour of North Wales and a visit to the Spanish-style village of Portmeirion. This unique coastal development, the brainchild of architect Clough Williams Ellis, was designed and built around 1925 and replicates the villages on the Spanish coast that Clough frequented and which, seventy-five years later, still provides that magical atmosphere made famous when it became the venue for the 1960s TV production of *The Prisoner*, where Patrick McGoohan played the leading role in the series that now has a cult following. Today the village that nestles below wooded hillsides with its Castell Deudraeth (Castle on the Beach), white-painted Portmeirion Hotel nestling on the waterfront and lighthouse perched high on the hilltop is a major tourist attraction specialising in Portmeirion china and pottery.

September saw us attending the National Kidney Federation Annual Conference in Blackpool. Again the Daimler was put to good use, and our three-day stay at the Hilton Hotel was an opportunity to meet again many of those that we had met at the twenty-fifth anniversary celebrations.

Ever since Maria's operation, her sisters in Argentina, Spain and Madeira had been anxious about her health and were looking forward to seeing her again. With these concerns in mind I arranged a two-week holiday in Valencia with her sister Regina. There were two reasons why we chose Spain as our first venture abroad since the operation. Firstly there was the excellent health service available in Spain and Valencia in particular; and secondly I knew that Regina would ensure that Maria would be well looked after while in her home, which was very convenient for shopping, walks and entertainment. On 18 October we flew out, returning two weeks later having experienced a wonderfully relaxing holiday with Maria waited on hand and foot and me having an opportunity of reading half a dozen novels.

Since we had ruled out Maria travelling to Argentina, the only solution was to bring her sister Julieta to Cardiff, so without telling the rest of the family in Cardiff, I proceeded to organise flight tickets for Julieta and her granddaughter Karina, who had just celebrated her sixteenth birthday, to visit us for four weeks covering the Christmas period. Having arranged for them to collect their flight tickets from the Air Italia desk at Buenos Aires Airport, Maria and I drove to London Heathrow to meet them on 6 December. Karina, who we had last seen as a young girl of eleven, had grown into a striking young lady who was experiencing all the problems of a teenager experiencing her very first boyfriend, while Julieta as always was delighted at seeing Maria once more and talked incessantly as the Daimler whisked us westward along the M4 to Cardiff.

The following Sunday we had arranged for all members of the family to be at Cranmer Court for what we had termed a pre-Christmas lunch, and it was only after all ten members had arrived and had been served their first drink of the afternoon that Julieta and Karina made an entrance from the bedroom where they had been hiding. Needless to add that the celebrations went on throughout the afternoon and late into the evening, since one characteristic of the Leca family that I had long recognised was its ability to party and enjoy.

The following weeks saw Julieta and her granddaughter being taken to numerous family gatherings at her other sisters' houses, and as my guests at the Probus Club Christmas Luncheon. Cardiff has several such clubs, including the Probus Club of Cardiff Castle which I joined following my term as president of the Rotary Club of Llandaff. The Probus Movement is an established nation wide movement whose membership is restricted to retired professional and businessmen, many of whom were or are Rotarians, and whose aims is to promote and enjoy fellowship in retirement. Clubs hold morning meetings at monthly intervals addressed by guest speakers, while during the summer months various visits are arranged for members and wives to places of interest. An annual general meeting selects club officers for the ensuing year while Christmas is celebrated by a luncheon at a golf club or restaurant.

It was to the Probus Christmas luncheon held at the Llanishen Golf Club that Maria and I took our visitors from Argentina – an occasion that they and we will long remember for the welcome and hospitality and pleasure extended to us all. On Christmas Day we visited Julia and Peter for late-morning drinks and then on to Maria's sister Sandra's for lunch where twelve family members were present, and where the festivities continued until late.

It was obvious that the experience of four weeks in the UK and talking to her Cardiff cousins had a profound effect on Karina, and although initially she was telephoning and constantly talking about her boyfriend in Argentina, as the weeks went by the calls became fewer and fewer, so much so that it was not surprising when we learnt that on her return home she had decided that her priorities had changed and that she now wanted to continue her full-time education, go on to university and travel the world, and that boyfriends were not part of the plan.

On 5 January 2004 Maria and I said our goodbyes as Julieta and Karina boarded their flight back to Argentina.

Now that Maria had regained her health, although suffering from arthritis, it was time once again to venture abroad. In April we visited Valencia on what had now become an annual visit and where we celebrated Maria's sixty-fourth birthday. In June the Rotary Club of Llandaff celebrated its fortieth anniversary, with a dinner at the Masonic Hall in the centre of Cardiff when the Lord Lieutenant of the County, Captain Norman Lloyd Edwards, was the speaker and guest of honour.

October 2004 saw my three years as chairman of the Welsh Kidney Patients' Association come to an end, and on Saturday, 16 October at the annual general meeting held at the Seabank Hotel, Porthcawl, I handed over to the long-serving vice chairman John Reever. Since I felt a clean break was called for, I did not seek election as a member of the management committee and trustee of the charity, but in order to continue helping kidney patients directly I had decided to continue as a member of the befriending service team. At a conservative estimate, this involvement over the last two years has seen me addressing around sixty patients attending pre-dialysis clinics, when by outlining my experiences as a carer, firstly to a patient on peritoneal dialysis and then to one who was fortunate enough to have a new kidney, I hope I have been able to convey to them that kidney failure does not mean the end of a normal life and that there are prospects of a new life beyond dialysis.

On the Monday following the AGM we caught an Air Portugal flight to Madeira, staying at a time-share apartment in Funchal and sharing one of our four weeks' stay with Pamela and David who were revisiting the island having decided that Madeira was the holiday place for them.

Returning to Cardiff on 15 November I was soon involved in the various Christmas festivities of the Rotary and Probus Clubs, followed very quickly by the onset of 2005 – a year that saw my involvement in a project that in many ways triggered this resume of all my yesterdays.

Early in 2005 I was approached by the vice chancellor of the University of Wales Institute, Cardiff – or UWIC as it was known – with a suggestion that since I had worked in the colleges that now formed the institute for eighteen years and had written the history of further and higher education in Cardiff for my doctorate degree, I might consider writing a book outlining the origins and history of UWIC, which would be celebrating its thirty years of existence and ten years as a university institution in 2006.

Since all the work that I had been involved with when chairman of the WKPA was no longer, I viewed this suggestion as interesting and to a certain extent I was flattered by having been approached. Although my initial response was to say no, when I was approached a second time, and after several glasses of red wine at UWIC's Celebration of Achievement Ceremony held at St David's Hall in Cardiff, I relented, said yes and was later formally commissioned to undertake the work.

Writing any historical account brings back memories and this work was no exception. As mentioned in my Preface, there were memories of incidents that while difficult to introduce into the academic development that led to the formation of the institute, would nevertheless always remain in the forefront of my recollections of the years spent at the various colleges in Cardiff. Researching developments also required visits to the institution itself, its records library, minutes of the board of governors and its various committees, records of its response to government legislation, and the memories and assistance of those members of staff both past and present, old enough to recall their experiences of developments.

This aspect of the work took me back in time forty-four years to that day in 1960 when I first stepped into the then Llandaff Technical College as a new member of its staff. The site that now houses the administrative centre of UWIC was still familiar to me, although I had not walked the corridors for approaching thirty years and although now very different, any institution that attracts around 9,000 undergraduate and post-graduate students per annum, including over 500 overseas students from forty-two different countries all working and living up to its motto – *Gorau Meddiant Gwybodaeth* which translated means 'The Best Possession is Knowledge' is a fitting testament to what went before.

It was during one of many visits to the Llandaff campus that an incident occurred that to me illustrated how our yesterdays can return in an amazing fashion. As I drove into the car park at the front of the main building I noticed a photographer and a few reporters talking to a gentleman who obviously had some connection with UWIC. As I was getting out of the Daimler he left the group and came over, asking me where I had got the car and for how long I'd had it. I told him that the car's initial owner was Christopher Chataway and that I had owned it for around twenty-six years. He introduced himself as John Wyn Owen, the newly appointed chairman of governors and went on to explain that while working with Christopher Chataway in London in the late 1970s he had ridden on numerous occasions in this very same car. He regarded the event as an omen, I as yet another example of the past returning.

Being a scientist and not an historian I felt that this fact should also preface the work, and words taken from the preface to the Life of Sir Leoline Jenkins, 1724 founder of the Cowbridge Grammar School, the first school that I taught in, sprang to mind:

> A better artist, from such materials, might have raised a much better superstructure. Yet I hope, as it is a production only of leisure hours, and something foreign to the profession in which I

am particularly concerned, that it will be read with that favourable allowance, which has been usually made to such kind of composers, and is in some measure due to every thing well intended.

Christmas 2005 saw Maria and I invited to UWIC's Annual Carol Service held at Llandaff Cathedral, and where I was able to tell the vice chancellor at the reception that followed that this was the fiftieth anniversary of the first such service held in 1955, one year after the Llandaff Technical College came into being. By March 2006 and after hundreds of hours on the word processor, the work was completed and proofs were submitted to the vice chancellor and chairman of the board of governors for comment, approval and a foreword, which I felt was desirable. The foreword by Professor Anthony Chapman, vice chancellor and principal of UWIC reads as follows:

> Dr James Marsden was commissioned by UWIC to set down his own personal account of the historical origins of the organisation now known as the University of Wales Institute, Cardiff (UWIC). He gives a highly factual account of a complex historical pathway as illustrated in the diagram on the following page.
>
> Notwithstanding its factual and chronological nature, this historical account forms an important part of the UWIC archive of events. It adds considerably to our understanding of the history of the predecessor institutions which each played their own part in bringing about an institution which, in the early part of the twenty-first century, is now a significant force in south-east Wales. This account gives a detailed and rich picture of the courses provided by UWIC's predecessor institutions and an insight into some of the decision-making which proved fateful to the system of higher education now prevailing in this part of Wales.
>
> This account is not a political history, nor does it pretend to contain a deep ethnography. This is, however, not to detract from its usefulness.

By June 2006 the work was published and circulated to members of the Welsh Assembly Government, members of UWIC's board of governors, senior staff and those organisations affiliated to or working with UWIC. During the initial stages of my research a very important and personal event took place. On 26 July 2005 Maria and I celebrated our silver wedding anniversary and to commemorate the event I arranged a family dinner at the Copthorn Hotel with part of the surprise being bringing Maria's sister Regina and her daughter over from Valencia to join in the celebrations. None of the family in Cardiff had prior knowledge of this, and it was a great surprise to all when they arrived on 20 July after being picked up from Bristol airport following their flight from Valencia. On the 26th sixteen members of my and Maria's family sat down to dinner at the Copthorn Hotel, the only absentees being David and Melissa, who were unable to travel due to the twins born the previous March.

Regina and her daughter returned to Valencia on 29 July after Maria and I had promised faithfully that we would make a return visit to see them in August 2006 – a promise that we duly kept.

As 2007 dawns and I record the final paragraphs of this record of my life and experiences over the last seventy-five years, I can but wonder at the enormity of the changes that have taken place in society as a whole and how these changes have impinged on my life and those of my generation.

The type of farming that I grew up in and which my family loved is no more, since the pressures imposed by the need to increase food production during the Second World War and later by the Common Agriculture Policy of the European Community has now been furthered by the needs of the multinational supermarkets with buying powers against which the small farming unit has little or no chance of surviving.

In healthcare, I recall visits to the local GP who had his surgery in a room in his house converted into a waiting area, consulting room and adjoining dispensary where various medicines were made up either by Dr Mostyn Davies or by his spinster sister, and where payment frequently took the form of a dozen eggs or a fresh chicken. The National Health Service introduced in the late 1940s was the vehicle of change with visits to the doctor and medicines becoming free, and with regional hospitals being built to serve the local community. Introduced by the then Minister of Health, Aneurin Bevan, MP for Ebbw Vale, this service was life-changing to the young families of the post-war period, but fifty years later and with an aging population is proving difficult to maintain. Through my experiences in caring for Maria during her various illnesses I experienced the modern Health Service at the point of delivery, and will always be thankful of its existence and the expertise of those who work in it.

In many ways education has experienced the greatest change over the last seventy-five years. The gradual but relenting demise of the small village primary school due to the fall in the rural population, much smaller families and with the younger members of such families leaving the countryside to seek work in the towns and cities. The total demise of the Sunday school centred on the local church or chapel. The demise of the grammar school where I and many like me received an academic base which at that time was second to none, and which enabled us to progress to university or to a skills based profession. The rise of comprehensive schools that in many instances do provide a broad spectrum of opportunity yet in many ways tend to ape their predecessors by concentrating on academic achievement to the detriment of very many less able pupils who would and could benefit from a more vocational approach. Coupled with these changes has been government policy of dumbing down standards in an attempt to increase success rates in these schools, and consequent entry to university and higher education. The resulting increases in entry to university education resulted in the grants system of student support becoming unsustainable, resulting in the introduction of tuition fees to be repaid by the student on completing his/her education and obtaining full-time employment. The increase in the higher education population also resulted in the establishment of institutes of higher education, polytechnics and the like from the technical colleges established in the 1950 and 1960s and their gradual evolution into university institutions, as depicted by the case of the University of Wales Institute Cardiff. Finally, the changes in society itself, changes brought about by a myriad of factors and influences, including the introduction of television into every home, computers, electronic mail and the internet, immigration and the diversity of religions, transport and the development of the international company with the ability to

330

move production and services to any part of the world as a means of maintaining or lowering costs and increasing profits. Such changes have, without doubt, influenced, and continue to influence, society and constantly impinge on my life and those of my generation. Had these changes not occurred then my yesterdays would in all probability have been very different, and in that respect I feel privileged in having lived through a time that will never be repeated. What of my and our 'tomorrows'? – I can but quote the frequent saying of my grandfather that 'Tomorrow belongs to no one.'

Printed in the United Kingdom
by Lightning Source UK Ltd.
134028UK00001B/511/A